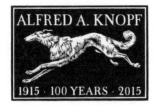
ALFRED A. KNOPF

1915 · 100 YEARS · 2015

I AM SORRY TO THINK
I HAVE RAISED A TIMID SON

I AM SORRY TO THINK
I HAVE RAISED A TIMID SON

Kent Russell

ALFRED A. KNOPF   NEW YORK   2015

THIS IS A BORZOI BOOK
PUBLISHED BY ALFRED A. KNOPF

www.aaknopf.com

Knopf, Borzoi Books, and the colophon are registered
trademarks of Random House LLC.

The following essays were previously published as follows:

"American Juggalo," "Ryan Went to Afghanistan" (subsequently reprinted in
Harper's), and "Showing Up" in *n+1*; "Mithradates of Fond Du Lac" in
The Believer; "Artisanal Ball" and "Island Man" in *The New Republic*;
and "Say Good Morning to the Adversary" in *Tin House*.

Library of Congress Cataloging-in-Publication Data
Russell, Kent.
[Essays. Selections]
I am sorry to think I have raised a timid son / by Kent Russell.—First edition.
pages   cm
ISBN 978-0-385-35230-7 (hardcover)—ISBN 978-0-385-35231-4 (eBook)
I. Title.
PS8618U757A6 2015
814'.6—dc23
2014025421

Jacket photographs by George Baier IV
Hand lettering by Janet Hansen
Jacket design by Peter Mendelsund

Manufactured in the United States of America
First Edition

For all Russells everywhere.

"But now, Grandpa was always comin' down on us. He said we weren't ready for when life attacks. He called dad a nothing-master. And a bluebeard. And fatty-tatties. And he called me a playboy man-baby. That made me imagine a crazy magazine. Dad tried to call his old friends. Local wizards, I'm sure, masquerading as store managers. But he hung up the phone slow, and sad. Dad said, 'The worst thing about living here is that you can only kill yourself once.'"

— BRAD NEELY

Write books only if you are going to say in them the things you would never dare confide to anyone.

— E. M. CIORAN

CONTENTS

I AM SORRY TO THINK
I HAVE RAISED A TIMID SON

1.

RYAN WENT TO AFGHANISTAN

On my eleventh birthday, my grandfather Alexei "Papa" Romanchuck crowned me with a standard-issue M1 helmet before an audience of my friends. "You'll grow into it," he said when the steel pot slid past my chin. "In seven years, I'm dumping you fifty yards from Virginia Key and seeing if you can't swim ashore with this thing on."

My birthdays were occasions for the men in my family to shower me with gifts from their branch of the military. My other grandfather, "Papa Lou" Russell, handed me a blue T-shirt with NAVY lettered in gold across the chest. He'd left his job teaching high school science in Sarasota, Florida, to fight in the Pacific Theater. "Old Papa, he stormed the beach when he was eighteen years old," Papa Lou said. To which Papa dutifully responded, "Well, those dirty Japs, they should be our slaves."

My father left the kitchen briefly and came back in with two small cardboard boxes wrapped differently from the rest. He handed them to my best friend, Ryan, who was standing next to me.

Before letting himself steal a glance at the boxes, Ryan swept his gaze around the room, to make sure it was okay. More so than my other friends, Ryan was in awe of these men. He looked from my nodding father to Papa, a blunt Russian who'd once had his marrow tapped by the cold of the Hürtgen Forest and so now was hunched over the kitchen sink, grumbling, a mild December draft blowing across the room from a window none of us assjacks would shut. Papa was shivering blue crab claws with huge, spatulate hands, the hands of a sapper who'd destroyed European bridges and built Eastern Airlines engines.

After him, Ryan set sights on Papa Lou, just as he was expeditiously dispatching my friend Filipe at a new set of Chinese checkers. Papa Lou had had a wife and three kids and was excused from the draft, but he enlisted anyway. He'd combed for mines in the beryl narrows between Japanese-held islands; "No sweep, no invasion" was how we used to greet each other. Presently, Papa Lou was hopping pieces—an endless zigzag Filipe followed like a tennis volley—while talking trash well beyond his foe's linguistic ken.

Finally, Ryan returned his eyes to my father, who, years ago, had taken him in as a de facto son. A series of car accidents and an addiction to painkillers had left Ryan's mother housebound; she rarely left her room except to stomp around late at night like a revenant. His father was a reformed hippie and failed movie producer; somehow he owned a high-rise condo in Coconut Grove, but little of his hustle money saw home. The rumor was that Ryan's grandfolks were loaded. It remained that—a rumor. Sometimes an uncle checked in. But, otherwise, the boy was on his own.

"First, Ryan opens his presents," my dad said.

I didn't mind. Ryan and I did most things together. A few days before, we'd shaved each other's heads, to cement our pact that when we grew up, I'd be a marine and he'd be a fighter pilot. People said we looked even more alike then—two pee-wees ripe with baby fat, grinning milk-teeth ramparts, our pale scalps shining.

Ryan tore at his favors. Inside: model planes, an F-14 and an F-16. They were brushed steel, weighty and detailed. He scaled them with flat palms, unblinkingly.

Then my father started the parade of gifts for me. He loved this. He'd leave the kitchen and walk back in theatrically, bringing with him old ammunition boxes and camo gear he'd bought at a surplus store he referred to as Earl's House of Crap. My favorite, and the one I put on right away, was an olive T-shirt featuring a hideously grinning death's-head. The skull had feathered wings with tips that curled up, as though flexing, and a streamer behind it that read AIRBORNE—DEATH FROM ABOVE. More gifts followed—MREs, a compass, a canteen—before the grand finale: the *Marine Corps Common Skills Handbook*.

He's a small man, my father, about five-four and thickly built. He likes to joke that they only admitted him into Vietnam because he stuck lollipops under his heels. He seldom wears a shirt, and the sun has cured his skin poreless. His head's horseshoe bald, with one tendril of graying brown hair lying across it. Until he gets upset, whereupon it falls next to his face and flails, always a step behind, like a gymnast's ribbon. His gray eyes are very nearsighted; when he joined the Navy ROTC at Vanderbilt University, he had to memorize the eye chart beforehand to pass. By the time of his honorable discharge, he ranked a junior lieutenant. He captained the swift boat that would later become John Kerry's. His orders were to stand apart and instead of a weapon wield his men like matériel.

My father never did weigh the pros and cons of becoming a sailor. In his time, service was expected of every young man. Especially so in our tribe. (After Papa Lou passed away, my father went through Lou's cache of genealogical documents and found the records of one paterfamilias Russell: officer in the Continental Army, "the Little Iron Man" his affectionate sobriquet.)

So, my wanting to be a marine came as no surprise to the men in my family. I'd simply understood what they had: that dress blues awaited. There was but a single mold for me to fit, like how biscuit honey has its bear.

I chose the marines because they were always the first to fight, and because they were a part of the navy. Since I'd never been much of a boater or fisherman, I figured the marines might make up for my deficiencies in the eyes of my father. My father, whose gift of their handbook made me giddy. I wanted to read it all right there. The table of contents seemed to me a delineation of the things I'd do later in life. I flipped through it with Ryan looking on and everyone else dicking around with the rest of the gear. It had charts and diagrams explaining things like *How to Identify a Weapon of Opportunity*, *What Is the Responsible Use of Force?*, and *How to Apply a Splint to a Fracture*. I've kept it to this day, and I consult it often.

After cake, the men stayed in the kitchen to drink, and we boys retreated to the dining room to have our Nerf-gun war. The dining room was perfect: at one end was a large entryway with two walls to take cover behind, and at the other was a carpeted three-step staircase that made a serviceable trench. My mother threw a quilt over her crystal. Then it was on.

I took command of the trench, and Ryan the walls. We rarely hit each other. When we did, nothing happened, nobody died. Our war made more noise than sense. I stood to the side of the trench with my Nerf chain gun and belched foam arrows that drifted past the enemy in sad arcs. I would never notice Ryan until it was too late, when I'd see half of his face poking out from behind the wall, and *thwunk*, a dart right in the neck. It stuck there, fast, because Ryan licked the cups.

In 2005, both Ryan and I were living in Gainesville, Florida. I was enrolled at the University of Florida, and he was attending classes at its feeder school, Santa Fe College. He lived across town in a house he shared with two brothers, casual acquaintances from Miami.

One night, while he napped in the living room, plainclothes police officers arrested the younger of the brothers in the front yard. He'd been selling marijuana from the house. As the police cuffed him, he yelled for Ryan. Ryan woke, saw men with drawn weapons approaching the house, and went for an AK-47 he'd purchased legally at a gun show a few weeks prior.

For a very long minute, there was a standoff. When the screaming subsided long enough for the men to announce, *Police!*, Ryan threw down his weapon and was arrested. He was charged with attempted aggravated assault on a law enforcement officer with a firearm.

Ryan told me, "I remember standing there, just being in a Mexican standoff with everybody, how exhilarating it was. One of them asked if I was in the army because I had my hair short, and I was aggressive with the assault rifle, and I was behind cover. He said I made all the right choices. 'What are you, in the fucking army or something?'

"Everything I did after that moment was boring. Everything I did didn't mean anything. Everything was in slow motion after that. Nothing compares to the thrill of gunplay.

"I kept thinking about what that dude had said. I thought about how I could redeem myself. I was a shitbag. All I cared about since high school was drugs, alcohol, and tits. I didn't care about anybody except me. My dad had spent forty thousand dollars to get me out of jail. He put the house on a second mortgage. I was going to trial arraignments without a job.

"Then I really researched what was going on in the wars and stuff. We're in two wars; I didn't know what these guys were dying for. I wondered, how do I re-create the excitement from that night? How do I become an honorable man like your father and your grandfathers? How do I do my part?

"Our country was in a war, so why not me? I called my lawyer, asked him, 'Do I have to go into any more arraignments?' He said, 'No,' so I asked him, 'Can I join the army?' He goes, 'If they take you, I don't see why not.'

"I couldn't join at first. I hadn't been acquitted yet, so I had to get a criminal waiver. I had to be interviewed by a lieutenant, a captain, a colonel, and a lieutenant colonel. One of them asked me, 'So you're the guy who pulled guns on cops? I've never been to jail, that's one thing I haven't done in my life. Welcome to the army.' They were hurtin' for manpower. They just wanted meat for the grinder.

"I enlisted without telling my dad. I was living at home while the court case was going on. Everything was fucking up. He would've never let me go; I would've never had his blessing. The day I enlisted, I came home to tell my dad.

"He goes, 'What the fuck are you talking about?' He tried to convince me not to go. He said, 'These wars are bullshit. Don't die for their bullshit.'

"He said, 'I'll give you five thousand dollars right now if you don't join.'

"I said, 'Dad, this is something I have to do.'

"He said, 'I'll give you fifteen thousand.'

"I said, 'Dad.'

"He said, 'I'll give you forty thousand dollars to not die for their bullshit.'

"I said, 'Dad, I don't care about the money. I need to do this.'

"He said, 'When you die for them, you're going to regret it.'

"I went to sleep. The recruiter came to pick me up the next day."

"That's why I joined, to go over there and bust heads," Ryan told me when he got back. "When I was actually over there, it wasn't how I thought it'd be. It wasn't romantic. Not noble or ideological. You weren't fighting for your country. It was a group of guys in the mountains trying to kill another group of guys in the mountains. You and a group of guys who are like you, fighting against a group of guys who aren't like you. In the midst of all this, civilians die because of you. People are killing kids. Are these people a threat to the United States of America? Nah, dude, they don't even have shoes.

"These people don't know that we want to help them. They see us in their mountains and go, 'What the fuck?!' The guys who died didn't die for America, they died for Afghanistan. Afghanis don't give a shit about us. They don't give a shit about their corrupt-ass government. They play both sides of the fence. Guzman got blown up on a mission we weren't even supposed to go on. I'm sitting there eating an MRE as he's dying, and I don't know it.

"I'm the crazy guy? I am. I want to get the bad guys. I still do. The older guys who were in real wars, they'd tell us, 'You're in the right division, wrong war.' Nobody gives a shit you're doing this except the guys next to you—your friends, your brothers. It's not a war. It's a gang war."

October in Miami is when the heat breaks and the rain stops. Skies are bare, and palmettos wave goodbye to the last bit of bluster coming out of the Caribbean. The afternoon of Tuesday, October 12, 2000, was mild and breezy. I reveled in the weather when I came out of my last class of the day. I'd been a high school freshman for a month, and my father and I had worked out the transportation scheme: I was too close to the school for the bus but too far to walk, so every day he'd drop me off and pick me up in the parking lot of an abandoned bank across the street, thereby avoiding the tangle of cars and moms at the front of the school. After the first two days, the process of coming and going went quickly and wordlessly; I'd be out of the car before it had come to a complete stop, and I'd see him pull into the bank as I walked out of school. This kind of precision and efficiency quietly thrilled my father.

Ryan and I were attending different schools. I was at the local public one; Ryan's grandfather was paying his way at an all-male Jesuit academy, for the discipline. Ryan *did* learn discipline there. He would tell me horror stories about the place: how it was a penitentiary atmosphere, how a new kid got sodomized with a blue Bic pen, cap on, in homeroom, and how there were three things a freshman could do to survive: make good with one of the groups of guys who preyed on one another; make yourself a clown or a bitch and offer yourself up that way; do neither and accept that you will be tested every day. The other boys from our Catholic middle school did the first two, Ryan said. He did the third.

And practically every day for four years, someone tried him, said or did something and dared him to fight back. If he didn't, if he demurred even just once, they'd all smell blood, and it'd be over. He came home with cuts under his eyes from seniors' class rings, and whenever his mom was conscious, she'd throw a fit because he'd stopped telling her the truth about why he was fighting. When he tried, she wouldn't believe him. She'd ask how Jesuit priests would allow that to happen. He'd tell her that they knew if they interfered, 1,400 hormonal savages without a skirt to chase would turn on their captors. Then he went into his room and did push-ups, sit-ups, and pull-ups while waiting for the next day. Everything extra came off of him. After the first month, his knuckles looked like kettle corn.

We still saw each other a lot after school. Sometimes he'd pick me up, loaded on his mom's painkillers. Sometimes I'd walk over to his place. One time, I opened the front door, and there he was in his white boxers, both barrels of his grandfather's shotgun in his mouth. He took them out, looked me dead in both eyes, and asked, "Is it loaded?" in the same tone he'd ask, "Is it hot outside?" When I tried to answer, he took a step closer and screamed, "But is it loaded?!" He gobbled the barrels, wrapped his big toe around the trigger, Hemingway-style, and squeezed. The chambers clicked. He gargled laughter.

Five more times he'd do this to me. But not once did I try to wrench the gun from his hands. I was always afraid that, this time, it really was loaded.

But on October 12, 2000, I was walking toward our car wondering why my father was in the driver's seat. The day before, he'd let me drive the short distance home, for practice. I expected him to get out and switch to the passenger side, but he didn't. He stayed where he was, ball cap and purple aviators and both hands on the wheel. I got in, and he started driving, and then without turning to me he said, "Arabs attacked a destroyer today. The USS *Cole*. Hit them in the galley as sailors lined up for lunch. Cowards."

He always wore his sunglasses while driving, but on this day, his lenses lent him an especially dizzy watchfulness. His head was swiveling; I couldn't be sure of what he *wasn't* looking at. The man knew from vigilance. He came into this world 364 days after the Japanese sneak attack on Pearl Harbor. Even casual mention of Japan or the Japanese still prompts my father to mutter things like, "It was a Sunday morning," or "In their beds," or "On the toilet." To him, the bombing of the USS *Cole* was the call to war. September 11 would only ratify how he'd felt a year prior.

What he said next I can't remember exactly. The words came as such a shock to me. Again, he'd never actively pushed military service on me. It was just part of our lives. Sitting through the Army-Navy football game despite a blizzard in Philadelphia; vacationing next to his old naval base in San Francisco; numbering our dinners and rotating them (J-5 = steak and potatoes); explaining to me philosophies he'd worked out but couching them first: "In the immortal words of Lieutenant Commander Ralph M. Strainey . . ."; helping me sew the official seal of the United States Navy on the left side of my backpack and the official seal of the United States Marine Corps on the right.

Yet that day he said, *I don't want you thinking about the military. It hurts me to say this. I believe in the military as an institution. But I don't want you fighting their war. You're too valuable. Let their own sons fight for them.*

I tried to rebut him. Tell him how what he was saying went against everything he believed about civic duty. How the military serves a president who's been democratically elected by fellow citizens. How you can't make your tax dollars go only to the programs you like, and how it's just as absurd to serve only for the "good wars." He answered me by talking politics and Vietnam.

He left the main part unsaid, but it's something he says implicitly every time he refuses to eat until I've finished my own meal, or won't hand over the keys until he's filled the tank, or doesn't leave the house until I wake up. What he's saying is, *A parent's duty is to protect his child. A parent is relieved of this duty only in the grave. I could never forgive myself if you were hurt or killed and I could have prevented it.*

I said nothing more on the ride home. The car was Papa Lou's, a white Grand Marquis. He'd left it to my father. The thing was a boat. Its paint had gone fibrous from the elements, same as happens to Plexiglas in a hull. If you ran your hand across it, you'd come away with a half a dozen shards that your body couldn't dissolve and were painful as hell to remove.

They had e-mail in Afghanistan. Once in a while I'd receive one from Ryan.

TUES JAN. 15 16:31:01 EST 2008

i got a letter from you a couple of months ago. but it was destroyed before i wrote back to you. i remember it was in computer text, not very intimate, but still appreciated. i prefer instant email myself. i just told the story to my buddies the other day of when we were playin foot hockey in your driveway and i hit a wicked fast slapshot into your nuts. the following moments after the impact were hilarious. as i get older and make new memories its easy to lose track of all the good times weve had, especially childhood times. i remember you wanted to be a marine and i was gonna be a fastmover pilot. its funny how fate molds you to serve your purpose. im lookin forward to the day where we can knock back some brews on a daily basis without me havin to go back to some war. cant wait to be a long haired degenerate drunk again. take care brother . . . Ryan.

FRI FEB. 08 17:37:23 EST 2008

hows life brother. hope youre happy and shit. spring is comin soon, all kinds of crazy rumors are circulating the platoons. suicide missions and international incidents and such. hope none of them are true. i realized that i had left bragg exactly 1 year ago today. cant believe that they deploy you for this long. 15 fuckin months. i seen two cherries straight outta airborne school at a FOB a couple of weeks ago. i used to be them. im not that kid anymore, i left him in the sand a while ago. been a long fuckin time here. even when i was home i knew i was comin back. next time i get to stay for good. i dunno how thats gonna feel. depression is hittin everyone real hard here cause its past the point where we shoulda gone home. everyone doesnt give a fuck unless they are gettin shot at that second. my morales pretty shitty but im always okay. no women no alcohol no food. fuckem . . . Ryan

THURS FEB. 28 14:04:52 EST 2008

hey brother. shits about to heat the fuck up real soon. i just wanna get it done. the way home is straight thru em. cant believe its been

4 years since high school. time flies by. seems like yesterday i enlisted. gonna be 2 years come march. looking forward to comin home in may God willin. leave will be from june 4th thru july 6. we gotta stay under observation for a while and do some psych bullshit so i dont blast myself and others. then all-american week and division review. the 4 brigades gotta compete against each other for a week. boxing, combatives, basketball, running, live fires. i think ill compete in combatives or live fire. havent made up my mind yet. youve been like a brother to me all these years, and your old man like a second dad. cant wait to crack open some brews at your house and pass out on the carpet without a weapon. fuck. peace.

"First they try to get you to reenlist in Afghanistan, because the bonus is tax-free. Then back at Bragg, they try to get the dudes who aren't going to reenlist because they want to have a life, have a family, go to college. They try as hard as they can to get them.

"A few months before my time was up, they'd bring me to meetings even though I'd long since told them I wasn't going to reenlist. They said, 'You can get all this money, you get all this great camaraderie. You really gotta make this decision.' Then, a few weeks before I was out, the meetings went, 'You're not going to make it on the outside. You're going to live with your mother. You're abandoning all your brothers. What are you, a pussy?'

"They try to alienate you; you're the guy trying to get out at that point. 'Oh, he's not a team player.' Some guys are so fucking brainwashed when they're over there—this is all you know. You don't even know what the civilian world is like anymore. You're in the zone. The army is all there is."

.   .   .

I was home from college and Ryan was home, more recently, from the clink. It was two months after the incident with the police in his front yard. He'd gone to court and been acquitted of aggravated assault.

The first thing he did when he came over that night was hold his fist level to my face. "You see this shit?" he asked. There were runnels of blood flowing from his knuckles down the grooves between his fingers. "Fucking, I'm squeegeeing my windshield at the Shell station, and a homeless guy punches me in the back of the head."

I was sure there was more to the story, but I didn't press. This was Ryan, after all. Ever since we hit puberty, it seemed to me, my share of bad luck and tough circumstance had been diverted onto him, as though a jetty had sprung up between us, piling it all on his side. I took him into the kitchen, where the house lights were on.

My dad was standing on the far side of the kitchen island, shirtless. I'd told him Ryan was coming over, so he'd arrayed plates of leftovers on the counter. Ryan had been rangy before high school, a starved thing, but now he was threaded with muscle. When he looked upon the food, his receded eyes rippled shallowly within their apron of brown.

This was the first my dad had seen of Ryan since he'd gotten out of jail. (He was the person Ryan used his one phone call on.) My dad kept his arms crossed so his biceps would look more parabolic. He beheld Ryan, grimaced, and cocked his head to the right. His tendril of hair slipped loose and dangled next to his ear. "Come on, Ryan. You can't be getting into more fights, not now." He handed him a clean plate. When we were in elementary school, my dad used to pack my lunchbox with an extra carton of two percent and a second sandwich—processed turkey, American cheese, yellow mustard on white bread—for Ryan. A sweating glass of milk was waiting for him now on the kitchen table. Next to it was a baseball cap embroidered with VIETNAM: I WON MY HALF.

"Kent doesn't eat leftovers. He's too good for them," my dad teased. "Survival school, Kent. You pluck a pigeon, boil it, and share it with fourteen guys—you'll eat anything after that."

Ryan sat down with a heap of arroz con pollo, aka C-3. My dad brought out a bag of tortilla chips and put it on the table, too, just in case. "How you been for real, though?" he asked.

"I got kicked out of community college the other day, for fighting," Ryan said, and dug in.

My dad fingered the hat. "You ever seriously thought about the military? I think it might do you some good."

"No, sir, not in a while I haven't."

"Armed forces teach you discipline. Which rules out people like this shitbird here," he said, thumbing in my direction. "What with the running and the waking up before noon. Plus, you're given responsibilities no one gives young people in the civilian world anymore." He glanced at me quickly, then back to Ryan.

"I tried to get Charlie, Kent's old babysitter's son, to think about the navy when he was your age. All the women in his family went apeshit. They thought I was trying to get their baby killed. He's in prison now."

I'd never heard my dad talk like this. His arms were still crossed, but he sauntered to the head of the island.

"When I was in the navy, the armed forces were the only places that were integrated. It's a meritocracy. Nobody cares that you didn't go to college or had to spend a few weeks in jail.

"When you come back, it's not like that in the civilian world. But, I'll tell you, you'll have things they don't. One's the discipline. When I got back, I went to the University of Florida's law school and did the six semesters one after the other, boom boom boom, no summer breaks, because I had that discipline.

"The other's that you'll own this country. The draft dodgers, the guys who can sing 'O Canada' by heart—they can't tell me shit. When you come back, you own this country more than they do. You're a shareholder."

Ryan bobbed his head, chewing.

"You'll know what duty means. That's for sure. Have the guy next to you trust you with his life, okay, and you'll learn to embrace him more than you do yourself."

Ryan swallowed, said, "I'll think it over, sir," and then bent back over his plate.

My dad turned to me, uncrossed his arms, and daubed his hair into place. I picked up some dishes and took them over to the sink, but my old man pushed me out of the way and said he'd do it.

"Eighty-second Airborne is the most elite conventional unit in the army, not counting Special Operations or Special Forces," Ryan told me when he got back. "So every year that he can, the president comes and reviews us. This was in 2008. Twenty thousand guys standing in formation at Pike Field in Fort Bragg. We're talking guys doing two, three, four, five tours already.

"George Bush is up on a podium, giving a speech. A couple guys start booing, then dozens, then hundreds, then thousands. Command sergeants and first sergeant majors are screaming, 'SHUT THE FUCK UP!' and punching guys in the back.

"Everybody knew these wars were bullshit. All those dudes over there saw their friends die. They had to murder noncombatants. For what? Going fifteen months at war, eleven months back, stop-loss, violated contracts. One of my higher-ups lied to my face; he told me I was being stop-lossed. I had to go to the civilian bureaucracy to hear I wasn't. I mean—I had my ace in the hole, the doctor's note about my mom and how I needed to care for her. But, still, I was disappointed. I'm a sergeant now. I would never lie to my soldiers like that."

After six months in Fort Bragg, North Carolina, Ryan shipped off to Afghanistan. I was in my junior year of college. He'd given me the address of his forward-operating base, a bit of reconditioned Soviet concrete still stained with blood. I decided I'd write him a letter.

It took me two weeks to draw up a rough draft. I had no idea what to tell him. I couldn't imagine that he'd want to hear about things like parking tickets and football games. But then, maybe that was exactly what he wanted to hear. I didn't know whether I should handwrite it or not—we'd never been sentimental about anything, but I thought handwriting it might show that I was really taking time out. I didn't know how to word the thing. Should I speak in the language and memories of our best times, middle and high school? Or would he prefer I be the college junior I was? I had no idea how to talk to him anymore.

After several drafts, I decided to just type the thing casually and in one go. I wrote about what was happening with the family, and how I was doing in classes, and what our friends were up to now. I told him that when I saw him over Christmas, I'd take him to a hockey game. I closed by telling him that I loved him, because I did, and I'd never said it before. I didn't want to miss what could be my last chance to say it.

The day I mailed the letter, I went to the very house where Ryan was living when he got arrested. His roommate was out of jail and having a party. A dozen-plus of my childhood friends were crowded around a keg in the backyard.

Someone had parked a car back there and was blasting bad hip-hop out of it. Dudes shouted over a beer pong table that splayed on four uncertain legs like a newborn giraffe. The spread boughs of a big live oak hid the sky, but a lattice of white Christmas lights stood in for stars. Wet, dead leaves stuck to everything. A kid who used to be my partner in Spanish class was trying and failing to light a fire in the fire pit. Two guys raced around the outside of the house in some kind of beat-the-clock drinking game. One of them tripped, fell, and vomited.

I'd thought of my nonservice as my individual decision. The men in my family who'd served before Ryan had done so in either the draft era or a time of national muster. It was what boys did. But now, with a volunteer military, my decision not to serve was simply another choice I was free to make, like choosing not to go to church. It was the sum of my conscience, my ambitions, and my own best interests.

As for Ryan—I thought he'd made the best choice available to him. Service would straighten him out and give him money for school. It was a way of getting his life together. He hadn't told me why he enlisted, but it wasn't exactly hard to figure out, either. He'd failed his way into rank, another poor college dropout in trouble with the law.

But that night I went up to my friend Dennis, who knew Ryan, who'd had Ryan over for parties and had invited him to play football every Saturday for ten years, and I told him that right now, as we spoke, Ryan was huddled somewhere in the thawing Hindu Kush waiting for the Taliban to regroup and attack.

Dennis's eyes glazed in an instant. They seemed to sheathe themselves with a membrane. "Man, I'm sorry to hear that. That's too bad." That was everyone's reaction when I went around, proud but scared, talking about Ryan: "That sucks, but he'll bounce back." As though this was an appendectomy, something to get out of his system.

I was disgusted by these people. But, I thought, this is what he's defending, right?

I proposed a toast to Ryan, to his survival. Dennis countered, "We should probably be praying for the Taliban. They're gonna need it. Ryan was born for that shit."

I thought: He's right. I once was riding shotgun in Ryan's car when some teens going the other way over a two-lane bridge threw a hamburger that splocked onto his windshield. A whole, unbitten McDonald's twenty-nine-cent hamburger. I laughed at the absurdity. But Ryan pulled an eight-point turn and chased after them. He drew a machete from under his seat. In my head I begged the teens, *Keep going, oh God*, because I knew Ryan might kill them. They escaped by running a red light.

If anyone should fight the Taliban, I thought, it was that man. If it's between him and me, he should go every time.

We settled on *L'chaim* and kept drinking.

Ryan was in Afghanistan for fifteen months between 2007 and 2008. He was stationed a thousand meters from the Pakistani border, his objective to kill or capture any noncoalition forces crossing the Durand Line in either direction. Days, he patrolled mountains. At night, he went on raids and ambushes. Sometimes, he gathered intel on suspect villagers before kicking down doors, his finger on the trigger.

He carried the biggest gun, the SAW, squad automatic weapon. When a group of guys shot at his group of guys, or when he thought they had, he got up and raked their position with hundreds of 5.56-millimeter rounds. His job was to lay down covering fire, lick things with a lead tongue. Later, he'd tell me that combat happened subconsciously. No thoughts, only effervescence. This feeling of a million fizzes rising one on another. I've since wondered: Is that what unconditional love feels like?

It was on Ryan's tour of duty that the Taliban turned to

improvised explosive devices. IED incidents and deaths in Afghanistan increased 400 percent during his deployment. One such incident involved his friend and squadmate Juan Guzman, who was killed while patrolling a small Afghan town in a Humvee. Ryan at the time was back at base.

"As shit was winding down, random people started sending me stupid e-mails asking me stupid shit. I was disgusted with them. I didn't want to talk to them. I had this sense that I was different than everybody. I was like, *You don't understand, so don't talk*.

"But I also thought that I had *less* entitlement to this country than everyone else. I feel like America's this big circle, and I'm outside the big circle looking in on it. I've been away for so long doing weird shit in a weird country. I see everybody and how they act and I don't understand. People treat me different if I tell them I was in the army. I like to sink back and be in the crowd, so I don't tell anyone I served."

Before moving back to Florida, Ryan did a semester at DePaul University in Illinois.

"I was in my German class, and the girl sitting next to me pointed to my KIA band for Guzman and said, 'What's that?'

" 'Nothing.'

" 'Is it a bracelet?'

" 'No, it's something else.'

" 'Seriously, what is it?'

" 'It's for my buddy, he got killed by Taliban.'

" 'I didn't know you were in Afghanistan.'

" 'You never asked.'

"She thought it was such a big deal I didn't tell her. Her name's Emily. We used to be German partners. I used to walk her to the subway and shit. After that she sat away from me and found a new partner. Maybe she thought we had nothing in common, or she disagreed with me going over there. Whatever.

"I can't study in the library because every person who walks by, I have to raise my head from the textbook and evaluate them as potential threats. I can't sit in the middle of the library. I sit in the corner with my back to the wall, with good lines of sight and proximity to an exit. I'm completely paranoid now. I don't carry a firearm here only because it's illegal to do so in Illinois. I know that's not normal. But I've seen so many lives snatched from seemingly nowhere. I learned from that. I'm not going to be a victim."

We carry two cases of Corona to a condo pool, Ryan wearing his boxers, his unlaced army boots, and his dog tags. His high-and-tight is growing out. His show muscles have receded into the lean, predatory symmetry of the rest of him.

We recline against the ledge in the shallow end, grandstanding our empties on the steps out. Our conversation is stilted and awkward; we need three beers to limber up. "Fucking Afghani Bedouins, man. Those guys are badasses," he tells me. "They kill anyone who messes with them, us or Taliban."

Story goes: His patrolling squad approaches a small tribe of Bedouin in a valley in eastern Afghanistan. Things are tense. There's mutual mistrust, and everybody's slung with guns. A baby cries out, and Ryan's squad goes on alert. They search the tribe for the baby but see none. The baby screams again, this time joined by a few others. Then a soldier screams, because he's found a baby. "In the fucking hair, dude. They strap the babies to camels under all the hair, to keep the sun off them. They had, like, eight fucking babies strapped on that camel."

Ryan kneels in the water, only his head above it, and looks to the sky. His tags are ringed with black rubber, and they float in front of him like an ineffectual tug. He tells me how his squad-mate from Texas talked the Bedouin into letting him ride one of their horses, and how the Texan rode it hard into the distance, dust trail kicking up, into a no-shit sunset. For once, the whole squad was at ease, watching the cowboy do what he would've done back home.

I ask Ryan a question I've been thinking a lot about lately: "Why was it you and not me?"

"Why would you waste a rich life full of potential? Jesus, Kent. Don't waste the best of America on this bullshit war. Let the guys with criminal records go. Jesus."

Ryan has blood bruises on his face from a bar fight he got into the other day. They're globular and asymmetrical, as if even his skin's fatigued. It happened while he was playing pool with a guy from his platoon. When we were little, we used to split a pair of Everlast boxing gloves and whale on each other in the front yard, the righty exchanged every other round.

"What about your kid, when you have one?"

"Absolutely not. Never. Fuck that."

"What if your lawn's under attack?"

"Then I'll be his fucking squad leader. If that's the case, I'll sacrifice him."

"What if al-Qaeda has a bunch of Pakistani nukes?"

"If al-Qaeda wants nukes, that's their fucking problem. People are gonna have nukes. People are not gonna like America. People are gonna have different forms of government. Does that mean we have to go over there and destroy them? No. That's un-American.

"But you keep sending guys like me over there? Without knowing what we go through? We may start fucking your shit up. First over there, then back here."

He drinks his beer to foam in three gulps. "To be honest with you, I really hope some *Red Dawn* shit goes down. Because I'll be ready. I'll pick the family up in the pickup, start handing out guns."

"Stark and uncomplicated," I say. "Can't wait."

"Some Chinese higher-up is gonna have a really hard fucking time with Manati Avenue."

"That little white house, third on the left."

"Going out in a blaze of glory while costing some general his stars? Hallelujah."

I've always had to be light-footed when discussing World War II with Papa. I never knew where I could take the conversation, or when I might overstep my bounds and set something off. Past times, I've asked the wrong question and sent him hurrying out of the room. He and Ryan, though, they're on the same wavelength.

Sitting on the lawn after Christmas dinner, they speak to each other in a kind of clipped army Morse.

"Cold where you were?" Papa asks.

"Yessir. Paktika Province, Hindu Kush mountains. Waited up there for bad guys to cross from Pakistan. At night you had to huddle naked with three guys to stay alive."

"In the woods, the wind was worse than the Germans," Papa agrees.

"Socks. It's about keeping your feet dry."

Ryan has on a hooded sweatshirt, my grandfather an old gray windbreaker. Both wear long pants and closed-toe shoes. The temperature is above eighty.

The conversation switches to lighter things. My grandfather remembers emancipating a cottage's silver, and throwing its owner off a bridge when he objected. "We was the victors," Papa explains.

The three of us are lined up in rattan chairs—my grandfather, myself, Ryan, all facing forward—and the veterans' voices are meeting over me. I feel snug. *At liberty*, like a boy who can swagger into a place because Dad or big brother's right behind him.

This bantam privilege—knowing you've been given leave to see without fear of being seen—it's the absolute best feeling in the world. Until the day it's not.

"They use IEDs because otherwise it's not fair," Ryan says. "You get rich Saudi teenagers coming to the mountains, thinking it's an adventure. I'd flank them, and they'd still be firing one-handed over a rock. Just kids, you know?" Papa nods, and levels his gaze on his hands on his knees. "At night at the fire base sometimes I'd look through my nods—night vision—and see these fuckers—pardon." Ryan stands up and pantomimes a blind person stepping tentatively. "See these guys coming up the mountain for us." Now he pantomimes holding a rifle. "We got an infrared beam that only we can see in our nods, and I'm painting these blind bastards right in the face." He laughs a little, and so do Papa and I, because he pantomimes the sightless Taliban again. "So I'd let them do a little of this before I put the steel to 'em. Pink mist, you call it."

I leave them to it and walk into the house to get another beer for Ryan and another whiskey soda for Papa. My dad turns from the dishes and admits, "What Ryan's seen, I can't even imagine. I'm just so relieved I didn't get him killed."

9/18/13

I've taken off work to fly out and visit Dad in San Francisco. Yeshiva University, where I am employed under the table as a factotum-cum-Shabbos goy. Not literally under the table, of course, but kind of: the subbasement, where I fix copiers, clean labs, and answer lost students' questions about the way to the mail room or going unmarried past twenty-five. I found this gig postcollegiately, after thinking long and hard about Officer Candidate School. I could do the push-ups and sit-ups, no problem; it was running two miles in twenty minutes that gummed me up. I didn't think the army would let me do it on an elliptical machine.

I applied to roughly thirty thousand NYC-based jobs via Craigslist. The fact that no one stole my identity made me feel worse about myself. I was turned down by the likes of the Central Park Zoo (maintenance man), a blind Iranian scientist (orator), and a tour company (pizza cicerone). YU were the only ones to call back. They treat me kindly enough. I get to emerge every couple of hours to wash toner off my hands and see the sun.

I told the faculty that there'd been a minor family emergency, which was not untrue. Dad was dying, according to Dad. Again. Still.

"What is living but dying?" Dad says, and has said, for as long as I myself have been breathing.

He insists that this is it, though. The big one. I know it is not. Cannot be. He will be released from this coil only when taking the lot of us out with him, we've decided, my sisters and I. That's the only time he's fancy-free—behind the wheel, with his babies on board. Then, everyone and no one is safe. It's both terrifying and not, having him as your ferryman. I can certainly think of worse ways to go out than: wheels on air, Russells a-scream, the Taurus chassis leveling into parabolic free fall.

I'd be inconsolable were he to actually die without me, however. That is a future I can't even begin to fathom. Talk about your wide-ass gyre. Though I take heart from the fact that, like all your small, skittering, chitinous creatures, he is hard to kill. Always have. Have, in fact, watched the man: walk through a sliding-glass door; unwittingly barehand a copperhead; set his commemorative Donkey Kong shirt on fire while stirring a pot of Hoppin' John in the bright a.m. I was in the vehicle when he got T-boned by a cerulean F-150. I was not when he did likewise, loaded, to a cocaine cowboy's yellow Lamborghini. I have seen him close a door on his own face.

After every injury, physical or otherwise, he yelps a "*Shit!*" and is fazed, but he does not accept help or consolation. There *is no* help or consolation. Suffering itself is the point. Shame is medicine, and to drink enough will cure you of anything.

It's the kind of worldview a mental-health professional could dine out on, a lot, at expensive brasseries. But he will never go to a mental-health professional. Mental-health professionals are the black helicopters of the self, dangerous interlopers to take cover from and bust back at. Suggestions that he "talk to someone" come across like grenades rolled into the officer's tent.

No, in this family we shit on the talking cure. We consider

psychology to be the hero's grave. We rub dirt into what pains us, and then we walk it off.

As a result, I have come to fetishize opaque brutes. Adventurers, gunfighters, all the dumb rollicking killers. Dudes for whom torment and doubt are inconceivable (or at least incommunicable). Homer's sublime dolts, gloved in blood and not wanting to talk about it.

"Nostalgia" is a dirty word, I know. Sentimental, retrograde. It's the sound ignoramuses make when mewling after what was false in the first place. A blank check issued to weak minds, the cashing of which ends up bankrolling bad history. Total duh.

But fuck, man. Consider any guy who captured your attention, who gave you the (metaphoric) dick tingles. Likely, there was something in him that was unhinged to his advantage. Likely, he was in some way opposed to the kind of man we're supposed to be now: the kind who understands himself, explains himself, acquits himself—the kind who, ultimately, never makes memorable gesture numero uno.

Doesn't that guy sound like a dildo? Aren't legends forged (*forged*, not recorded) by the kind of man who lives in the world in such a manner that, unbeknownst to him—and, really, he couldn't give a good goddamn either way—his days become his credentials?

Because me, personally—I have had it with all these stories about anemic ephebes and their disquiet. I do not want to make a reasonable being my object of adoration.

Which is why I polished off yet another Daniel Boone biography prior to whipping out my laptop on this red-eye flight. (Dad having suggested the seat, 36F, after doing his research on Seatreviews.com. "You get a lot of legroom, but you gotta be the guy who opens the emergency door. You're strong enough to do that?")

In his lifetime, which spanned from 1734 to 1820, Daniel

Boone blazed the first trail into the West through the Cumberland Gap, explored the territories of Florida, Ohio, and Michigan, defended frontier towns during the Revolution, hunted game on the level of an extinction event, and spurred hundreds of thousands of Americans to settle in Kentucky and, later, Missouri. At one point, 358 monuments to the man existed in this country. The number of us who have claimed his descendancy—staggering.

Whatever instinct it is that attracts you to what encourages you—an instinct that comes from feeling at home in the world—Boone didn't have it. Short and powerful, pony-built, he ran away from home after killing one of his father's horses in a jumping accident. His father had beaten him then, in the Quaker fashion, beaten him until Boone asked forgiveness. *Canst thou beg?* his father huffed between strokes. Boone was silent, leaving his father free to close the matter at his leisure. Once his father had exhausted himself, Boone lit out for the wilderness.

Semiliterate, Boone could hold a long rifle in one hand and take the head off a nail from distance. He won renown for his marksmanship, as well as his ability to track game like an Indian. He cared little for himself and took ill-advised risks. In so doing, he bungled into history. He served as George Washington's teamster during a campaign that saw the future president twice shot off his horse. Boone ignored every warning and became the first to chance an unauthorized American settlement west of the Appalachians, getting one of his sons killed by Indians in the process. Another he would bury in a mass grave following the 1782 Battle of Blue Licks, and this after reproving him, "I did not hear your name when they were beating up for volunteers. . . . I am sorry to think I have raised a timid son."

Boone was a frontiersman, which is a latter-day euphemism for "unrelenting opportunist." He tramped around the native element looking for unclaimed resources, things to exploit before moving on. He bushwhacked, schemed, and hustled—mapping land, running a tavern, harvesting ginseng—but really he was something of a loser. By middle age, he was a bankrupt deadbeat on the run from the law.

The one thing he was truly good at was pushing farther into the woods to kill for flesh and fur. Boone spent almost all of his borrowed time doing this, hunting peregrine. It kept his family decent while simultaneously keeping *him* away from *them* for months at a time. There was something salvific in it: the separation, the descent into a more primitive state, the regeneration through violence. He was still hunting and trapping well into his seventies.

If you read the few primary sources, you start to get why. Boone feared something. It's the same something feared by any ass-kicker who finds himself in medias res, hacking through the thick of it, knee-deep in the dead. He feared that, were he ever to stop, the mind he needed to keep trained on a target might instead turn on him. So, Boone came and went on his hunting trips. His shirt and shoes were always blood-soaked, and he'd have a nice present for the kiddies upon his return. But he never did stay for long.

I took a break from journalizing to use the in-flight Internet to confab with Lauren. As always, she is oracular. Our middle-sibling keystone.

Lauren: jesus, dad's insane
me: what'd he do

Sent at 11:28 PM on Wednesday

Lauren: just reflecting
me: yeah

me: what made you think of that this time?
Lauren: just like
how there are no fucking answers?
like a lot of shit happened we know nothing about?

Lauren: for instance
remember how he told us that fucking BODIES
would come up from the GROUND
if it rained too hard
me: yeah
Lauren: and i remember sort of uncritically accepting that as fact
me: no doubt

me: how long do you think that lasted
dad-programming
Lauren: what do you mean
me: like, the way dad programmed us so that
for instance

when the afternoon thunderstorm rolled in, our minds ran the
conditional
IF (SIT BY WINDOW) THEN (STRUCK BY LIGHTNING)
IF (TAKE A SHOWER) THEN (STRUCK BY LIGHTNING)
IF (PICK UP PHONE) THEN (STRUCK BY LIGHTNING)

Sent at 11:36 PM on Wednesday

me: i actually don't know which if any of those is untrue

Sent at 11:37 PM on Wednesday

me: i'm saying, when do you think you stopped taking him at his
word?
Lauren: mmm unclear
in high school, maybe

Sent at 11:38 PM on Wednesday

Lauren: but i think thats normal adolescent stuff
like i dont think its dad-specific
i think once you're able to not be totally dependent on your
parents
you start to receive them a little more critically
me: well, sure
Lauren: once you realize no one knows really what the fuck
they're doing
me: but by then you're also not under the command of dad

the unrelieved captainship of dad
on the USS WE R FUKT

Sent at 11:39 PM on Wednesday

Lauren: what are you talking about.
we are all still under the command of dad.

Sent at 11:40 PM on Wednesday

Lauren: do you remember this one time
we stayed in a hotel for a while
on miami beach
with just mom?
me: when dad was on a bender?
Lauren: i believe that was what was going on

Sent at 11:42 PM on Wednesday

me: yeah, i vaguely remember that
i vaguely remember all that stuff
that time was, for me, like sleeping through turbulence
i remember coming-to a couple of times
terror goosing me
unseen forces jouncing me
but then ultimately falling back asleep
confident that we'll either get to where we're going, or we'll go
down in flames

Sent at 11:44 PM on Wednesday

Lauren: but like why wouldnt we go to papa's house?
me: no room?
shame?
Lauren: didnt want him to know where we were?
and of course
there's a literal fucking hurricane coming
while all this is going on
me: yeah
Andrew
the too-easy metaphor
Lauren: i know, shit

Sent at 11:50 PM on Wednesday

me: did you find out anything more about why dad is hesitant re:
going with me to ohio?

Sent at 11:58 PM on Wednesday

Lauren: ok
so
a few different threads on why no OH
first, to paraphrase
he thinks you are a silver-tongued lie jockey who condescends to
his subjects
related, he suspects your only aim is to flush his ancestry, shoot
them in their american-dreamdomes
making yourself look better than them, through them
obvi
second is the fact that there were only like 3-4 lived years in OH
during which he was cognitively able to form memories

he was there from ages 1-8
also, those memories, while in and of idyll
he does not consider to be particularly important or interesting
so, while the first thread seems to suggest there's some shame-
grist (potentially) for your fucking irresponsible moneymill
the second is just true

Sent at 12:03 AM on Thursday

Lauren: when do you pay me?

Sent at 12:04 AM on Thursday

me: goddamnit.

Sent at 12:05 AM on Thursday

For some time now, I have been trying to convince Dad to go with me on a trip to Martins Ferry, Ohio. I want him to show off the block he grew up on, the places that formed him.

The closest I've managed was a brief tour via Google Maps' street view. In the still frames, I saw a lot of boarded-up buildings on Main Street, and what looked to be the smoldering ruins of an idealized past. It was so bleak there that Wheeling, West Virginia, was directly across the river.

I suppose we *could* go to Sarasota. But Sarasota now is no different from any other stretch of exurban gooch connecting major Florida shitholes. It certainly isn't the place he's wistfully described as "a true kid's wonderland," this mix of wire-grass

South and primeval swamp, where he spearfished in the Gulf and was conversant with the freaks across town at the Ringling Bros. winter camp.

I want the ancestral homeland. I want to drive from California back East. And when we get there, after maybe a good number of side quests and misadventures, I want to find the graves of my namesakes, Kent and James Russell, the uncles I never met. I want to look for Papa Lou's parcel, too, because Dad *mailed* his ashes and never followed up. He doesn't know whether or not his own father is out there in the ground.

More than anything, though, I want to dowse for the wellspring that is feeding the fiasco of our character. I am homesick most for the place I've never known.

2.

AMERICAN JUGGALO

I'd been driving for seventeen hours, much of it on two-lane highways through Indiana and then southern Illinois. Red-green corn sidled closer to the road until it stooped over both shoulders. That early in the morning, a mist was tiding in the east.

I figured I had to be close. A couple of times I turned off the state road to drive past family plots where the houses were white, right-angled ideals. Rising from many of these plots were incongruous humps of grass—homespun cemeteries. I wondered what it would be like to grow up in a place like this. Your livelihood would surround you, waving hello every time the wind picked up. You wouldn't be able to see your neighbors, but you'd for sure know who they were. You'd go to one of the Protestant churches seeded in the corn, take off your Sunday best to shoot hoops over the garage, and drink an after-dinner beer on your porch swing, certain of your regular American-ness. And one day you'd get buried feet from where you lived, worked, and died.

Doubt about this trip unfurled inside me as the odometer crawled on. I couldn't have told you then why I was doing it.

Back on IL-1, I glanced to my right and saw an upside-down SUV in the corn. It must've flipped clear over the stalks nearest the road, which stood tall and undamaged. The SUV's rear right wheel—the whole wheel—was gone, but the axle still spun. Stumbling alongside the wreck was a dazed kid in a Psychopathic Records fitted cap. The fingertips he touched to the side paneling seemed to keep him from pitching over.

When midwestern bugs hit your windshield, they chink like marbles. When I'm feeling indecisive in a car, I mash the accelerator.

When the hip-hop label Psychopathic Records released its seventeen-minute trailer for the eleventh annual Gathering of the Juggalos, a four-day music festival, five people I knew sent me links to it. I suppose that for them it was a snarker's Holy Grail: everyone involved in the video had such a boggling lack of self-awareness that the whole thing bordered on parody. "The Gathering has fresh and exciting shit to do all around the fucking fizzuck," the trailer went. "One hundred rap and rock groups! Helicopter rides! Carnival rides! Seminars! . . . And if you like midgets, we got midgets for you." Mind you, I had no idea who or what any of this was.

The trailer featured bedraggled white folks and nary a complete smile. "Fresh-ass" was used as a compound modifier denoting quality. Willis from *Diff'rent Strokes* would be there, and Vanilla Ice was going to sign autographs. There'd be wrestling all night, four nights in a row.

I could understand how some might find joy in making fun of these people and their "infamous one-of-a-kind" admixture of third-rate fun fair and perdition. But I was also impressed by the stated point of the thing: "The real flavor, what separates the Gathering from every other festival on the planet, is the magic in the air. The feeling of ten thousand best friends around you. The camaraderie. The family. And the love felt everywhere throughout the grounds. You'll meet people, make future best friends; you'll probably get laid. And you'll realize that the family coming together is what all of this is really about."

I did some hasty groundwork on that boon the Internet and found out that juggalos are: "Darwin's biggest obstacle." "A greasy, fat teenager with a Kool-Aid mustache and no friends who listens to songs about clowns in his stepmother's double-wide mobile home when he isn't hanging out at the mall food court." "They paint their faces, are aggressive, travel in packs, abide (supposedly) by a simplistic code of rules, and tell all those non-juggalos that juggalos live a happier and freer life." I learned that *Saturday Night Live* spoofed them on the regular. There's a band called Juggalo Deathcamp. "Illegal Immigrants Can Stay, Deport the Juggalos" is a statement that 92,803 individuals on Facebook agree with.

Who were these people? Why did everyone hate them so?

"Juggalo" etymology is this: Insane Clown Posse, the founders of Psychopathic Records, were performing in front of 1,800 at the Ritz in Warren, Michigan, in the early '90s. Violent J, one half of the Posse, was doing "The Juggla," a song off *Carnival of Carnage*. When he rapped the chorus, "You can't fuck with the Juggla . . . ," he asked, "What about you, juggalo? Are there any juggalos in here?" The crowd went nuts and the term stuck.

No definition exists. Nowhere in Psychopathic Records' discography do any of their artists—not ICP, nor Twiztid, nor Blaze Ya Dead Homie, nor Anybody Killa, nor Boondox—attempt to delineate what a juggalo is or believes. The artists themselves self-identify as juggalos, but when they rap about juggalos, they do so with awe, incredulity, and more than a little deliberation.

From ICP's "Welcome to Thy Show": "We just glad we down with them, hate to be y'all / and have a juggalo shatter my skull for the Carnival."

From Violent J's interview with *Murder Dog* magazine: "Juggalos started with ICP and now it's grown into its own culture. It's still very much a part of ICP, but there are other groups that juggalos follow. A juggalo is not just a fan base of ICP. A juggalo is a way of life. . . . The juggalos is very much like a tribe. It's like this wandering tribe who gather every year at a sacred place to have a ritual. It's an ancient thing for humans."

ICP are Violent J and Shaggy 2 Dope, a couple of white minor felons from the working-class suburbs of Detroit. In the early '90s, the two of them dropped out of high school, donned clown face, and founded both Psychopathic Records and a mythology called the Dark Carnival. Without getting too deep into it: The Dark Carnival comprises six studio albums, released between 1992 and 2002, known as the Joker's Cards. With each Joker's Card—*Carnival of Carnage, Ringmaster, Riddle Box, The Great Milenko, The Amazing Jeckel Brothers,* and *The Wraith*—ICP disclosed more of their Carnival and its murderous personalities and attractions. They envisioned a kind of big-top kangaroo court run by vigilante carnies. A darkly righteous expo that traveled from town to town and blew up racists, tortured wife beaters, bled pedophiles dry, and consigned the wealthy to hell.

From Violent J's memoir, *ICP: Behind the Paint*, which reads a lot like Bukowski's *Ham on Rye:* "Every kid who came through the line was just like us. They looked like us, dressed like us, talked like us and all that. NO!!!! I'm not saying that we influenced them and their style; I'm saying that they already had the same style as us. We were all just different forms of SCRUB!!!! We were all the same kind of people! We were all the world's UNDERDOGS. We were all pissed, and ready to do something about it."

In the early days, this "something" sounded a lot like class warfare. For instance, there's this, from the liner notes to *Carnival of Carnage:*

> If those of the ghetto are nothing more than carnival exhibits to the upper class, then let's give them the show they deserve to see. No more hearing of this show because you can witness it in your own front yard! A traveling mass of carnage, the same carnage we witness daily in the ghetto, can be yours to witness, feel and suffer. No longer killing one another, but killing the ones who have ignored our cries for help. FREE PASS FOR THE GOVERNOR'S FAMILY! Like a hurricane leaving a trail of destruction, the ghetto on wheels! My views may be ugly, but so are the bloodstains on the streets I roam. If there is no change soon tickets will be issued to . . . The Carnival of Carnage.

This was more or less of a piece with the greater gangsta rap ethos of the early '90s, albeit espoused by two white clowns. But after *Carnival of Carnage*, ICP focused their creative energies on rapping about new nemeses and gory set pieces for their Dark Carnival; fanciful descriptions of retribution took precedence over politics. J and 2 Dope became like superheroes (at one point producing their own comic book series), and their slant-rhymed fantasies of comeuppance stood in for mobilization. If anything, their political beliefs could now be described as apocalyptic.

Or at least that's how some juggalos have perceived it. In 2006, one juggalo named Jacob Robida attacked three men in a Massachusetts gay bar with a hatchet and a gun, fled to West Virginia, kidnapped a woman, and drove to Arkansas, where he killed her, a police officer, and himself. In 2008, two Utah juggalos armed with a knife and a battle-ax attacked a seventeen-year-old, hacking at him twelve times. A juggalette from Colorado got her juggalo boyfriend to stab her mother to death. Two Pennsylvania juggalos took a boy into the woods and slit his throat in 2009. Police in Utah, Arizona, Pennsylvania, and California consider juggalos a criminal gang. So does the FBI.

The man in the ticketing trailer told me someone would be by shortly with my press pass, which I had lied to get. Nobody assigned me to go to the Gathering of the Juggalos, and I couldn't have said why I was standing there in the buzzing heat at the entrance of Hogrock Ranch & Campground, a hundred-plus acres of cleared land in the Shawnee National Forest just outside tiny Cave-In-Rock, Illinois. Next to me was a shirtless kid named Squee. I'd helped him carry a gunnysack down the steep declivity that connects the overflow parking to the campground. I'd said, grinning conspiratorially, "Let me guess: This shit's full of beers, right?" He'd said, "Fuck your beers, dude, we're smoking that weed. This shit's full of Powerades. Gonna sell these shits."

Squee rapped on the trailer's window ledge and told the ticketing man, "Uhh, I lost my car." "You lost your what?" the ticketing man asked. "My hoopty." "Can't help you." Squee turned to some other kids who were getting their bags checked at the gate and said, "Shit, I was in a tent with four juggalettes—sounds good, right?—Camry keys in my pocket, getting my drink on, my brain on. Now I can't find that shit." He glared at the kid next to him and said, "I told you it was a stupid idea to get that fucked up on the very first night, Randall."

Sandy the PR agent, my age and attractive in a round-featured midwestern way, rode shotgun in a golf cart that skidded to a halt in the dirt in front of the trailer. She handed me a lanyarded, laminated card that had the dimensions of a child's placemat at a chain restaurant. It was emblazoned with the Psychopathic Records mascot, the Hatchetman, and the letters "VIP." I'd never been credentialed before.

"Charmed, I'm sure," Sandy said, reaching her right arm over her left shoulder for me to shake from the back of the cart. At the wheel was a freckled child. "This is Justin. He works here, kind of." Justin turned to me slowly. His smile was wide and shingled with loose baby teeth. He floored it.

We bounced down the dirt pathways that web Hogrock. "This is normally a biker camp," Sandy said, "but sometimes also a Baptist kids' camp. This is the third straight Gathering here. Every Gathering's been in Michigan, Ohio, or Illinois. Seven thousand went to the first; twenty thousand went to the last. This business is a day longer than Woodstock."

Tents sprouted from every inch of available flat land on either side of the path. Pup tents, two-person tents, bivouacs, walk-in affairs with air-conditioning. Back in the woods, red tarp domes showed between trees like pimples under hair. Next to most were dusty American cars filled to the windows with stuff: beers, empty motor oil bottles, liters and liters of Detroit's bottom-shelf Faygo cola, pallets of Chef Boyardee, chips, chocolate, powdered Gatorade. Ruddy juggalo faces poked out of tent flaps at the approaching burr of the golf cart, adding to the surreal feeling of touring an encamped American diaspora.

We drifted past the seminar tent, the second stage, the autograph tent, the freak-show tent, the adipose food booths. The sky was as dully off-white as the inside of a skull. I'd read that these four days would range in temperature from ninety-six to a hundred degrees. Sweat-wise, I was already beyond recall.

"I did the whole Gathering last year," Sandy said. "I'm not staying past sundown tomorrow. I hope you brought something green, or an orange." Justin slalomed around shirtless juggalos. Seen from behind, most had broad, slumped shoulders and round, hanging arms. They were not stout. These people were grubbed with fat. They looked partially deflated. You think I'm being cruel, but these were the most physically unhealthful people I'd ever seen. "Because if not, you're shit out of luck. Unless you especially love carnival burgers, or fried curds from out the back of someone's RV."

We visited a swimming hole nicknamed Lake Hepatitis that was the kelly green of putt-putt hazard water. A waspy helicopter you could ride in for forty dollars. A trailer full of showers, a wrestling ring, and the half-mile-long valley that held the main stage on one end and a small fair at the other. It turned out that Justin was the son of Psychopathic Records' VP. My credential flapped in the false breeze, whining like a musical saw.

Justin braked hard on a narrow bridge that spanned a parched creek. There was a backup of cars looking for open campground. Not more than twenty-four inches in front of us sat twin girls on the rear bumper of a white minivan. They couldn't have been a day over fourteen or a biscuit under 225. They wore bikini tops, and the way they slouched—breasts resting on paunches, navels razed to line segments—turned their trunks into parodies of their sullen faces.

The air here was dry and piquant. Cigarette and pot smoke convected, chasing out oxygen. One of the girls called out to Sandy, "You're really pretty," emphasizing the "You're" as though being pretty were suspect. Juggalos swarmed the bridge, and when the traffic stopped, they closed in, hawking whatever they had. Hands shot into the cart, holding cones of weed for fifteen dollars, glass pipes for ten dollars, bouquets of mushrooms for I don't know how much, Keystone Lights for a dollar, single menthols for a dollar. A clutched breast was pushed through the fray and jiggled; a disembodied voice demanded a dollar.

Then somebody screamed, "WHOOP, WHOOP!"

Understanding how this sounds is important, as it forms a refrain to the entire Gathering. A single "WHOOP, WHOOP!" is like a plaintive, low-pitched train whistle Dopplering from afar. The *O*s are long, and there's a hinge between the first "WHOOP" and the second. You sort of swing from one syllable to the next.

The crowd fortified the call, returning it deeper and rounder. "WHOOP, WHOOOOOOOOP!" Sandy overturned her handbag, found oversize sunglasses, and put them on. "Just say it. Just do it," she said. Thinking myself a funny guy, I did a kind of Three Stooges "Whoop whoop whoop!"

Which I know now was wrong. "WHOOP, WHOOP!" is juggalo echolocation. Its not pinging back means trouble.

The twins screamed, "Show us your titties, bitch!" at Sandy. A tall guy with a massive water gun screamed, "Man, fuck your ride!" and sprayed us with a stream of orange drink the pressure and circumference of which made me think of racehorses. A "FUCK YOUR RIDE!" chant went up and around the crowd, and garbage was thrown. I would describe what kind of garbage, and how it felt to be the object of such ire—but I had so much garbage thrown at me at the Gathering of the Juggalos that showers of refuse became commonplace, a minor annoyance, and describing one would be like describing what it's like to get a little wet on a winter's day in Seattle. Justin, bless his heart, floored it, parting the crowd with the derring-do one is capable of when one's father is running shit.

"Shit," Sandy said. "Shitbagging shit."

Justin grinned. "That was your first Faygo shower, dude."

They dropped me off in an empty field. I never saw them again. Thenceforward I returned every "WHOOP, WHOOP!" with gusto.

.   .   .

Blender named ICP the worst artists in music history. I'm sure you won't find many music fans or journalists who disagree. And yet, according to Billboard's independent album charts—and ICP has been independent since they left Island Records in 2001—their album *Forgotten Freshness Vol. 3* peaked at #10, *The Wraith: Shangri-La* at #1, *Hell's Pit* at #1, *The Calm* at #1, *Forgotten Freshness Vol. 4* at #4, *The Wraith: Remix Albums* at #9, *The Tempest* at #2, and 2009's *Bang! Pow! Boom!* at #1. Twiztid has had one #1 independent album, two at #2, and one at #3. Dark Lotus, the quasi-mystical supergroup made up of ICP, Twiztid, and Blaze Ya Dead Homie, has charted at #3, #4, and #6.

As of this writing, ICP alone has two more #1 indie albums than both Arcade Fire and Elliott Smith; three more than Arctic Monkeys and the National; and four more than the Yeah Yeah Yeahs and the White Stripes. I understand that may be hard to believe. You likely can't name a song by any Psychopathic Records artist (except for maybe ICP's Internet-famous "Miracles"). They don't have singles that play on the radio, or in hip bars, or on the stirring trailer for *Where the Wild Things Are*. Only Insane Clown Posse has made it onto the Billboard Hot 100—in 1997, when they spent five weeks on the charts, peaking at #67, with "Santa's a Fat Bitch."

Psychopathic Records peddles horrorcore, a hip-hop genre spawned two decades ago that narratively and figuratively incorporates all kinds of horror-film tropes: hyperviolence, grue, moralism, Rube Goldberg–style faces of death—and all of it set to samples from, say, *Creepshow* or *Zombi 2*. According to Jamie Madrox of Twiztid: "Think of it as if there was a *Halloween* or *Friday the 13th* on wax, and Jason and Michael Myers could actually rap. This is what their vibe would sound like."

The germ of horrorcore can be traced to the Geto Boys (influential beyond their appearance on the *Office Space* sound track), several of whose lesser-known songs first integrated the aforementioned stuff. But it was Esham, a Geto Boys contemporary from Detroit, who was the first MC to build his persona exclusively around the horrific. He inspired the Insane Clown Posse, who in turn inspired the Psychopathic family.

Horrorcore had its big national moment in the mid-'90s, when the Flatlinerz and Gravediggaz were charting and ICP's *The Great Milenko* went platinum. Yet the sound still defines Metro Detroit and much of the Rust Belt. There's Esham and the Clowns, of course, but there's also King Gordy, Prozak, Twiztid, Marz, Blaze Ya Dead Homie, J Reno, Rev. Fang Gory, Freddy Grimes, Troubled Mindz, Defekt—even Eminem can be considered horrorcore-influenced, on account of Slim Shady's onomatopoeic chainsaw revs and gore-focused gaze.*

Since ICP, many if not most horrorcore acts have been white. As has been their audience. All but one of the artists on Psychopathic, which is based in bourgie Farmington Hills, come from Michigan. All are white or Native American. Psychopathic pulls in ten million dollars a year and has its own wrestling federation, energy drink, and film division.

Wending my way to the park entrance from where Sandy and Justin dropped me off took three hours. The golf cart had created a compact and navigable illusion. The campsite was shaped

---

* ICP and Eminem had a long-running beef that began in 1997, when Eminem was a little-known battle rapper about to release *The Slim Shady* EP. He was passing around a flyer at a club re: his release party. The flyer read, "Featuring appearances by Esham, Kid Rock, and ICP (maybe)." Eminem handed one to Violent J. This being the first time the two had ever met or spoken, Violent J objected to Eminem's presumptuousness. After that, barbs went back and forth. Eminem called ICP talentless; ICP contended that Eminem was a commercial product masterminded by Dr. Dre and MTV. They recorded a parody of "The Real Slim Shady," entitled "Slim Anus."

like a bone-in top loin, its paths marbling it as randomly as fat. I realized I hadn't packed any water, or bedding.

I had imagined, what with the Gathering being a music festival, that I'd be able to slink around anonymously. I was immediately disabused of this notion. I was the only person not wearing black or red. I was the only person who did not have Psychopathic Records iconography tattooed somewhere on his body. My hair, ridiculous as it was—both fro'ed out and sopping in the humidity—marked me as exceptional. The juggalos who hadn't shaved their heads completely had shaved everything below their crowns and braided the rest into rigid tendrils that zagged upward like the legs of a charred insect.

Everywhere I went, juggalos stopped what they were doing to track me with spotlight eyes. Their heads moved in time with my stride, the way man or beast will do when a threat is sensed. For four days I would have to fight a strong urge to break into a jog.

I decided to follow one of the dry creeks that no longer reach the Ohio River. I moved between trees on the bank, walking until I realized I was amid a dozen people facing the creek in a staggered formation of lawn chairs. Somehow I hadn't noticed what they were watching: one man breaking tube after fluorescent glass tube over the back of another man who lay prone in the creekbed. When the tubes popped and tinkled, they released jinnish poofs of talc. I thought maybe the other guy was drunk. Then the assailant moseyed to the back of a rusted panel van that canted down the bank. He pulled out a T-ball bat vined with razor wire. I actually said, "Oh, no!" He knelt over the other guy, pulled his head up by the hair, and started gouging his forehead with the bat. Someone in the chairs spoke up, said, "Pin his ass, Darryl." I moved on.

I walked by a pavilion whose purpose I couldn't immediately discern. Women danced naked in cages, and there was a stage fronted by picnic tables. Both stage and picnic tables were being stood on by a lot of people. A master of ceremonies emerged from the onstage crowd, screaming a station identification into a microphone—WFuckOffRadio, Psychopathic's own—and that it was time for the contest. I didn't see any hands go up. It was just: two beer bongs were handed to two dudes who put the hoses to their mouths before two other dudes poured a plastic 750-milliliter bottle of gin into each funnel. I found myself shaking my head *no* while applauding slowly. After the bottles were emptied, the dudes were allowed fifteen seconds to recoup. The naked ladies had stopped dancing and were gripping their bars tightly. Only cicadas zapped the silence. Then began the second leg of the contest, which involved a third dude—this time chosen from a show of eager hands—jumping onstage to kick one of the gin-drinkers in the crotch, and then the other, and so on, best-of-three-falls style. The last man standing was given a goodie bag smaller than the goodie bags I'd received at the end of mediocre birthday parties. The crowd lined up to high-five both contestants, "WHOOP, WHOOP!"s all around.

When I finally arrived at my rental car, panting and glazed with sweat, I threw it in reverse, feeling a most acute despair. The Hardin County sheriff stopped me at the Hogrock egress. Caprices and Grand Marquises illustrated with Psychopathic Records decals sat passengerless on the shoulder. Two deputies were ducking juggalos into a paddy wagon. The sheriff ambled up to my window, leaned in to appraise me, and waved me on. I was still full of paranoia and phantom guilt when the wind whipped my VIP badge across my neck, drawing a faint line of blood. I drove to the next town over, to buy beers, because I needed them.

A few words on horror, and why some people like it:

I've never seen *Citizen Kane* and don't care to, but Kane

Hodder is the best and only Jason Voorhees in my mind. I have no idea what *Casablanca* is about, but I can give you rundowns of *Cannibal Holocaust*, *Cannibal Ferox*, *Sexo Canibal*, and *Anthropophagus*. Or if cannibals aren't your thing, *Demoni 1* and *2* and *Demonicus*. I need to scan down to number fourteen, *Psycho*, on the American Film Institute's list of our hundred best movies to find one I've actually watched.

"Serious" film strikes me as absurd. It's bowdlerized life. Filmic drama asks me to care about loves, losses, supposed triumphs—things that together amount to the chiseled dash connecting my birth to my death on my tombstone. To me, the modern horror film has more to do with first-world existence as it is lived today. In the modern horror film, we no longer come together to defeat an existential threat, gaining knowledge of and confidence in ourselves along the way. Altruism is not rewarded. Even the most self-sacrificing character will be killed off, often for laughs. One protagonist, if any, makes it out alive by becoming more brutal than the monster. He trades debasement for survival, which is short-lived—because of course the monster comes back, for the lucrative sequels.

In horror, characters are stripped of everything they think they know and believe they are. Education and privilege mean nothing. Security is a delusion; today is the last day of the rest of your life. You, what makes you *you*, your blemishes and singular characteristics, will disappear in an instant. Stalking everything you do is death, and all that matters is how furiously you go out.

Back at the Gathering, with my quivered tent on one shoulder, my book bag packed with water and Luna bars on the other, and a suitcase of Natural Light in hand, I went looking for a spot to camp. I had picked up a map and program from the ticketing trailer, so this time I knew where I was going. Along the way, I took note of the license plates I saw: Illinois, Wisconsin, Michigan, Indiana, Ohio, Iowa, Nebraska, Kentucky, Missouri, Kansas, Oklahoma, Colorado, New Mexico, West Virginia, Pennsylvania. Over the course of the Gathering, I did not see any plates from Florida, nor did I meet anyone from Miami. I *did* encounter dozens of juggalos from Ohio, even one from Martin's Ferry, my dad's ancestral home. My mom's people hail from New Castle, a cluster of mining concerns and fireworks factories in western Pennsylvania, which also happened to be well represented at the Gathering. I myself had never been this deep into the Midwest before. As I was driving here, thumping regularly over I-71's asphalt panels, not quite equidistant from cultural capitals on both coasts, I imagined my rented red Kia a blood cell not driven but recalled to a heart.

One enterprising juggalo matched his stride to mine and asked if I wouldn't like to touch his testicles for five dollars. I hastened my search. Finally I picked a spot adjacent to the parking lot in the "Lost Ninja Clan" area. ("Ninja," I learned, is the diminutive form of "juggalo," e.g., "What up, ninja?") Having never camped before, I spent twenty minutes flexing tent poles and accidentally launching them like javelins. I heard a soft voice behind me ask, "Need any help?" I turned and met Adam.

Adam was from Detroit. He was shorter but more solidly built than me, and as pallid as the disinterred, with fine black hair and black eyes. He pronounced short *a*'s with the nasal/ pirate accent Michiganders swear they don't have. His red and black Blaze Ya Dead Homie basketball jersey exposed an homage to horror-movie serial killers tattooed over powerful arms. A full-color Leatherface swelled on his right bicep while he put my tent together, a Kool puckered throughout.

Adam was camping with his brother twenty feet away in a canvas lean-to. They both worked irregular shifts at an auto plant, which was why they could come. This was Adam's third Gathering. He was disappointed the rest of his friends couldn't make it. "That's okay, though," he said. "I've got ten thousand friends here."

I knew then and there that I should stick to Adam like a journalistic remora. But it was hot and I'm awkward, so I shook his hand, told him I'd catch up with him later, and crawled into my tent, happy to have a space that was mine alone.

I turned on the lantern end of my emergency flashlight and started jotting impressions. The heat, light, and cicadas made the experience not unlike lying inside an incandescent bulb. It wasn't long before I dozed. A "FUCK YOUR FACE!" chant roused me from half sleep; I checked the program and couldn't be sure if it was coming from the Psychopathic Records Karaoke Tournament or the wet T-shirt contest hosted by Ron Jeremy. Then I was asleep.

In 1992, my parents went into real estate and its law and began making money. Almost instantly—my mother had been in the business three weeks, my father a little longer—I was pulled out of Boys and Girls Club baseball and enrolled in a tennis academy on a private island. I received a new wardrobe of tiny white shorts, white polos, white loafers. My parents bought a conversion van, with a TV and VCR in the back, and took us on long vacations to ominously named Blue Ridge precipices, "Mount Exsanguination" or some such. There were art lessons. Nintendos, plural. A family portrait was taken and mailed with season's greetings, four months ahead of Christmas.

We were at our first Dolphins game, a preseason game, marveling at the champagne and chicken fingers in the luxury suite, when one of the many TVs cut in with news that Hurricane Andrew had made an unanticipated ninety-degree turn to the west. It was going to intensify into a Category 5 storm between the Bahamas and Miami.

Police cruisers rolled through our neighborhood and ordered evacuation as Biscayne Bay crawled over the seawall. Except for what fit into duffels, we each wrapped our favorite belongings in a heavy-duty garbage bag that was left on top of our beds. They're eerie even in memory, polypropylene sarcophagi. We piled into our van with our dogs. We raced a fast and black sky inland to Papa's.

We rode out the storm in my grandfather's bathroom, the safest part of his cinder-block house. We took turns standing on the lip of the filled bathtub to look between the slats in the boarded-up window. First came a five-hour block of destruction, after which my family, along with the rest of the city, went outside to tour the damage. Miami was leveled, cast yellow. It seemed to quaver inside of the eye's half hour of anxious peace. I was seven years old, desperate to run from building to building and sample the damage. I felt a kind of fluorescent joy. The liberation of disaster. Then came five more hours of bookending storm. My dad looked ill, haunted, like the ghouls in *Evil Dead*. He kept sweating and making jokes about losing everything in the drink. When it ended, my parents drove me and my sisters straight to the airport.

My mother had called in a favor from her extended family in New Castle. My sisters and I were going to live there for a while. Before we boarded that plane to Pittsburgh, we had no idea we had cousins. They were the family my late grandmother left when she and Papa moved to Miami after World War II. Papa had heard there were jobs there for fishermen, which he was not—but anything was better than a coal mine.

My sisters and I stayed in the drafty empty nest of my great aunt, a fierce nonna recently widowed of her long-haul-driving husband. She was the cook at the bar-and-grill our cousins collectively owned and operated. They all pitied us for having fallen to them from a higher station. They went out of their way to treat us as they thought we were accustomed—they bought me a Game Boy, a New York Yankees hat, and Michael Jackson tapes. September in Pennsylvania got too cold for the clothes I'd brought, so they took me to the consignment shop and sprung for a Teenage Mutant Ninja Turtles sweatshirt. On it, Raphael challenged any and all to c'mon, try it! I asked my cousins how that first word read, and they said it was "see-mon."

It wasn't until we came home to South Florida that I understood our home had been destroyed. Twelve feet of storm surge had washed over it. Only half of what remained was habitable. When school started back up, the district mandated that my sisters and I be taken out of class once a week and put in a support group, where we colored in pictures of newer, better homes. For Christmas we covered the water damage with gift wrap. My dad was jobless within the year.

We rebuilt our house with insurance money, sort of, and remained there for decades, leaks, mold, and zoning codes be damned. We never lived as high as before the hurricane or as low as immediately after it. When I got back from the Gathering, I learned that my parents had closed on a deal to sell the house to the neighbors. Then they put their stuff in the van and lit off for California. The neighbors demolished the house posthaste.

I was awake and jackknifed in my tent after a juggalo hollered "WHOOP, WHOOP!" right outside it. Those in the vicinity returned the call, and it redoubled on the trails, an aural telegraph relaying the A-OK. Security stayed near the front entrance; juggalos were very much in charge here. Adam and his brother were gone. I'd slept for five hours, and now it was early evening. The bigger acts were beginning their sets, and everyone was making their way to the main stage.

The setting sun made candy floss out of the clouds. A kid leaned against a tree and faced the procession with this sign: NEED COKE? SHOW ME YOUR OPEN BUTT CRACK, GIRLS. The helicopter had not stopped—nor would it stop—buzzing 'Namishly overhead.

I paused at a carny food booth to buy a cheesesteak. I took my sandwich to a large wooden pallet to sit and eat, but I was shooed by a child huckster who was using it as a stage. "What up, fam. Help a juggalo get home. Three dollars for one kick, five dollars for two." He wore a red jumpsuit and had braids like dead coral. On the back of his jumpsuit was the Hatchetman, Psychopathic Records' logo and Kokopelli. The Hatchetman is a cartoon profile of a guy with a big head, the aforementioned braids, and a goatee, who's running with a hatchet in one hand. Over the course of four days, I saw the Hatchetman stitched onto shirts, pants, cheer shorts, bikini tops, beanies, caps, and shoes; I saw it shaved into heads and chests; and I saw it tattooed on so many pounds of lacquered flesh—on arms, shoulders, and forearms, over the avian bones on the backs of hands, across necks and asses, in the lee of breasts, on calves, clavicles, and feet.

A topless woman wrapped in the Canadian flag walked up next to me to watch, her boyfriend behind her. She noticed the VIP signboard around my neck.

"What makes you so special?" She was ghost-colored, but her eyes were blue to the point of looking colorized.

I stammered something about maybe trying to write about the Gathering. Then I asked if they'd met any other international juggalos.

"Fuck yeah we have," the boyfriend said. He was bullish, his head shaved. "Finns, Australians, English, Japanese." He was from Windsor, Ontario, right across the border from Detroit. He'd been waiting ten years to go to a Gathering. He wanted to know: "You going to shit all over us like every other newspaper?"

"They want to shut us down," the woman added. "If this was political, they'd shut us down."

Her boyfriend leaned in: "Look, dude, there've always been juggalos. It's just, before ICP, nobody gave us a name. We were just walking around in Bumfuck by ourselves, you know? But get us all together? Tens of thousands of us? And everybody wants to shut us down." At this I nodded, but I didn't know who "everybody" was; overall, the Gathering seemed more ignored than persecuted. "Just tell everybody the truth, ninja," the boyfriend said. "Tell them what we're like. Maybe when they read it, they'll be, like, 'That's me, that's where I belong.'"

A man working a barrel grill paid his three dollars and had his kick. The kid didn't even need to catch his breath before reprising his spiel. "Man, I was a punter in high school," the griller said, shaking his head. "I heard them shits pop."

The valley that held the main stage and carnival was filled with juggalos. After sunset, the only light came from the stage and the winking bulbs of the Octopus, the Swinger, and the Hustler. I lingered in the light of the rides, scribbling notes and drinking the Nattys I'd brought. Several worse-than-mediocre acts came and went from the stage, and the juggalos chanted "FAM-I-LY" at the ones they liked.

I felt it necessary to get more than a little buzzed that night. The nigh-illegible notes I took in the rides' glow became suffused with a false and beery insight. After one of the cars in the Hustler rained solid waste upon me, I wrote, "In another time, these people *still* wouldn't have belonged to unions, or the Elks." When a group of teens who hid their faces with bandannas passed me by, I wrote, for reasons that remain inscrutable, "Ohio is SHAPED LIKE AN ANCHOR!!" and underlined it hard enough to tear the page.

I also wrote that juggalos seem far more comfortable around black people than your average middle American, and I stand by that. There were a handful of black dudes at the Gathering who weren't performers, and their interactions with juggalos were some of the most natural black-white interactions I've ever observed. It was just guys talking to one another.

By the time Naughty by Nature took the stage, I was good and drunk. They kept spouting malapropisms like "We're glad to be at the juggalo!" and "Much love to the ICP posse!" As with the rest of the non-juggalo rappers performing at the Gathering—including Tone Loc, Warren G, Rob Base, Slick Rick, and Coolio—they were clearly in it for the money. All I wanted was to hear "Hip Hop Hooray," but they kept demanding that I and everyone else chant "WHITE BOYS!" first. Meaning Naughty by Nature misunderstood their audience. They saw the crowd as another mass of white boys, same as at every other gig they'd played over the past two decades, and they betrayed a little passive-aggressive weariness. The juggalos around me seemed mostly confused. Their collective, grumbled response could be summed up as: "These guys don't understand that we're just like they are, or like they used to be, before they made money."

I was a white, middle-class teenager, but where I'm from I was the exception. My Miami high school was five times the size of the average Florida school and 80 percent Hispanic, 10 percent black, 10 percent other. Most of the student body qualified for free or reduced-cost lunch. My friends were Cuban, Nicaraguan, Haitian, Brazilian, Panamanian, Colombian, Bahamian, Mexican. Few of their families could be considered solidly middle class. They were working-class immigrants, born overseas or else first-generation American.

Assimilation is a fascinating thing to watch happen. The

metaphor of the melting pot is pretty spot-on. Over time, immigrants' original cultures are rendered, and they take on the essence of ours. That's what stewing does—it takes disparate ingredients and imbues them with a single general flavor. In Miami, most people I knew assimilated. They put on polo shirts and said "dude" and drove circles around malls on weekends. They affected middle-class white adolescence, with quite a few cultural tics. (For instance, their Super Bowl parties included *croquetas* and boner grinding.) As an American, you have to believe that's something everyone strives for, becoming the "we." You feel good seeing it. You're a little affronted if someone doesn't strive for that inclusion.

In my high school, the kids who assimilated had a derisive term for those who didn't: *ref.* Short for *refugee.* Fashion could be reffy, as could hair, mannerism, inflection, you name it. The assimilated kids picked on refs, who were considerably poorer. They screamed "INS!" and waved lit matches around refs' oiled hair. The refs never protested. They shoaled along walls and stared straight ahead, always maintaining the same imperturbable expression.

Me, everyone mostly ignored. Sometimes I got pushed into the hydrangea bushes and called white boy. Sometimes Latinas feigned interest in me while their unseen *novios* busted guts behind lockers. But, foremost, I was an anomaly. And, at the risk of sounding ludicrous, I never felt white, except by default. White America was very far away. It was a nation my parents expatriated from; like my Cuban friends, I figured that one day I'd get to visit my homeland. The glimpses I caught on TV or in movies were bewildering. Ski teams? Blond cheerleaders? Battles of the bands? We had a hip-hop showcase, with the final coming down to a Hot Boyz clone vs. a Dead Prez ripoff. Our school's homepage looped Trick Daddy's "Let's Go." Our senior class song was "Tipsy" by that one-hit wonder J-Kwon.

· · ·

In the night I was roused by three juggalos attempting to enter my tent. I struggled to hold the zippers together, hissing "Go away!" until it became an incantation. "The fuck is up with this ninja?" said one of them. "We just want to pass out, ninja," said another. Sometime later I woke up needing badly to pee. The tent's zippers, broken now, wouldn't budge. I guzzled a bottle of water and used it as a receptacle; this I did every hour on the hour for three hours. I missed Coolio's 4:30 a.m. set but could hear it anyway. The juggalos finally came to rest at dawn. The cacophony they made—burps, coughs, hacks, pukes—sounded like a bodily orchestra tuning up. A sleepy "WHOOP, WHOOP!" followed someone's long brown note.

After tearing a hole in and birthing myself from the tent, I went on an early-morning circuit of the grounds. The nearest port-o-potty had been blown up in the night. RVs that also served as mobile tattoo parlors were opening their doors at 7:30. The treetops in the distance made a rampart against the sky.

I stopped at the Spazmatic Energy Sauce pavilion to mix a tube of coffee crystals into a bottle of water. Juggalos in various stages of undress slumped everywhere over everything. A young mother led her son to the other end of my picnic table. He sat down to breakfast on an elephant ear and grape Faygo. His mother pulled the tab on a can of beef barley soup. She rubbed an eye with the heel of one hand and sipped from the can with the other. Hanging from her neck was a homemade advert scrawled on torn cardboard that read $2 FOR BIG ASS TIT-TIES, $1 IF YOUR A DOWN ASS NINJA. She lit a menthol and took a swig from her son's Faygo.

The mother was in a bikini top and her son was shirtless, a yang of black paint smeared on one side of his face. They were probably a combined thirty years old, yet stretch marks mottled their bodies. Fat dangled in dermal saddlebags as empty as the calories that made them. Again, I bring this up not because I'm body-snarking, but because I've only ever seen these physiques in places—the Bronx; Liberty City, Florida; New Castle—where dinner comes from either Burger King or the convenience store.

The son razzed me with a tongue full of violet pulp. I smiled at him. Then he "WHOOP, WHOOP!"ed and Pollock'ed his remaining Faygo all over me.

Whether my open notebook had triggered some kind of antischolastic mania in the child, I'll never know. But he managed to soak it so thoroughly that only days later, after several hours under a blow-dryer in a Washington, Pennsylvania, motel room, could the notebook be opened again.

The rest of this essay's grist was scribbled in cryptic shorthand on folded paper towels in a goddamned hurry.

I went to the Boondox, Insane Clown Posse, Anybody Killa, and Blaze Ya Dead Homie seminars. "Seminar" is the official name for these sessions, but it's maybe the wrong term. They're more like shareholder meetings. The artists stood on a dais and explained themselves to hundreds of juggalos gathered under a tent, sweltering in hay dust and pot smoke. Boondox set the tone, saying, "We wouldn't be shit without you." Audience participation stretched for hours; comments ranged from "When are you coming to my town?" to "Can I have a hug?" to "You don't even know the names of your own songs, you cock," to "I'm proud of the way your attitude has improved." Juggalos challenged artists to chugging competitions, and beat them. Glass pipes of innumerable colors and fungal shapes were passed from the audience to the stage. Someone fired Roman candles into the tent's folds, an exceptionally bad idea. In front of me among the crowd at the back of the tent, two men explained to a third how they had just hitchhiked their way back from the Hardin County jail. A range-finding water balloon popped in the dirt a few feet behind me. Violent J of ICP summed up my predicament: "You could have a camera crew, or documentary people running around; you could take pictures, interview ninjas; but you can't possibly know what it's really like to be part of this family unless you're a part of this. That's like . . . that's like . . . hearing about love, and actually being in love. Those are two different ma'fucking things, right? Well this is love, right here. This is real love amongst each other in this bitch." As he spoke this, some juggalos with a trebuchet on a distant hillside pegged me right in my face with a Faygo-filled balloon.

I had hoped to find Adam at the campsite around lunchtime. Maybe have a few brats, laughs. No sign of Adam. Ate a few chocolate Luna bars, soft and fecal-looking in the heat. Immediately regretted it.

There was one ATM on the premises. It might've been the only ATM in Cave-In-Rock. It was the plastic, stand-alone kind you get flaccid bills out of at bodegas and strip clubs. I saw no one else use it. It was its own little island in a glade that included the Psychopathic Records merch tent. The usage fee was five dollars.

For twelve hours every day, the merch tent thronged with juggalos. I watched them buy T-shirts and CDs, but also caps, cowboy hats, ski masks, hoodies, basketball, football, baseball, and hockey jerseys, tongue studs, comics, posters, wallets, belt buckles, fingerless gloves, flip-flops, shorts, and dresses, all in every conceivable size and color. Except for PROPERTY OF PSY-CHOPATHIC RECORDS onesies; those were available in black only.

I wondered, How is the merch tent doing such a brisk business without anyone having to use the ATM?

The answer is that the Gathering of the Juggalos is a free market in every sense. Aside from Drug Bridge—which even the security guards called Drug Bridge—juggalo wares were on sale anyplace you looked. RVs doubled as tattoo parlors and greasy spoons. Cardboard signs affixed to tents advertised kush, chronic, and 'dro. I still don't know what ketamine is, but I said it out loud once and was pitched to lickety-split. Reese's Cups, fan fiction, electronic cigarettes, oil paintings. I saw gasoline bartered for acid tabs. The juggalos I spoke with believed that making money this way was preferable to having a real job, was the *American dream*, basically, despite the fact that they lived demonstrably worse lives than people with real jobs. Still, one juggalo told me, "Dog, I came here broke and hustled a thousand dollars."

The second evening, I locked myself out of my rental car. I asked the first person I saw if he had a slim jim. He did, and fifteen seconds and thirty-five dollars later, I was back to getting waters out of my trunk. As I headed to see Warren G, a guy driving roughshod in a golf cart spotted me and pulled a U-ey. His handpainted sign read TAXI RIDES $2. "Hey, my man!" the guy said, pointing to my VIP pass. "Where'd you get that?" I explained that I e-mailed ahead of time and made arrangements with Sandy, the disappeared PR agent, and that actually the VIP pass entitled one only to free golf-cart rides on the first day of the Gathering. "Yeah, I don't care about all that," he said. "I'm riding in this golf cart, you know what I'm saying? Which I stole, you know what I'm saying? And they see that shit around my neck? Dog, I could get in anywhere!" Off in the distance, Warren G was launching into "I Want It All." "Dog, I'll make it worth your while. Money . . . or, you know, drugs." I declined.

When I reached the main stage, I took a water out of my

book bag. A horrifically sunburned albino limped up to me, squinting, and asked, "How much?" I didn't know how to explain that I wasn't selling my waters. But he was in a bad way, so I charged a dollar. The bottle was still hot from the trunk, you see.

I took off my VIP pass once, to blend in, maybe get the juggalos to open up. Within three minutes, security guards materialized, and they threatened to take me to "juggalo jail." Standard admission was $150, and juggalos were sneaking in, they told me. Where was my wristband, or my commemorative sheriff's badge celebrating the release of "Big Money Rustlas," Psychopathic's Western homage? I stammered and jangled my VIP lanyard. Then they all bought balloons filled with nitrous oxide from a guy.

The nights at the Gathering were black as space. If you didn't have a flashlight to sweep trails with, you were bound to twist an ankle. On the plus side, I could plop down with the burnouts and scrawl blind notes without anyone noticing.

That second night, a carny stabbed another carny in the stomach, and Tila Tequila was pelted with debris until she bled, but I was elsewhere, watching Tom Green perform in the seminar tent. (Prior to his set, two juggalos in the audience fistfought for half a minute before onlookers chanted "FAM-I-LY! FAM-I-LY!" The fighters stopped and slinked away, shamed.)

I say "perform." Tom Green bounded onstage and got belted with a hot dog. He was then offered two separate bong hits, one of which he accepted; the chant was "TOM SMOKES GREEN!" Any joke that required a setup was interrupted. Someone shouted something about Drew Barrymore that seemed to hurt him. A juggalette to my left started to laugh at a joke, paused to vomit, and resumed laughing. Tom tried to do a bit about technological dehumanization, with gags about text messages and porn, but he was chanted down. It was very uncomfortable in there. More things were thrown. Juggalos had power over a famous person and they knew it. Eventually, Tom Green was performing like a jester, quick to start one joke only to abandon it for another, hoping both to please and not get murdered.

He ended with a monologue about how everyone on Twitter had begged him not to come, but that since his post-cancer philosophy was carpe diem, he wanted not only to come but to prove everyone wrong about juggalos. This was answered with raucous "WHOOP WHOOP!"s.

I heard that, later, he tried to save Tila Tequila from her bombardment by jumping onstage to draw juggalo fire—to no avail.

After sleeping for maybe two hours, I got up on the third day and went to see the actual Cave-In-Rock. It's a fifty-five-foot-wide, hundred-foot-deep cave scoured into a cliffside by the Ohio River. For more than two hundred years pirates, counterfeiters, horse thieves, and murderers used it as a natural refuge and ambush. The river floods it from time to time, which is why it's so cool and loamy inside, smelling of equal parts fecundity and decay.

I was reading the teen inscriptions (VINCE DID ALLIE X RIGHT HERE), not finding any that were juggalo-related, when a mother and her two daughters entered the cave. The mother, who spoke with a deep Midwest twang, said she lived forty-five minutes away but had never brought her girls here. We're liable to do that, she said—spend our lives missing the beautiful things right in front of us. She had the blue eyes and curdled face of a 4-H beauty queen gone to seed.

I fibbed and said I hadn't heard of the Gathering but was passing through on my way home from a friend's. She offered to pray with me right then and there. "Right here and right now to know you are saved," was how she put it. "This wasn't a coincidence. You and me here today. Don't write it off as one." My nods were bogus, like a drinking bird's. Behind her on the Ohio the *Shawnee Queen* puttered by, and some old folks waved. She said she was sorry to say it, but I could die just as easily as her sister did at seventeen. Wherever I was going to, I could just die. "You will stand before Jesus Christ. You will." She squeezed her girls' hands, and they said, "You will be judged by our Lord and Savior." The woman asked me to consider living a life like hers, said she'd leave a CD for me on my rental car's windshield. Then she left.

My clothes were geologic with overlapping sweat rings. I smelled like trench foot. The shower trailer at the Gathering was out of the question. I took off my boots and jumped into the Ohio River. I promised the woman I'd listen to her CD, but I don't know what I did with it.

On the third night of the Gathering I finally found a perk associated with the VIP badge: access to the handicapped persons' viewing platform. I stood behind paraplegic juggalos, juggalos on crutches, a little-ette (his term) with a prosthetic leg signed by the entire Psychopathic roster, a blind juggalo, juggalos suffering from various twists and sprains. One woman tore her meniscus during Brotha Lynch Hung but joined us on the platform rather than go to the infirmary; she refused to miss Blaze Ya Dead Homie's set. Her face, and the faces of her husband and two children, were painted in the style of ICP's Shaggy 2 Dope.

The handicapped used the height advantage to rain Faygo on those below. I used it to watch the crowd in the minutes before the sun set. Every third face was painted. Juggalos flew homemade banners announcing their area codes. They did drugs, they moshed, they diced the air with their hands while rapping along to Axe Murder Boyz, two Colorado brothers signed to Psychopathic's sublabel, Hatchet House. Amid the thousands was someone waving a used car lot–size American flag with the Hatchetman sewn over the stars.

The good liberal definition of the underclass is something like: black and brown, struggling but persisting, systematically disadvantaged but dignified, living for the dream of becoming We. Americans don't have a hard time explaining white poverty because Americans rarely try to, even though most poor people in this country are white. If you're white in this country, it's taken for granted that you're part of We.

Not all juggalos are poor. Many bristle at the accusation. But a lot, maybe most, are. In the last decade, the Midwest experienced the largest upswing in poverty in the United States. A third of the country's poor now live in suburban Middle America. Still, you'll never hear a juggalo use the term "white trash."

It's an old term, "white trash," older than the United States of America itself. Its roots lie in the seventeenth century, when "lubbers" and "crackers," these formerly indentured and escaped white servants, formed their own communities on the outskirts of the Chesapeake tidewater region. These whites flouted the colonists' nascent cultural mold, disrespected their ideas of property, color, and labor. The mass of men thought them boondock curios, except during political and economic crises, when they considered them criminal savages.

"White trash" nowadays is a contemptuous term. It implies that one had all the privileges of whiteness but squandered them; one's poverty is one's own fault. It's a shocking term, because it suggests that even without unions and factories, class in America is real, and it cuts across racial lines. But mostly it's a useful term, because it has no set definition. It's protean. It's for when the majority of white people want to delineate what they are by saying, "What we are *not* is them."

Juggalos say anyone's free to become a juggalo, but I don't know about that. I think it's more like: they weren't born into the respectable middle class and didn't see a path that led there, so they said fuck it. They tattooed the Hatchetman on their necks and allied themselves with a fate they couldn't escape. They would be stigmatized for this white poverty, this woeful inability to move and change, to be free radicals, so why not embrace it, make it known permanently and up front? You can be a juggalo, or you can be white trash—the first term is yours, the second is somebody else's.

One juggalo in particular caught my attention right before it got dark. Onstage, the Axe Murder Boyz were closing out their set, rapping the coda to their modest hit "Body in a Hole": "And it ain't no friends, and it ain't no girls cuz I'm by myself, and I got this hole in my backyard / I've been digging it for a year / I can't cope with my own fear / Voice I hear has all control, so / I beat you in the head with a hammer and leave it stuck in your skull then I put your body in a hole."

The juggalo was threading his way laterally through the back of the crowd like an unraveling hem. He was decked out in Axe Murder Boyz merch, and he carried with him a milk crate brimming with plastic 1.5-liter bottles. The bottles were uncapped and filled with gray water. Periodically he set the crate down, grabbed a bottle, and chucked it skyward as hard as he could. A liter and a half of wastewater weighs 3.3 pounds. Some of that streamed off in flight, but not much. Fellow juggalos in the front were packed too tightly for any of the bottles to miss. If they weren't knocked to the ground, the victims reacted the same way: First, they took a few moments to allow their eyeballs to recenter. And to consider what had just happened. Then they looked around for the cause of the pain. Finding no evidence, they picked up the leaking bottle and hurled it in a cardinal direction.

The kid in the AMB gear skipped close enough to the platform that I could hear him yelling "FUCK THE FRONT! FUCK THE FRONT!" as his bottles netted the air. The Axe Murder Boyz closed their set by shrieking, "Fuck the whole world except the motherfucking juggalo family!"

I was disappointed with myself for having missed both nights of Flashlight Wrestling, and this despite the program's adjuration to "FUCK YO SLEEP grab a six pack a bag of that fluffy green a flash light and join us ringside." But I was ready for BloodyMania 4, the biggest event of the Juggalo Championship Wrestling circuit.

I showed up early, a few minutes before 1:00 a.m., yet the three sets of bleachers were already full. When I sat down on the grass, I was quite surprised to find I was next to Adam and his massive twin brother.

"Adam!" I said. "Where've you been all week?"

"You are so uncomfortable, ninja," he said. The flood lamps were chaffed with bugs, so light flurried about his face like TV static.

"Dog, we know you're uncomfortable." He didn't look at me directly; his eyes were strabismic. He was probably quite high. He had a sweating phalanx of beers on the dead grass in front of him. "We seen you walking around all the time, never sitting down. 'The Orbiter' is what we call you."

"It's because I'm writing about this. I'm going to write the good juggalo story, give you dudes a fair shake." I pulled out my wad of etched Brawnys. "I want you to help me. Tell me, will you ever stop being a juggalo, or is it like the mafia? How come when you guys start listening to Psychopathic, you stop listening to everything else?" A bit of a gulp and then, "Why does everyone hate you?"

"Nah, man, I'm not going to speak for us. I'm not going to be no spokesperson. There are so many juggalos, and, like, you don't know me."

The Weedman and Officer Colt Cabana entered the ring. Officer Cabana was the heel, so he took it to the Weedman in the early going.

"Do me a solid, dude. No juggalos will talk to me because I'm not a juggalo." Officer Cabana was using his baton on the Weedman whenever the referee's back was turned. The crowd demanded redress.

"Bet it's not that they don't like you, but cuz of this," Adam said, flicking the enormous VIP pass around my neck.

Contrapuntal chants flared up: "YOU'RE A BITCH!" and "WE WANT BLOOD!" Adam's brother keeled over onto the grass.

"It's like, we'll never read what you write about us. You can write whatever you want about us, and everyone's going to believe it. What difference does it make what I say? You've got the power. Plus, I give no shits."

In the bleachers, juggalos stood and gestured emphatically at Officer Cabana. Each painted face sang its own curse. None was comprehensible, but all together the juggalos looked like a frontlit audience of nattering holy fools.

Officer Cabana climbed the top rope and told the crowd, "I am the law!" Juggalos hailed him with whatever was at hand. Full beers, chicken wings. A dead fish landed several feet short. I watched a mother take a shitty diaper off a baby and hand it to a man who spun it like a discus over the ring.

"What you should write, though," Adam went on, "is why do, like, motherfuckers in New York or whatever—how do those motherfuckers think they're better than me if, like, making fun of me is still okay with them? You know what I'm saying? It's like they think they know me, and, like, know what's best for me, is what pisses the fuck out of me. Motherfucker, not everyone wants to be you, you know what I'm saying?"

The Weedman began his comeback when someone hustled him a joint from the bleachers. I was exhausted.

"You know, I always wanted to be a professional wrestler," Adam said.

A juggalo on a bicycle shadowed me on the ten-minute walk back to my tent. Out here, the night sky was unlidded. The moon seemed Zambonied. Did you know our moon is the only one in this solar system to have been created out of its captor planet? It's true. Billions of years ago, something the size of Mars slammed into proto-Earth and kicked up detritus that conglomerated into the moon. Much of the detritus came from that Mars-size projectile, but the moon and the earth are more alike molecularly than they are different. It's that the moon is this ashen doppelganger. They say it smells like spent gunpowder.

Before I turned off the path, the juggalo on the bicycle kicked me in my ass and said, "Fuck off!"

That third night a huge midwestern thunderstorm finally rolled in and inveighed. I had to sprawl like a starfish to keep my tent on the ground. Purple lightning lit the inside of it like thoughts in a head. Outside, three guys from Rochester sat around a sheltered fire and talked about the juggalette they had slept with in succession. "I fucked the shit out of that bitch," went one.

"Listen to me, I sound like a proud dad, but that preteen pussy was doing some very fucking adult shit," went another. I don't think I can convey how terrified I was of them seeing the coal of my cupped flashlight as I transcribed their conversation. I consider myself a connoisseur of low-pressure systems, and I was impressed with this storm. Serious midwestern thunder unfurls. It made me think of dead fists blooming.

At dawn I pulled up my stakes in the rain. The low moon was still visible. I would miss the Insane Clown Posse concert that caps off every Gathering. On my way out of the grounds, four juggalo hitchhikers ran into the path of my rental car. I did not slow down, and they jumped out of my way.

The teenage girl behind the counter at the lone two-pump station in Cave-In-Rock had angled a boom box so that it blasted Taylor Swift at the door. I lurched in, sopping and rank, my legs sheathed in mud. She was all freckles and crinkled church dress. After so many juggalos, I thought she was a seraph.

"The pump won't stop, so be honest," she said. "Are you part of that thing? Are you honest?"

I told her I was leaving it.

"We don't like those people," she said. "Those people aren't like us here."

Ten minutes after deplaning, I had two voice mails from Dad:

"*Kent, goddamnit, it's your father. The degree of difficulty here is quite large. Call me back.*"

"*Kent, Jesus,* upstairs. *Are you* upstairs? *The plan was always* upstairs, *departures level. Oh Christ, the meter maid.*"

Every time I visit, I have hopes that my soufflé of good humor will stand for longer than it takes to drag a suitcase to the curb. And, every time, that soufflé immediately, flatulently collapses.

He didn't bring the Taurus to a stop. "Who're you sexting?" he asked as I jogged alongside the car, my eyes on his supplementary messages. "Or are you looking up porn already?" I slid in, reached across the gearshift, slapped the top of his head, hugged the man.

"Here, take this." He handed me a 24-ounce Coors Light in my old insulated lunch box. "This is a pain in the ass for *some* people, you know."

On the way back, he nattered incessantly. Exasperatingly. Misremembered local history and recent commercials he's liked and Mom's newest efforts in her campaign to disenfranchise him, often shoehorned into the same sentence. I honestly wonder sometimes if he needs to talk like sharks need to swim.

"San Francisco, man. The city that meant the end of America. Where else would an old sailor want to live?" He turned to look out the driver's-side window. He pointed toward his former naval base with one hand and his former favorite bar with the other. "Back before it was pink shirts drinking claret, you understand." I reached for the unattended wheel but was batted away. "Beer for a dime, mixed drinks for a quarter.

"Which reminds me—I want you to get that scholarship shit out of your Ryan article," he said. "I didn't have a scholarship at Vanderbilt, okay? I don't want people thinking 'stolen valor.' My two years wound up before I saw combat, so I re-upped and went to fight *my* war of *my own* volition.

"I know it's your job to be a nibshit—but you have this habit of identifying me in stories and then misreporting the truth." I pitter-pattered thumbs against my phone to get this down. He said, "Stop it with your nibshit machine. This is important."

Lately I've gotten the sense that he is as horrified by the course of my maturation as I am. Maybe not *horrified*. But I suppose he and I both were wrong to think that this would shake out any other way.

Because this seems to me inborn. An inherited distemper. At first—seven years ago? ten?—I'd wake up feeling a few degrees foreign to myself. This I ascribed to hangovers; I choked down a BC Powder and walked it off. But now, I look in the mirror and see the transformation completing itself, to my shock and awe, à la *Teen Wolf*. Now, I am become Dad, destroyer of beers.

"What're you . . . ah . . . working on in your spare time these days?" he asked some moments later, pausing like a hostage negotiator waiting for his men to get in position. "Something other, actual people might be interested in?"

I waggled the tab from my Coors, folded it into a microshank, and stabbed it into the top of the can, to smooth and enlarge the pulls I was taking. "Eh," I said. "Fuck 'em."

That right there's the problem. This insoluble callousness—this gall—at my core. An agglutinated little pebble of ambivalence, fatalism, correctional laughter, obstinacy—the dregs of what I figure normal people discharge over time, and with relative ease. A psychic kidney stone.

All of us Russells behave like we're in the throes of passing it. But the relief of passing it is inseparable from the long, horrific, painkiller-necessitating struggle of passing it. This kidney stone is also sometimes referred to as Life.

I am so spiteful. I see recollective Sunday brunches among friends, and I want to walk up to them and ask, *You're all best buds? Really? You're all ready and willing to bear the weight of love's deep and diffuse obligations? Oh, word? It's not just that you've self-selected from this sinking ship the people most amenable to your personal brand of resentment and narcissism—your mimetic desire—to float on in a life raft together over bitter water for at least as long as supplies last?* Then I chokeslam myself through their table.

I am so purposefully divisive. Especially in my ill-fated relationships with the similarly self-sabotaging people I gravitate toward. A dog barks loudest at its own reflection, as they say. Do they say that? They should.

My theory has been: human beings are not meant to go hand-in-hand the whole stretch of the way. Or even part of the way. Always to have sympathy, always to be accompanied, always to be understood—that sounds fucking *intolerable*.

My praxis has been: carry around a soda can poured with rotgut.

I cannot help but chirp, smirk, and nod—and then relish the blow when it comes. This way, other people are never near enough, nor real enough, to affect me. This way, it's just me and my refusal. Which, like a mouthful of blood, or grain alcohol, has a taste I've come to acquire.

"What you do . . . it's like birthdays," Dad offered. "You know how I feel about birthdays. Birthdays and writing about your family—these things should only be celebrated when the person involved is a child, or retarded."

I used to smile at the stories he'd tell about preschool aides approaching at parent-teacher day. *We're afraid he's poorly socialized*, they'd admit. *He only plays at playtime when we threaten him.* Which was true. I liked to huddle inside a giant ceramic planter that was shaped like a teacup.

Dad would wave away the aides. He'd pat my head, pick me up, put me on his shoulder, and off we'd go.

"That's what I'm worried about. You guys," he said as our car crossed into Marin County. "Don't get me wrong—young people have always been thieves, dissemblers, and opportunists. But your generation? You guys seem . . . egregious."

I guffawed, a little too loudly. Then, as one, we declaimed this new sharing economy. Where agreeableness is popularity, and popularity value. Where well-being, both financial and emotional, depends on the esteem of others. On the traffic driven by their Facebook posts and retweets; on their appraisal of my like- and dispensability.

On the opinions of others, Dad gave his own: "They're dumbshits."

On the interest of others: "They're nibshits."

The Russell character being both solace and disease of isolation, you understand.

But as soon as we walked into his and Mom's rented one-bedroom, I found myself caught again in the push/pull of the old relationship. I was trapped by parental gravitation. I was tracing my old trajectory as a filial satellite. Breaking free was hard if not impossible. Escape velocity: high.

For instance, not a moment after dumping my dirty clothes into the hamper, I could hear Dad singing out in falsetto, "O precious baby boy! Your sandwich awaits!"

When I walked to the kitchen counter, he was up to his third knuckle in the mayo jar.

"My man, I'm dying," he said.

"The hell you are. Gonna bury us all."

"Nope. This is it. This is the end." His voice was trebled with congestion. He says he's been phlegm-glutted for over a month now; he's convinced Mom brought back some riverine pestilence from a rafting trip proposed by her brother that he refused to go on.

Mom had by that time retreated to bed, beat as she was from another eighteen-hour day spent ironing out contractual real-estate minutiae. It's been this way since Hurricane Andrew. Mom would come home late; I'd bury my face in her shoulder pad, ask, "How was work, Ma?" She'd answer, "Work was work." Then she'd spend the rest of her night working at the kitchen table, winning that bread. Weekends were for cleaning and teaching Sunday school.

"It's all over but the buryin'," Dad said. He removed himself from the jar and finger painted the crust of a ham sandwich. "Sweet death, come take me soon." He handed it to me wrapped in a paper towel. "Me and all the other mayonnaise-loving, Ernest-Tubb-listening-to whiteys out there. Our time is done-zo."

I've been told that right before my delivery date, Mom was bumped from the room she'd reserved at Jackson Memorial Hospital. A boatload of pregnant Haitians had just landed. Emergency cases. They'd risked their lives crossing the Florida Strait in tubs so they could see their babies born in Miami. And born they were, a great many of them, all at once. This was a huge boon, it turned out, because were it not for the refugee fruitful, and had my mother had me when she'd planned to, I would've split her uterus. She and I both would've died en route to the hospital.

Before me, she'd miscarried twice. Imperious men who strode about converting their will into law, I think they would've been. Bizarro-me's, with a gift for languages, and thick cocks. They were never more than clouds, though; weather on a screen. They got washed from drain to sewer stem to deep blue sea.

I, however, was delivered early via emergency cesarean. December 19, though she wanted my birthday nearer JC's.

Mom was unconscious for the whole thing, of course. When Dad tried to behold my delivery, shit-housed, with an eight-cell boom box pressed over his head, blaring "Born in the U.S.A."—he was bounced.

I've also been told that on that day, I fit right into the crick of his arm. The warmth I gave off was geological, he said. A heat that made me seem some figurine shot straight from the center of the earth, hot and still pliable. He handled me as delicately as possible so as not to misshape me as I cooled.

That would become his prime directive. A native strain of the Golden Rule: I will leave you free to do what you might like to do, but I expect you'll do the same for me. Imposition being not just bad parenting—worse, it's un-American.

Ergo, I was free to do what I wanted. Which meant I did nothing. Left to my devices, I did what was most convenient and most selfish. Napped a lot, joined no clubs. Dated nobody and volunteered nothing. Didn't really read, write, care. In fact, I can so little recollect what exactly I *did* in my adolescence that I'm supremely suspicious of any dude who can.

I had a group of four friends; that much I remember. In middle and high school, we spent every weekend together. We all could smirk but not smile. We played roller hockey badly, and downloaded snuff films from early file-sharing sites. We were not nerdy. We were aloof. Bored enough for badness. We liked to get faded and do violence to matter.

Actually, that's one thing—the day Columbine happened. I can recall discussing it during eighth-grade religion class at St. Hugh. Sister Patricia was dumbfounded by Ryan. Like, jaw-dropped. She'd asked what we were feeling about the news. Ryan raised his hand and—this being when Coloradoans were still fleeing in lines like ducklings on TV—said, "Just judging from what they're saying, it's not only shotguns the shooters are using."

We knew what was coming. The "circle time," the separate, compassionate grillings. One of our group was himself something of a duster aficionado, so he got it worst. Juan liked to take milk-naked photos of himself. On these he'd doodle varicose, H. R. Giger–style dongs before distributing them. On everything else, he doodled *Waffen-SS* sig runes. He was kind of a Naziphile? Which, even now, it's like—Juan, bro, you're full-blooded Cuban. *What're you doing?*

The nuns' memories were long. They brought up the fact that when asked to name our lunch table (so it could be included in the wheel of chores), we christened ourselves after a machine pistol. They brought up the fact that in fourth grade we'd eagerly swapped paperback novelizations of the first-person shooter *Doom*, a video game that Harris and Klebold were reputed to love. (Did I remember writing a poem about the game's sequel, they asked, and then *produced the original poem*.) They tried to turn us on to books like *A Wrinkle in Time* or *The Giver*—but, lame.

Obviously, we didn't *condone* the act. We didn't condone it, and we knew it was wrong. We understood how it could *happen*, sure. But we also considered the killers pussies. For succumbing to the pressure.

Regardless, to the nuns we fit the description. Every class

has one(s) like us who does—a boy, often white, who is not quite rounding into shape but will be given the benefit of every doubt. *He'll put it all together, at some point* seems to be the consensus. There is a general love or craving in him—you can see it in his eyes—but it has not yet found its direct object. So, to protect himself, he has it manifest as hurtful apathy.

Still, this apathy is more or less benign in the grand scheme. The worst it did in me was get me suspended on prom night. Filipe and I must've been some conspicuous-ass needles in that particular haystack. (Granted, it should've been my third suspension—grounds for expulsion—but the second one had been expunged. Turned out that partaking in our same bender during a class trip to Orlando was the class president–slash–football mascot. And we had the pictures to prove it.) When my high school principal, a creeping shit-sucker if there ever was one, begrudgingly handed over my diploma a few weeks later, he smiled for the cameras while whispering in my ear, "Lay off the booze, eh, you son of a bitch."

The only one of us I ever was a wee bit scared of was Jake. Jake would order rifles online and mean his racial slurs when he said them. He went on to Jesuit high school with Ryan, but he didn't fistfight. He seemed rather to move about like a violent decision that was in the process of making itself.

Later, he became the second of the group to pay a prostitute to take his virginity. The second to enlist, too. But his blond hair and Lurch-like personage made him perfect for the honor guard. He didn't go overseas. He was one of the twenty-one guns saluting our war dead at Arlington.

I know that Juan left a trail of scag vials and bad checks and got himself locked up. Filipe took the high road and became a banker in Brazil. But I don't know what's become of Jake. We didn't keep in touch. Last I heard, he was bussing tables at a North Florida Outback Steakhouse. I worry. He wasn't lucky enough in his early life to have developed the capacity to metabolize love. I'm fairly certain that without it, he today is cold pride and latent rage wrapped up in an unfeeling vessel. A homegrown IED, waiting to go off.

I'm fairly certain of that *now*. But at the time, we were all of us blind to the elephant in the room. No one wanted to try touching it, much less describing what he felt.

Dad was mummifying the leftover ham and bread in four layers of Saran, for freshness. He swaddled clingwrap over clingwrap, the contents obscured like prey caught in silk.

I went, "There's this spider that, right before her babies are big enough to leave the nest? She lets them eat her. Just lays herself down, allows the fruit of her egg sac to skitter all over, inject digestive venom."

"Uh huh," he said, knitting hands, not looking up.

"Their development ends with her getting *eaten* from the *inside out*. You see what I'm saying?"

"That you are an assholing know-it-all."

He palmed his one long tress of hair across his head. It had been dangling past his neck, looking like a broken feather in a one-feather headdress. I was reminded then of his funerary imperatives, which have evolved suchly:

In middle school—"Look, I've been trying hard to croak on a Wednesday. I know you've never taken the garbage out in your life—but Wednesday's garbage day. When I succeed in my task, okay, just break my legs so you can fold me over and close the lid."

In high school—"When I die at this ball game, just put my shades on my face, cross my arms, and leave me be. But *after* you've made sure to get the car keys and wallet out of my pockets."

College—"Any one of you tries putting me in a home—forget about it. I'm grabbing the gun and disappearing into the swamp. Happy hunting, assholes."

And then, right on cue, he said, "It is the duty of the old to die. So, take whatever you want: pens, underwear, the TV. All I ask in exchange is that you take my ashes to Point Bonita or some shit. Just don't do like Donnie in *The Big Lebowski*. Really get me in the water."

I poised my hands above the laptop's keyboard and asked, "Right. We'll get to that bridge when we cross it. But first: What, *exactly*, is gonna be lost when you are gone, would you say?"

He turned his head and scowled down his shoulder at me. He asked, "What, *exactly*, are you typing?"

First thing next morning, I tried to watch a Louis C.K. clip the Internet was telling me to watch. "You need to build an ability to just be yourself and not be doing something," his bit goes. "That's what the phones are taking away, is the ability to just sit there. That's being a person. Because underneath everything in your life there is that thing, that empty—forever empty."

"SHHHH GODDAMNIT!" Dad said, at a volume far louder than YouTube. He looked to the ceiling and waited for the upstairs neighbors to stomp. This is his telltale conscience. Of course, no one ever stomps. Up there, they're just graceless.

Sticking to my splendor of morning has never been easy. On school days, Dad would pace up and down the hallway counting down *FIVE MINUTES!* and then *THREE MINUTES!* as Karen, Lauren, and I hustled into the plaids and loafers we'd laid out the night before. He wore dark aviators and stood cross-armed next to the idling car while we grabbed what could be carried, as though rushing from a fire. St. Hugh was less than five minutes away.

We were never late. Not once. Not even on days when tropical storms blew in and "driving" to school involved spraying heavy wakes that capsized other commuters' rubber rafts. When we pulled up to the main building, we wouldn't need to push the car doors open; yank the handle, and the wind took care of the rest. Sister Kathleen would emerge with her arms up and splayed, a touchdown of disbelief. The black flame of her coif danced on the howl as she exaggeratedly mouthed the words "RUSSELLS, GO HOME."

One time, in high school—*the* one time, and an unavoidable one at that, as Dad had to take Lauren to look at state schools—he entrusted the job to Karen, who was herself home from college. Naturally, Karen overslept by twenty minutes. She roused me by pushing me clear out of bed, in her underwear, shrieking *"FUCK, KENT, RUN!"* When Ms. Feldman failed to notice me slinking into second-period English, I was more than astounded. My faith was rocked. Negligence had exposed me to the punitive intelligence that runs the universe and . . . nothing had happened.

What did we think would happen? What did he tell us would happen? Long ago, the stress of it gave Karen an ulcer. In the endoscopic image, it looked like the planet Jupiter. I was four years old and absolutely certain that the gastroenterologist was Bob Saget. I saw Bob Saget in the face of every tall white man, as I loved not only *Full House* but also *America's Funniest Home Videos.* Every Sunday night, after church and dinner, Mom would get back to work, and the rest of us would sandbag ourselves on Dad on the couch and watch the latter show. Dad would be at his rip-roaringest then, sloshing loud laughs as father after father got whomped in the dick by his kid.

Later that morning, he was in an athletic crouch next to the television, using his crippled right pinkie to point out a blob of Yuletide-colored rain whorling over the Midwest. He got that pinky crimped irrevocably while blocking a spike during a volleyball game at a rehab facility. Game was probably just as sweatily homoerotic as the one in *Top Gun*, only with more dry heaving.

"Yeah, you wanted to be driving down there right now, right, asshole?" he asked, gesturing at Ohio.

This bullheadedness tickled me greatly. I probably wouldn't be so hard up about going there otherwise.

"Let's do it," I said. "Once the rain clears out, the heat should be gone. *Blam*—perfect."

"Aww, hell," he said. He pinched his rosy gin blossom and exhaled, effecting some kind of decompression. "All you gotta do is call up the Ohio Chamber of Commerce and have them send you a fucking videotape.

"Look, I was out of Ohio by eight years old. I went back once, when I was fourteen. Ohio in the fifties—Jesus Christ, it was so goddamned boring you just wanted to pour yourself with gasoline and light a match. I made my life elsewhere, you understand.

"In fact, I'm sort of mad at my parents for wanting to be buried there. Though now that I'm away from the swamp, I can sort of understand it. Anyone from the North does not want to be buried in South Florida. Your bones get sucked through the limestone. Completely recycled. You become a part of fountain drinks and toilet flushes. A horrible place."

He's right, of course. But I don't like non-natives talking trash. He may have moved there, lived there, been deformed by the place—but he's not *of* there. He wasn't Miami, Florida, born and raised.

Miami is America's Samarkand. It is a borderplace, a porous frontier that seems to be both seat of culture and lawless zone. Economically, it is a bright, shiny mirage. The city exists insofar as it reflects the appetites and fantasies of people arriving from the north and west. (And, to a lesser but exponentially increasing extent, those coming from south-by-southwest.) Lots of chrome curves and billowing white. Tits like tan dirigibles, and the best sunsets on the East Coast.

But there's something about Miami that's . . . at odds . . . with the rest of the nation. It's a melting pot, yes, but more than New York or L.A. it is sort of . . . uniquely fucked up. Out-of-towners can't help but alternate between pining after the place and passing judgment.

Many if not most people outside Miami misapprehend just what the city is about. They come, and implicitly they believe that because this is their equatorial getaway from where real lives are lived, the living in Miami must be simpler, less real. It's the classic tropical syllogism: the place advertises sun, leisure, and repose; you come and experience sun, leisure, and repose; therefore, the locals must know nothing, really, aside from sun, leisure, and repose.

For our part, Ryan and I tried to combat this misapprehension by driving around tourist hot spots and smash-and-grabbing whatever was on hand in rental Sebrings. But there *is* one thing tourists have gotten nearly right about Miami, and it's couched in the old jape that goes: *What's so great about Miami, other than the beaches, is it's so close to the United States!* The implication here is that Miami is this weird sovereignty in but not of America. This is true, in a way.

The chicken to that joke's egg is the stereotype of the Miami Person. The Miami Person, as far as I've gathered, is a balking, Judeo-Latin alloy of dress shoes, jeans, dress shirt half buttoned, white gold—and vacuousness, gaucheness, childishness, ill temper. The stereotype is, I think, meant to be repellent in a cautionary way. *Here's a person who is unlike your typical American*, it implies. *Here's a person—an alien—who isn't really a part of your union, and who seems fine with that.* There's some truth to this, too.

For all intents and purposes, Miami is the capital of the Island of South Florida, which runs 110 miles from West Palm Beach to Homestead. This island separates Everglades National Park from the Atlantic by as many as 20 or as few as 5 miles. The populace is a true crazy quilt. In Miami, half the people are foreign-born, and about three-quarters speak a language that isn't English. She is the sixth-poorest city in the nation, Miami, yet one out of every ten of her citizens is a millionaire. People coexist, but on mutually unintelligible planes: Cuban Miami, Haitian Miami, white, black, Nicaraguan, Colombian Miamis. The place is so spread out, and traversed only by private automobile. People can and do drop from their lives anyone with whom they choose not to associate. And since people are so strange and separate, they understand one another only in general. If they have to interact, they do so from a sort of ritualized stance. They believe each other to be their antipodes. How they define themselves is as wrapped up in this opposition as is muscle around bone.

It's been ten years since I lived in Miami, and three since I stayed more than a few days. This guilts me to no end, for though Miami is a young city with few long-standing ties, her sons are doting. To leave is considered a kind of betrayal. The vast majority of my old friends and acquaintances never did. There were a few besides me who moved out of state, but from what I heard, they came back looking ailed and grizzled; malarial, as though the place had borne something into their blood.

Which is to say: the Island of South Florida is also hermetic-feeling. Mainly because of its monsoon climate, the only one in the country. The weather patterns in South Florida are most similar to those of the Amazon, central Africa, and Southeast Asia, meaning that there are only about three weeks per calendar year when oxygen needn't be ginned out of the thick air like seeds in cotton. The rest of the time, the simmering out-of-doors might as well be the surface of some furnace planet; equatorial Venus.

In South Florida, plants grow malignant fruit, and are studded or spiked. (In my neighborhood, we'd check under the kapok tree every week for newly fallen branches, because they made excellent maces in our rock fights.) Ditches never drain, and galaxies of stinging insects float through them. So many people drown in the canals and morasses bordering roads that citizens are encouraged to drive with metal stakes in their glove boxes, to shatter windows from the inside. There are hurricanes, tornadoes, and floods, of course. Exotic snakes in car engines; weeds pushing through cement by main force. Mesozoic cockroaches that can *fly*. There, ocean-land air masses rub together like excited hands and produce quiverfuls of the country's deadliest lightning. I was once caught out on Papa's fishing skiff in one of those lightning storms. We each grabbed our ankles and aimed our asses at the heavens. If you're going to get struck by lightning, that's where you want it, right in the austral kisser. We stayed that way for only a minute, though, smelling ozone and having our hair mussed, because everything in South Florida fills its moment entirely and then vanishes.

It's the nature of the place. It's hothouse America. It's so hyperfecund. It abides nothing. As soon as a tree sprouts or a house is built, the environment conspires to bring it down. It's tropical entropy, the sped-up cycle of birth and decay.

Dissolution is key. Miami will have you believe that not only can the worst happen—it's probably marshaling itself in the Atlantic. Or else it's percolating through your walls like mold, or yawning beneath you like a sinkhole. What's dread, what's paranoia, when the ground you're standing on might fall away at any moment?

.   .   .

"Situational awareness," Dad was saying, still next to the TV, snorting and blowing to clear his nose. He caught a Rorschach blob in his left hand, pantomimed a little *olé!*

He was planning the logistics for our trip to an upcoming Oakland A's baseball game. The news so far had told him that: 1) There was someone shooting at cars on the 101; and 2) Oakland, crime-wise, was doing what Oakland does.

"Head on a goddamn swivel." He bobbled his in example. "Look at the size and shape of me—I didn't get to seventy-one by accident."

Ever since Dad quit smoking a few years ago, he's back to being stout through the middle like a capital D. His color is still that of overmilked coffee, which he pounds to get through the day. He is exactly *This Tall* → tall enough to ride rides.

He's maybe an inch or two shorter than my favorite hockey player of all time, Theo Fleury. Christ, I loved Fleury. I used to watch him on TV with a bagged loaf of raisin bread in my lap, stoking a huge new hunger, me leaning against the shuttered footrest of my father's Larson-model La-Z-Boy, the one sized expressly for short people, because if I sat on it my knees would be all up in my face. Fleury was the only All-Star who might have been of distant relation. Not only did he seem to whir through the legs of bestriding defensemen, insurgent, on his way to score goal after goal—he also brooked no shit.

Behind the play, Fleury would slash Achilles, give a nice spear along the glass. If an opponent came at him, he would pike his hockey stick and dare the challenger to come through it. When the action was whistled dead, he'd crane his neck and chirp at goons he really had no business giving the red-ass. I'd mold my mouth while watching him, try to feel out his words. In these moments, Fleury's brows would open up and away like launch silo doors. His eyes showed a horseshoe of sclera above the green irises, a crazy amount of white. And he would nod nonstop, agreeing wholeheartedly with whatever the big guy was saying—couldn't wait for it, in fact, the mutually assured destruction.

Fleury is part French, part Cree, five feet six inches tall. He spent his childhood in Russell, Manitoba, a moony snowscape of 1,500, with his alcoholic father and bedridden, depressive mother. His time he bided at the rink. "It was like I belonged somewhere for the first time," he wrote in his autobiography. "For me, it wasn't a fantasy. It's not like I dreamed of getting in the National Hockey League; I was getting ready to go into the NHL."

Fleury was sent to a nearby hockey school after neighbors and family friends raised the money. There, he met a coach who told him he had the talent to make the pros in spite of his size. Later, when Fleury was in his mid-teens, that same coach recruited him onto his junior team in Winnipeg. In junior hockey, Fleury realized, "I had to protect myself, and the best way to do that was to have people believe I was crazy. This was my competitive advantage. I didn't have size, but I was volatile. Teams found out that they could beat the shit out of me and I would not back down. I made the choice to live by the sword."

Fleury roomed with a billet family, but his coach demanded he stay overnight with him two or three times a week. These nights, Fleury would wrap himself with his blanket as tightly as possible and cry himself to sleep. "He'd wait until the middle of the night, and then he'd crawl around the room in the dark on his hands and knees," Fleury wrote. "He had the blinds duct-taped to the windows so no light could get in. It was the same every time. He would start massaging my feet and I wouldn't move, pretending to be asleep. He would try to come up higher, but with that blanket wrapped so tight, he couldn't get at me. [He] convinced me that, if not for him and his help, I would not be going to the NHL. As far as I was concerned, the reason for my whole existence was to make it to The Show. It was all I had."

When I was eight, after Fleury had recorded his second hundred-point NHL season, I sent away for a life-size poster of him. Along one edge of the poster was a rule by which you could measure your growth. My notches on it were regular if closely spaced until the period between my senior year of high school and my sophomore year of college. That's when I had growth spurts and finally crested the thing.

The reason I shot up was a mild case of Marfan's syndrome, a genetic disorder that affects connective tissue. Long story short, I retained my small-person core but wound up with taffied limbs and thin joints that waggle through all 360 degrees of motion. Also, I have an inverted breastbone—a sunken chest; you could serve salsa out of me—which means that, eventually, my aorta will weaken and dilate, and time or a hard blow might cause my heart to stop.

Accordingly, I'm trapped in that juvenile stage when one feels as though he's a tiny pilot berthed inside his gawky vessel. (*Splice the main brace! Something the topmast! Christ Jesus, proprioception!*) My shit's all out of whack. My hands never grew, so they're furtive-looking. My feet did, but they're a hindrance, dry-land flippers. I don't believe I ever relearned how to walk correctly. I lollop with my legs out in front of my hips, until my shoulders begin to slide toward the ground, whereupon I pitch my carriage forward, restarting the whole dynamic. People tell me that this gait calls to mind a lone baker trying to carry a monumentally tiered cake, or Bernie from *Weekend at Bernie's*. When I glimpse my reflection in storefronts and subway windows, I'm astonished—I'm taller than people! I can't help but continue to see from a truncated point of view.

Now, popular misconception has it that Napoleon was short. He was not. The confusion can be traced to the British press of that era, who lampooned Napoleon by depicting him as tiny in cartoons. In fact, Napoleon stood five-foot-six, a good three imperial inches taller than average back then.

Which is interesting, because in 1908 a psychoanalyst named Alfred Adler based his theory of the inferiority complex, aka the Napoleon complex, aka short-man syndrome, on his supposition that Napoleon thirsted for power and conquest and was in general the Western world's dread retributive agent all because his ass was short.

According to Adler, Napoleon was short and thus felt physically and spiritually inadequate. He compensated for this feeling of inadequacy by inventing a goal—a world where he had power, respect, *puissance*—and directing his every effort toward its realization. He was very successful in his pursuit of this goal, for a time. But, as his life (and winter campaigns) made clear, pursuit is one thing, overpursuit something else.

The Napoleon complex is not included in the American Psychiatric Association's *Diagnostic and Statistical Manual of Mental Disorders.* The book says there's no empirical evidence suggesting that shortness correlates with aggressiveness or any other behavioral anomaly. Today, psychologists consider the Napoleon complex a social stereotype, the kind of thinking that lives on through post hoc rationalizations like "He was a little ball of hate, of course he was, that poor, tiny man."

We've had one nonseasonal portrait taken, the Russells. I was fourteen, my sisters sixteen and eighteen, my parents on the windward side of middle age, Papa and Papa Lou hanging on. Last chance together and all that. We drove down to Sears in our funereal best. We ordered ourselves in front of a slate curtain. We stood there clutching one another for a minute and a half. Then the photographer, who had been shielded behind a giant plastic clown's face, addressed us through its toothless grin: "One a y'all need to step forward," she said, "because y'all the *same damn size.*" No one did. Dad and I refused to stand on phone books. Thus pictured, we looked like an intergenerational police lineup called in for a crime a classy dwarf committed.

As a clan, we are pygmoidal. This doesn't faze the women. The men, however: smallness becomes us.

Papa sometimes behaved as though the membrane separating his self from the outside world was more tightly conscribed than it ought to be. Whenever he thought someone might permeate it, he decked them, or pulled a knife. (It is for this reason that my family's business is no longer welcome at Alan's Drugs, the Hyatt Regency Miami, or the carpet samples section of Poe's Hardware.) He did not much care for my mother and uncle's abbreviated fame as the Florida State Circus's *Rolla Rolla Romanchucks!*

Papa Lou was more resigned about his stature, albeit in a strangely appealing way, as though he'd been spiritually footbound. A favorite story was how his son, my dad, once confided to him on an all-clay diamond, "I'm a little worried about my size, but I think I can become a major league baseball player." Dad *was* a great ballplayer; in most tellings of this story, he'd just teed off on future All-Star Dougie Corbett when they both were teens in Sarasota. He had the mind for the game for sure. But Papa Lou's response was "Start running as fast as you can." Then he outran his son, my father, backward, laughing in his face all the way.

Dad has in his attitude some of both my grandfathers'. Rationalizing a kerfuffle in a subterranean line at Six Flags Over Georgia, he screamed: "Guys like me, in Vietnam, they used to hold us by our ankles and dip us in the tunnels! Who else but little turds do you think gets sent in to flush people out? What do you think that does to you?" Another time, I watched him slide into a seat on a bus that was bracketed by two spectacularly fat men, saying, "In survival school, I listened to Jackson lose his shit in the solitary box next to mine. Tried to talk him down. I was comfortable, though. Could've made a goddamned nest in there."

He refuses to wear boys' sizes and so gives all new pairs of Costco slacks to my mother to hem. In crowds, he puffs his chest and fixes his face but walks too fast to be called assured. He has about him a forest-floor anticness. Not like he's harried, but like he senses he's about to be. He measures himself by the tape of a world that, he believes, looks upon him with amused contempt and pity. "You know what you're allowed to be when you're under five-foot-five?" he once asked me. "A clown, or a crazy person."

When I started inching north of five-foot-four, something about my relationship with him changed. I'd find him sizing me up with a grin and a rehydrated glint in his eyes. During small arguments, he'd remind me: "I've got reach enough to shove one up your ass, believe me." Under the basketball rim in our driveway, he'd post up on me while shit-talking my heart condition, my arms up like *Huh?*, his pickax elbows chipping away at my unsteady foundation. It was around this time that I realized I had become my family's Goliath.

In his autobiography, Theo Fleury wrote, "My anger made me dangerous. When you're raging and you have absolutely no fear, you can do a lot of damage. That quality would really become a part of who I was on the ice."

On the ice, he slew-footed and cackled. Armored in his too-big helmet and bucket shorts, he raged like a Spartan baby once left for dead, back now on the warpath. He was exceptionally good at penalty-killing, playing shorthanded—trapped in his own end, chasing the puck as it skirted the boards, the anxiety mounting, the carrot he was after just out of reach.

He was in fact so good at this kind of tweaky pursuit that I came to suspect he had a Fleury of his own. An abridged little fucker who never gives a moment's rest. Frets you, bird-dogs you, forces you to do things you didn't think yourself capable of, and do them at speed. He's exhausting. When he's not in your face, his strides are shushing right behind you. He goads you with his stick.

The big knock on Fleury was that he had a penchant for committing bewildering penalties at key junctures in games. Such was his style of play. "I had always taken retaliation penalties," he wrote, "which were usually bad for the team but necessary for my survival. I was unrelenting. If I hit a big guy and he whacked me back, hoping I'd learn my lesson, I would come back even harder. I was ferocious. I had to be . . . If I let one guy take me out without doing anything about it, the next guy would be standing in line behind him. So I made no exceptions, even when the game was on the line. I couldn't."

Fleury was what hockey people call an agitator. As agitator, his MO went: Slash an opponent once, and the opponent would shake it off or else try to sell it to the referee. Slash him again, and the opponent would slash back, antagonism begetting antagonism. Slash him and his teammates at every turn, and they had no choice but to respond to Fleury as he needed them to. They came at him from all directions. They rode him into the boards with their elbows high and their stick blades higher. They hated him. And they were unforgiving.

Therefore did Fleury re-create the game in his own twisted image. The only possible style of play for him was one that had been filed to a needle point.

By the twelfth year of his professional career, Fleury had twice been entered into the NHL's substance abuse program. Of this time and the time preceding it, he wrote things like: "The night before we left, I called the Molson rep and said, 'I need beer.' . . . So we picked up twelve flats of twenty-four. We also picked up a Texas mickey—one of those 66-ouncers of whisky—

and I found a source who sold me a bag of weed the size of a toddler."

He also wrote: "I just stayed in that room and let my brain go swimming in Paxil, coke, two six-packs and a twenty-sixer of Grey Goose."

And: "I was torn between Drea, the New York stripper I had been seeing at the end of my marriage, and Steph, the stripper in Albuquerque."

And: "I knew I was a full-blown alcoholic drug addict."

By his thirteenth season, he was earning seven million dollars per year playing for the New York Rangers. He approached his stint in the league's biggest market as "a challenge, an opportunity to shove it up somebody's ass." He claimed that during his three years in the city, he failed thirteen consecutive drug tests but was not suspended by the league because he was a leading scorer.

During his fifteenth season, he was involved in a free-for-all with the bouncers at a gentleman's club in Columbus, Ohio. He was by then playing for the Chicago Blackhawks. After the incident, the Blackhawks placed him on waivers. No team claimed him. That off-season, he was suspended indefinitely for substance abuse violations.

Altogether, Theo Fleury appeared in 1,084 regular-season NHL games, scored 1,088 points, and was assessed 1,840 minutes in penalties. The only players in NHL history with as many points *and* penalty minutes are Brendan Shanahan (six-foot-three, 220 pounds) and Mark Messier (six-foot-one, 210). Fleury spent thirty-one hours, or about ninety-three games' worth of playing time, in the penalty box. Some might call such behavior self-destructive.

"The secret is that if you show the tiniest clue that you are intimidated or afraid," Fleury wrote, "you are finished."

His relationship with his teams' fans was such that one

night, when he was sent off the ice to replace a bloodied sweater, someone in the stands removed and threw down a Fleury replica jersey so he wouldn't miss his shift.

His relationship with other teams' fans was such that one night, as the crowd at Nassau Veterans Memorial Coliseum chanted, "Crackhead! Crackhead!" at him, he slapped his bicep in vulgar salute after scoring the game-winning goal.

But two years after hockey, in New Mexico, at dawn one day, Fleury "ran out into the middle of the scrub, screaming at the universe, 'Fuck you, fuckin' asshole-son-of-a-bitch. I've had enough. I can't take it anymore. Don't give me any more shit!'" He drove to a pawnbroker and paid him five thousand dollars for a pistol and one bullet. He returned to his home, loaded the gun, and put it in his mouth. "I sat there forever, shivering so hard the barrel was bouncing off my teeth. How did it taste? It tasted lonely."

He did not pull the trigger.

"It's not as if I'd felt this sudden urge to live. I still felt like shit and wished I were dead. I think that's why, after I ran outside and chucked the gun into the desert, I was screaming at the universe like a madman."

What we cherish as drive or will, the psychoanalyst Adler considered "but a tendency in the service of the feeling of inadequacy." Adler believed that every one of us feels inadequate in some way. We can't help it; we picked it up when we were young. It doesn't even matter if we really were inferior. It's simply the nature of this place to make us feel small.

Then what happened was we learned ambition, how to pursue a grander future. We thought up some goal. We thought, *It'll all stop once I grow up, once I make the NHL, once I get published, once I take over the world.* This goal—we ordered our whole lives around it. And we strove, relentless.

"[Your] goal is so constructed that its achievement promises the possibility either of a sentiment of superiority, or an elevation of the personality to such a degree that life seems worth living," Adler wrote. "It is this goal which gives value to our sensations, which links and coordinates our sentiments, which shapes our imagination and directs our creative powers, determines what we shall remember and what we must forget."

This was what I loved about Theo Fleury. What made him so inspiring to watch. Through sheer force of will, he shoved it up everyone's ass. Even in the twilight of his career, his Hall of Fame stature long since achieved, he played as if proving something. He was fired by a deathless engine he had to keep stoked. This was also what damned him.

Alfred Adler: "So many people are convinced that their ambition, which might more appropriately be called vanity, is a valuable characteristic because they do not understand that this character trait constantly dissatisfies a human being, and robs him of his rest and sleep."

Theo Fleury: "All was perfect in my world, and for me that was a problem. Because I had built my life on being the underdog. Being the one who said, 'I'll show you.' But all I knew how to do was manage the fight—once I'd won it, once I was at the top, I didn't have a clue. The only place I felt good when I was sober was on the ice."

After the NHL, Fleury joined the Horse Lake Thunder, a senior amateur hockey team that played out of the Horse Lake First Nation reservation in Alberta. They failed to win the senior amateur championship, the Allan Cup.

He joined the Belfast Giants and was voted 2006 Player of the Year by the British Ice Hockey Writers Association.

He joined the Calgary Vipers minor league baseball team in 2008 and played a few games as a utility fielder.

He formed a seven-member country-and-western band, singing lead.

He filmed a pilot for a reality show about his new concrete business called *Theoren Fleury: Rock Solid.*

And six years after his last NHL game, finally sober, he

petitioned for and was granted reinstatement into the league. He accepted a tryout offer with an old team. At forty-one, he recorded four points in four preseason games but was cut from the roster.

Did he ever figure it out, I wonder? How to content yourself with where you tap out?

3.

MITHRADATES OF FOND DU LAC

On the way were still more beers, the night being young in Fond du Lac, Wisconsin, and Tim's blood stanching where the cobra had bitten him. He wanded a good finger over the restaurant's menu pictures and told me, "If it was you, dude, you'd be dead in this Applebee's."

If it was anyone else on this earth, they'd be dead. The African water cobra that had tagged him two hours earlier is so rare a specimen that no antivenom for it currently exists. Yet cobra bite and lagers notwithstanding, Tim looked fresh; he was well on his way to becoming the first documented survivor of that snake's bite.

"Which reminds me," he said from across the table, taking out his phone so I could snap a picture of his bloody hand. "For posterity. After tonight, every book is fucking wrong."

It was on my account that he had done this, willfully accepted the bite. Even though we'd only shaken hands that bright winter afternoon in the salted parking lot of a Days Inn. Tim Friede, the man from the Internet who claimed to have made himself immune to the planet's deadliest serpents. I'd come to test his mettle, to goad him into an unprecedented ordeal: five venomous snakebites in forty-eight hours.

Around us, young people were getting unwound in a hurry. The hour was fast approaching when the restaurant would flip off the APPLE portion of its lighted sign, clear out the tables and chairs, turn the edited jams to eleven, and allow for twerking on the floor space. Our server returned with the beers. Tim looked up at her with his serous blue eyes, smiling, and said, "You never did card me. You have to guess." She demurred. He continued: "I could be your dad."

While Tim fumbled for an in with her, I considered the swollen hand he propped next to his head. Two streams of blood had rilled down and around his wrist bone, reading like an open quote. He was a dad's age, forty-four years old; that much was correct. But he appeared both grizzled and strangely boyish. He had an eager smile of small, square teeth and a platinum buzz cut. The skin over his face was very taut; it looked sand-scoured, warm to the touch. Scar tissue and protuberant veins crosshatched his thin forearms, which he now covered by rolling down the sleeves of two dingy long-sleeve T-shirts. His neck was seamed from python teeth.

The snake that had done his twilight envenoming was *Naja annulata*, about six feet long and as thick as elbow pipe. She was banded in gold and black, a design not unlike that of the Miller Genuine Draft cans we'd bought and then housed on our way to Tim's makeshift laboratory. When we walked in, the snake was shrugging smoothly along the walls of her four-by-two plastic tank. She was vermiform mercury. And she greeted us with a hiss, a sourceless, sort of circular sizzle, what one would hear if one suddenly found oneself in the center of a hot skillet.

Kissing-distance past my reflection in the glass, the cobra induced in me a nightmare inertia. Attraction and revulsion. She had not spirals but eclipses for eyes.

"I love watching death like this," Tim had said, leaning in, startling me. "Some nights I watch them all night, like fish. Mesmerizing."

The cobra was one of a $1,500 pair he'd just shipped in, Tim preferring to spend most of what he earns—working the 10:00 p.m. to 6:00 a.m. line shift at Oshkosh Truck—on his snakes. The thing nosed under an overturned Tupperware container while I checked her CV on my phone. Her venom? A touch more potent than arsenic trisulfide. Tim unlatched the front of her tank, reached in, and was perforated before he knew it. The cobra flew at him with her mouth open and body lank, like a harpoon trailing rope.

"Ho ho, that's just beautiful," Tim said, withdrawing his hand. There were two broken fangs stapled into his ring finger.

He picked up a beer with his other hand, cracked it expertly with his pointer. I glanced around at all the other caged ampersands—mambas, vipers, rattlesnakes—and I smiled. Rosy constellations of Tim's blood pipped onto the linoleum, shining brighter than old dead ones.

A little while ago, I was searching the web for the man who best embodied the dictum "That which does not kill me makes me stronger." I was looking for him who thought he'd succeeded in fortifying his inborn weaknesses. Who believed he had bunged the holes left by God.

I discovered Tim among the self-immunizers. The self-immunizers are a far-flung community of white, western men—a few dozen of them—who systematically shoot up increasing doses of exotic venoms, so as to inure their immune systems to the effects. Many of these men handle venomous snakes for business or pleasure, so there's a practical benefit to their regimen. A few prefer instead to work their way from snakes to scorpions to spiders, voiding creatures' power over them. Most seem to be autodidacts of the sort whose minds recoil at the notion of a limitation deliberately accepted—something I sympathized with, being myself an unfinished, trial creature. On their message boards, Tim talked the biggest medicine.

Their practice has a great old name: mithridatism. It comes from Mithradates VI of Pontus, aka "the Poison King." In his lifetime, Mithradates was the last independent monarch to stand against Rome. He tried to unite Hellenic and Black Sea cultures into a neo-Alexandrian empire that might resist the Western one. For a moment, he was successful. Rome was forced to march against and attempt to occupy the Middle East because of him. The Roman Senate declared him imperial enemy number one. A ruthless general was dispatched to search and destroy. Mithradates went uncaptured, hiding out in the craggy steppes.

Machiavelli deemed him a hero. Racine wrote him a tragedy. A fourteen-year-old Mozart composed an opera about him. A. E. Housman eulogized what was most remarkable about Mithradates:

> *They put arsenic in his meat*
> *And stared aghast to watch him eat;*
> *They poured strychnine in his cup*
> *And shook to see him drink it up.*

Like any despot, Mithradates inverted humanity's basic psychic task and made insecurity less, not more, tolerable. He trusted no one, and in anticipation of conspiracy and betrayal, he bricked up his body into an impenetrable fortress. Each morning he took a personal cure-all tablet that included things like cinnamon, castor musk from beaver anuses, tannin, garlic, bits of poisonous skinks and salamanders, curdled milk, arsenic, rhubarb from the Volga, toxic honey, Saint-John's-wort, the poison blood of pontic ducks, opium, and snake venom. His piecemeal inoculation worked so well that, when finally cornered, Mithradates was unable to poison himself. According to Appian's *Roman History*, he begged his guard to murder him, saying, "Although I have kept watch and ward against all the poisons that one takes with his food, I have not provided against that domestic poison, always the most dangerous to kings, the treachery of army, children, and friends."

The official recipe for his *mithridatium* was lost. But from Nero onward, every Roman emperor ingested a version of the Poison King's antidote. Some had thirty-six ingredients; others as many as one hundred eighty-four. Charlemagne took it daily, as did Henry VIII and Elizabeth I. The Renaissance poor had their generic versions. Oliver Cromwell found it cleared his skin. London physicians prescribed it until 1786. You could buy it in Rome as recently as 1984. It was believed to kill the helplessness in your constitution. It's our longest-lived panacea.

Tim is adopted. A cop raised him. Asked about his childhood, he offered: "I grew up fighting in the streets of inner-city Milwaukee." He once tried to reach out to his biological parents after one of his children was born dead, strangled by the umbilical cord. "I thought it might be some kind of genetic thing," he told me. "But I never found out. I couldn't get an answer out of them as to why they didn't want me."

What he'd wanted for himself was to be a marine, a Special Forces agent. But he broke his ankle in a car accident two months before basic training. He took a year off, reenrolled in basic, rebroke the ankle. He could never be Special Forces if he couldn't jump out of a plane, so he did the next best thing and became a high-rise window washer.

Ten years of window washing put him up to injecting snake venom. "Why?" he explained. "Because when you wake up feeling no pain, then you'll know you're dead." He began by injecting a dilution of one part Egyptian cobra venom and ten thousand parts saline solution into his thigh. He did this every week for a year. Then he upped the potency to 1:100, including in the mix Cape and monocled cobra venoms. From his journal of that time:

9-17-02
Small rise in fever, but started to
eat and drink. No painkillers yet,
but I'm barely hanging on. No one
was allowed near me.

9-18 to 9-23-02
To sick to take notes, just don't care.

9-24-02
This is the first day of puss release,
thank God. 3:00 p.m., puss release
with great pressure. Urine is clear,
no painkillers, no anti venom, no
hospital. 6:00 p.m., had second
puss release. Couldn't walk,
needed to crawl.

He was left with a six-inch-by-six-inch scar on his leg and an immune system with twice as many venom-specific antibodies as most people have regular ones. He's since repeated the procedure with mamba and rattlesnake venoms. He takes booster shots every couple of weeks. He has begun immunizing against the inland taipan, the deadliest terrestrial snake.

"There's no standardized guide to this shit. Everybody's different. I sort of wrote the handbook on self-immunization,"

Tim said, referring to a self-published PDF available on his website for twelve dollars.

"I'm separated from my wife of fifteen years because of this. I didn't change oil or cut grass or really be a husband or father. I was researching venom twenty hours a day. I had a thirteen-hundred-dollar mortgage. One day I came home and my wife had taken the kids. She had left." With her, he's maintained a kind of relationship; it's his kids, Tim admitted, whom he's lost touch with. "My wife was supportive, but I never needed her. Oh, she'd said, 'The snakes or me' before I lost our house. I was sleeping in a tent. My two kids are fifteen and six. But self-immunization is my entire life."

Snake venom is an astringent cocktail of ribonucleases, nucleotides, and amino acid oxidases that, once injected into prey through hollow fangs, immediately goes to work disrupting cellular function. It breaks down tissue proteins, attacks muscles and nerves, dissolves intercellular material, and causes metabolic collapse. The stuff is usually classified as either neurotoxic (if it attacks the nervous system) or hemotoxic (if it goes for blood components), because even though most induce both neuro- and hemotoxic symptoms, each venom tends to induce more of one kind than the other. Meaning the damage a venom does is species-specific. Snakebite is thus like lovesickness in that, each time, you're wrecked special and anew.

But there *are* generalities within the two categories. For instance: a potent, primarily neurotoxic venom will effect a quick death. Immediately after the bite, though, comes a lightness of being. Then an acute sense of hearing, almost painfully acute. Chest and stomach cramps next. Sore jaw. Tongue like a bed of needles. Inflamed eyes; lids closing involuntarily. The soles of your feet feel as if on hot coals. Numb throat. Blurred vision.

Then every fiber explodes in pain. From head to toe you are under a barrage of agonizing spasms. Neck, eyes, chest, limbs, teeth—searing, aching. The pain feels like a filament burning brightest before it pops. Then your vision splits. Everything splits. Then your muscle contractions are disabled. Your body paralyzes gradually and methodically, as though someone were going from room to room, turning out your lights. Your central nervous system is not able to tell your diaphragm to breathe. You fall down the tiers of a sleep that feels just and due, a reward.

In North America, only a few snakes—corals, elapids, and Mojave rattlers—are neurotoxic like the old-world killers, the cobras and mambas. The vast majority of venomous snakes here—the copperheads, the water moccasins, and the other rattlesnakes—are hemotoxic. Though their bites are less likely to kill, their venom, even if survived, often causes chunks of tissue or whole limbs to fall away. It dissolves you. But first you feel a flame bud and lick at the wound. Your skin tickles, pricks, and burns, as if in the process of crisping. Your lymph nodes distend and your neck balloons into a froggish sac. The venom is going from door to cellular door, pillaging. Blood from ruptured vessels escapes into your tissues. Your afflicted limb hemorrhages, enlarging to monstrosity. You sweat and go dumb. Your blood pressure plummets like barometrics before a storm. You see double, go into shock, and barf up everything. It then feels as if red-hot tongs have plunged inside you, to seek out the root of the pain. This is a living death. You witness yourself becoming a corpse piece by piece. You are barely able to piss, and what does come out is ruby red. You twitch and convulse. Your respiratory system is no longer strong enough to pump the bilge from your lungs. The foam you cough up is pink. And hours to days later, cardinal threads fall from your gums and eyes until, beaten by suffering and anguish, you lose your sense of reality. A chill of death invades your being. Your blood is thin as water. If you die, you die of a bleeding heart.

None of the above, I should say, is Tim susceptible to. He's been treated with enough neuro- and hemotoxic venoms that his Swiss-army immune system will respond to a bite by flooding itself with the requisite antibodies. These will patrol his blood, disengaging toxins like keys opening locks. He'll swell up, but he'll be okay—if there's *one* bite. It's *multiple* bites that might overwhelm him.

Still, he's worked hard to do this, to reconcile himself to the grand old foe.

Sifted flurries began to fall on the drive from the restaurant to the place Tim's rented since separating from his wife. We took my rental car because his rust-eaten Intrepid had no heat. Try as we did, we could not figure out how to change the Club Life satellite radio station.

"Here's one for you," Tim said, doing an economical frug in his unbelted seat. "'Venus' and 'venom' come from the same root—'love,' in Latin. *Venenum*. 'Venom' used to mean 'love potion' but over time came to mean 'poison.'"

I skidded us off the highway onto a lightless dirt road. I flipped on the brights and blinked several times to see if there was in fact more past the windshield than unspooling mud and velvet nada. The sputtering heater worked intensely when it worked. The rattle from the backseat meant the diamondback was up.

"Somebody's getting hot to trot," Tim said. He'd picked up this snake from a friend around the way. She was going to be the last one to bite him this weekend.

"What I'm saying is—" I began, and then stopped, having forgotten what I was saying.

"Snakes and love," Tim said. "Love and snakes."

"You fell in love with these beasts because why?" I asked. "They aren't pets. A snake doesn't know what a damn relationship is. The thing doesn't know your ass from Adam."

"No, no," he said. "With snakes it's cut-and-dried. They're like, 'I want to kill you, and you'll have to survive. I'm a badass motherfucker, and you need to be a bigger badass motherfucker.' And I'm like, 'You're going to kill me every single time, and I love you.' It's the best relationship I've ever had."

We jounced past huge barns pushed back from the road. They were hung with one high, bright light, and I felt drawn to each even as I thought of anglerfish and their bioluminescent lures. "But, bro," I said, "how can you still love them once you've become immune to them? You've hardened yourself to their serpentine wiles. Now what? It's like—like the difference between being in love and then being in a committed marriage."

"That's a good analogy," Tim said around the Marlboro he was lighting. The diamondback bumped its head along the seams of its plastic Bed Bath & Beyond container. She was not in time with the four-four radio beat. "But the snake is ten times the woman for me than the women are. Besides, this shit right here has to be a one-man show. You can't depend on that snake-woman, because she don't give a shit. She just wants to eat and shit and kill you in defense."

Tim told me which unpaved byway to look out for, and we rode on in silence but for the electronica/serpent mashup. With his swollen right hand he handled his cigarette ineptly, inserting and then removing it from his mouth the way an intern might a thermometer.

"But how great is it to be a human and do that? Beat that?" he said, and turned to point into the backseat. "To be one of the only people in history to beat you?"

And this is where I did not ask: Is it really evil that tempts?

Or is temptation more about thinking you've found the shortcut to utopia? I was actually very curious about what Tim would answer. Because, to me, the desire to divinize yourself has always been the most tempting thing in the world.

"Yuh-oh," Tim said into the backseat.

I heard the rattling afresh, and then Tim muttered something, and then the plastic lid on the case snapped shut.

"The venom," Tim said, "it gives me something I need. If I had the time and the money, I'd become immune to everything."

I pulled the car around hay bales and dead tractors and parked next to an unfinished guesthouse on the edge of a llama farm. Somewhere in the night, a windmill lamented oil. We put the beers and the whiskey in the cold-storage shed and went on inside.

A fox pelt and an ankle trap were nailed to the wall of Tim's foyer. There was no furniture. On the floor in the living room/kitchenette lay a sheetless full-size mattress. Drifts of books on animal tracking and mixed martial arts. Whey protein and fifteen-pound weights on top of a fridge that didn't work. A bran of roaches and plaster flakes, all over. Many delicate bones were laid out to dry on paper towels by the sink.

Tim put the rattlesnake case on his mattress. In the light I could see she was gravid with babies. Her poison head tracked me but not Tim as he approached a stereo and cued a skipping CD of Scandinavian heavy metal. We lisped beers and poured Gentleman Jack into them.

I crunched across the floor and picked up an old textbook on venom. I flipped to the middle, where there were color photos of hemotoxic snakebite gore: carmine fissures and scabby limbs. Tim walked over, pulled a bookmark from the later pages, and unfolded it. It was a letter addressed to him from the textbook's author. "Dr. Findlay Russell told me that I'd never be able to survive pure venom," he said, handing me the letter. Then he told me about antivenom.

Antivenom is no new thing. We've known about it for more than a century. Back then, its production was a simple if crude, painstaking, and resource-intensive process. Nothing about that has changed. Take an animal—usually a horse or a sheep because of their blood volume, but a shark works, too—and inject it with small but increasing amounts of milked venom over the course of several months. The animal develops antibodies in its blood. The animal's blood is then extracted and purified and made into a serum. The serum is injected into a victim of snakebite, and the purified antibodies ride in on hyperimmune plasma like cavalry over a hill. It works similarly to a vaccine, except the immunity it confers is short-lived. The antibodies are on loan, and their introduction doesn't spur the production of one's own immune cells.

The problem, Tim continued, is that even with antivenom available throughout much of the world, 125,000 people still manage to die from snakebites every year, most of them in Asia and Africa. This is because antivenom is a very particular drug. It must be stored at a constant temperature not exceeding 46 degrees Fahrenheit. It must be administered by a doctor under controlled conditions. And, in most cases, it must come from the species of snake that did the biting. This all presupposes things like reliable electricity, clean needles, expertise, and the money needed for five to twenty-five vials of antivenom, which in our country cost about fifteen hundred dollars each.

"The cure is in the snake," Tim said. "People are stepping on the cure. The cure is in me. And I want to develop a vaccine from it. I want to be the first person in medical history to develop a vaccine with no degree."

Tim walked into the other room and waved at me with his

bitten hand. It looked like a cheap prosthetic, the fingers curled and fused. When I shifted my weight to follow, the diamondback coiled into her S-shaped strike posture, rattling.

This other room was carpeted and clean. Tim had hung it with streamers of shed skin belonging to every snake that ever bit him. Inside a curio cabinet against the far wall were antique snakebite kits, tinned bunk that had never saved one life: chloroform, chlorinated lime, and carbolic acid; injections of ammonia and strychnine; tinctures of devil's dung; potassium permanganate, which was rubbed into sliced-open fang punctures as late as the 1950s. Kits like these were popular especially in Australia in the late nineteenth and early twentieth centuries. There, they were hawked by traveling salesmen who performed sideshow acts with deadly species. These men received so many defensive bites in which only trace amounts of venom were injected that, unbeknownst to them, they built up immunity. They thought they were being saved by the nostrums they'd cooked up in the bush and applied after every bite. They sold them; people bought them; they still died.

Tim showed me a photograph of one such showman, Thomas Wanless. In the photo, he's crouched in a dirt patch with a tiger snake clamped onto his forearm. Tim's marginalia read, "NO ONE HAS TALKED TO ME MORE THAN THIS."

Around us were turrets of books stacked on homemade shelves: *God: The Failed Hypothesis*, old leatherbound volumes of Darwin, *Calculus for the Practical Man*, *The Immune Self*, evolutionary biology, a history of self-experimentation entitled *Who Goes First?* I pointed out one called *The Beginner's Guide to Winning the Nobel Prize*.

He said, "I mean, if I do it, I do it."

Tim did not have a college degree. He did not have any formal training in medicine. "As much as school could help me, it's such a crock of fucking shit," he said. More than anything, he wanted a university to agree to study him, to find out what exactly is going on in his body, how it might be reproduced in an easily injectable form, maybe even underwrite the funding for the vaccine production agreement he has with Aldevron, an antibody research outfit.

But universities don't and won't, because of liability issues. They can't be affiliated with a layman whose only test subject is himself. (When the History Channel asked to feature Tim in an impressively ridiculous segment a few years ago, his one stipulation—that the network arrange for the University of Wisconsin to study him—was not met.) "If they backed this, and then I died, or I somehow led to other people's deaths? Well, what's that gonna cost them?"

Tim won't personally help anyone who wants to start self-immunizing. "Liability. All you gotta do is make one calculation wrong, and then my shit's done, too," he said. What he did to himself wasn't illegal. Even the Food and Drug Administration had given him the okay. It's just that this was not how objective research was supposed to be done.

"Bullshit," Tim said. "Mice, rats, sheep, equines—but no humans? There's no other recourse. Only humans know what a thing feels like.

"Whatever, though." He picked up a framed portrait of a former friend who had become the director of a reptile zoo and had gone on something of a smear campaign against self-immunization.* The glass was webbed from the center out, sug-

---

* This friend wrote: "There is no scientific evidence (published in a peer-reviewed journal) to back up self-immunization. [Bill] Haast is one example and therefore anecdotal. . . . You can still suffer severe tissue damage or death before your antibodies have time to do you any good. That's why it's called an immune response. Therefore, the benefit of such 'immunity' is slim to none."

gesting a punch. "They may got seventeen degrees, but the one thing they don't got is their hand in the cage. I just don't see why they have to cockblock me on this."

"Why would anyone try to stop you?" I honestly wondered.

"Jealousy. They're jealous of my ability to not get killed. And they hate me because I'm proving the books wrong. I'm proving *them* wrong. But that's the history of self-experimentation and immunology."*

So, having given up on academia, Tim was petitioning the government of Sudan for money. He had taken out a two-thousand-dollar loan to fly there in the summer.

"Sudan," I said.

He told me a Sudanese immigrant he worked with on the production line was going to introduce him to the minister of social affairs. Was supposed to have already, actually, when she was visiting Kentucky. But Tim's coworker's rental car broke down on the drive from Wisconsin. "Now, instead, I'm going to stay in Sudan for a week, get bit by mambas to buy confidence."

"That is crazy," I said.

"This is crazy? You just took a flu shot last week."

"I'm from Florida. I've never had a flu shot."

"What I have to have is a short nap on a long couch," Tim said. I went to fix us a couple more boilermakers.

---

* Some highlights: In 1803, Friedrich Wilhelm Adam Sertürner isolated the active ingredient in opium, dubbed it "morphine," and with three of his friends tried out ninety milligrams, or ten times today's recommended limit. In 1892, Max von Pettenkofer drank cholera bacteria and showed no ill effects. In 1921, Werner Forssmann threaded a catheter through his arm and into his heart, to see if such an intrusion would be fatal. (It wasn't.) In 1954, John Paul Stapp strapped himself into a rocket sled that nearly reached the speed of sound before making an abrupt stop. Because of him, we have seat belts. In 1984, Barry Marshall swallowed a petri dish of *Helicobacter pylori* to prove that bacteria could live in our caustic stomachs. Marshall and Forssmann each received the Nobel Prize.

When I returned, Tim took me on a tour of what he called his "peer reviews." They were printed-out Hotmails from scientists and one Nobel laureate. He'd framed some. Others he'd taped to the wood paneling. They were all polite and vague. "You are probably one of a few people who have immunity against snake venoms"; "I appreciate the studies done on you and there is no criticism." Each was a printout of the whole screen, not just the text, so there were a lot of perimeter ads for penis-enhancement pills and *Wedding Crashers.*

"This is as bad as it gets, with a good ending," Tim said, cheersing with a hand that was rooted with dried blood. Already the swelling was ebbing. "Write this down: If you can't do it yourself, well, then, what the fuck good are you?"

No man lived through a wider variety of venomous snakebites—if not more bites, period—than Bill Haast. "I've been bit more than one hundred seventy times and maybe almost died twenty or twenty-five times," he said in a 2007 interview, four years before his death from natural causes. "I don't count the little bites."

In his personal museum, Tim keeps a photo of himself with Haast, the most renowned modern mithridatist. ("I had to fill his gap," Tim said of the man.) Haast started self-immunizing in 1948, when he injected one part Cape cobra venom and one thousand parts saline solution into his left forearm with a number-25 hypodermic needle. He took a booster every three months and eventually upped his dosage to a drop of raw venom. Then he added Indian and king cobra venoms to the mix. No one could say what might happen to his liver and kidneys. One zoologist wrote to tell him that he wouldn't "give a plugged nickel" for Haast's life in three years. But there were no harmful side effects, no severe reactions except for some boils caused by Haast's refusal to use sterile solutions. By the time he was ninety-five years old, Haast was injecting himself weekly with a brew of venoms from thirty-two snakes and lizards. "I could become a poster boy for the benefits of venom," he told the *Miami Herald*. "If I live to be one hundred, I'll really make the point." He lived to be one hundred.

After stints as an engine tester, a bootlegger, and a cashier in a prohibition chophouse, Haast operated the Miami Serpentarium from 1946 to 1984. There, he charged the curious to watch him milk venom from cobras, kraits, rattlesnakes—all of the dread host. He didn't have a high school diploma, but he donned a white lab coat when doing extractions. Using no protective equipment, he handled up to a hundred snakes every day of the week. On Sundays, he'd release a fourteen-foot king cobra onto the front lawn and spar with it, feint and duck its strikes until he'd grabbed its head and subdued it. (It often bolted for the audience, there not being any issues of liability in those salad days, and he'd have to yank it back to him by its fist-thick tail.)

The Serpentarium was the culmination of a boyhood dream: encourage venom research by making it easy for scientists, especially those in the United States, to obtain all sorts of snake venoms from a reliable and knowledgeable source. "This venom has got to be useful," Haast said to his tearful second wife after he was laid up in the hospital by another bite. "It can't affect every nerve in the body like this and not be useful. It must be. Someday, someone will find a use for it."

Haast tried. He was leading a promising study on the effects of neurotoxic venom on polio when Jonas Salk discovered a vaccine. In the '70s, Haast and a Miami physician were using a venom-based serum called PROven to successfully treat more than six thousand people suffering from multiple sclerosis. When the FDA shut them down, they cited improper human testing.

Scientists and academics did not much love him. "It is hard to evaluate the significance of Haast's work because so little has been published," wrote one of his customers, a leading venom researcher. "He has certainly demonstrated that a human being can recover from a hell of a lot of snakebites." But the self-immunizers inspired by Haast cherish his work, most of all his long-out-of-print biography. (Tim referred to it as "my Bible.") In it, Haast is described as "a sometimes unapproachable and stubborn man" who "doesn't waste motions or time," who "hopes and plans for the best but expects the worst and is ready to accept it." He was "strongly individualistic with an almost innate sense of pride. He could never bring himself to ask anybody for anything, least of all to beg or plead."

Haast was made an honorary citizen of Venezuela after he flew deep into that country's jungle to save a snakebitten boy's life with a transfused pint of his hyperimmune blood. In all, he donated blood to twenty-one victims of snakebite; each survived. A letter from one, the director of the Des Moines zoo, read, "Each morning when the sun comes up, I think of you."

He ate meat on even-numbered days and seldom consumed refined sugar. He was fit and nimble till the end. Unusually youthful-looking. He claimed never to have been sick a day in his life, to have known neither the flu nor the common cold. He didn't even take aspirin. And he lives on as the self-immunizers' alpha, the apotheosis of how a man wins hard liberty and authors his own destiny.

Haast couldn't write much, though, for his hands were gnarly. An eastern diamondback bite curled the left one into a claw. A Malaysian pit viper ossified his right index finger. A cottonmouth bit the tip of his pinkie, which then turned black, lost feeling, and had to be clipped off the bone by his third wife, Nancy, who used rose pruners to do so. Nancy is currently writing Haast's updated biography, his first wife having left him before the Serpentarium opened, and his second having flown the coop not long after, saying, "I can't stand it. I can't stand it. I love you, Bill. I love you. But I can't stand it anymore."

It wasn't a full-blown hangover I had—more like a subcutaneous chafe. I could feel another sour me ruffling against seams that would've split had there been one more drink last night. By noon, I was on my way back to Tim's lab.

The lab was among the old industrial rind along the south shore of Lake Winnebago, in a disintegrating crematorium. Tim was waiting for me amid piles of snow-swaddled rubble outside. He had on the same dirty shirts and loose jeans. An open Pabst was in his hand. He introduced me to his best friend, Corey, who worked with him at Oshkosh Truck. Corey was brown-haired and haunted. His wide-set eyes seemed clear on their surface but marred below, and he wore both a black T-shirt and a trapezoidal mustache. He handed me a beer.

Inside, half a million dollars' worth of crossbred reticulated pythons spooled in rows and rows of tanks. They belonged to another friend, Gavin, who ran a tattoo parlor while mongrelizing new colors and patterns of snake on the side. They were vulcanized muscle, and they moved slowly if at all. The musk they gave off was hearthy, like wood chips and spoor; sedative, until one got wind of the antiseptic tang of chemicals used to clean up after a thousand digestive systems turning hard-to-swallow prey into boneless shit. This was where Tim slept after his wife left him.

We went upstairs. Under low pipes and cobwebs were many old sofas, and two plastic tubs with an alligator in each. "These were a gift to Gavin, from this guy, before he went to prison," Tim said. I asked what was going to happen when they outgrew the tubs. He pointed to a picket corral of unsound construction.

In the opposite corner, a doughy man in Sunday shoes was using both hands to rustle sheets of dead skin off a beaded lizard. Tim led us on past, and we entered the lab proper, a climate-controlled shed with room enough for eight tanks. Tim paid Gavin three thousand dollars a year in rent; cheap, compared with the five thousand he spent on the rats stacked in plastic drawers throughout the crematorium.

The lizard man's wife clutched a baby to her breast and followed us in. When she crossed the threshold, the newly interned western diamondback roused herself, admonishing. The wife decided to watch from the other side of the shack's one window.

Then a guy named Dan arrived with Tim's Mojave rattlesnake. The Mojave was smallish and decorated with tan chevrons. Here now, the most dangerous species on the North American continent. This Dan placed on the floor, to kneel and poke at.

Dan resembled nothing so much as a debased tax accountant. Five-five, wire-frame glasses, a dome Bic'd clean, but no front teeth. He regularly fed quarter-size plugs of Skoal through the slot in his mouth. "She's a sweetie," he said, swimming his finger in front of the rattlesnake's furrowed brow. She lifted her front third off the ground. "She'll sit on the hook juuuust fine."

Tim was crouching behind the Mojave, talking to me, when she turned and struck at his thigh. "Got only denim," he assured us.

Dan went to get everybody more drinks. Tim decided to take out the pregnant diamondback and practice with a new set of snake grippers ordered specially from Georgia. When he unlatched the box, the snake flowed straight up and out, a genie from its lamp. She was *ornery*. On the linoleum, she seemed almost overwhelmed by the forest of legs to snatch at. Tim tried one of the bigger grippers, speared her behind the head, but the diamondback wormed easily out from under it. She writhed and lunged about like a downed but sentient power line. Using a smaller gauge, Tim pegged her, picked her up, and held her out to us spectators. She yawned, her pink gullet bracketed by fangs winking drops of venom. Everyone in that room was, deep down, a misanthrope who had never quite lost his adolescent fascination with the death act, snake on rat, who maybe still gazed upon it with a sort of jealousy.

Dan returned with an armload of Steel Reserves and another woman. "I asked you if there was gonna be pussy," he said to Tim. "All I found . . . was this." Her name was Megan. She was a slim woman with a bulb nose and inky hair kept bundled in a red kerchief. Lacy with tattoos, she exuded a pheromonal benevolence. She was Corey's fiancée, and the night janitor at Oshkosh Truck. But before that, when she was jobless and adrift, Tim had loaned her money, provided her with a place to stay, and put her in charge of his rats. His wife once briefly kicked him out after finding Megan's colors mixed in with his in the wash.

During quiet moments the night before, Tim had brought Megan up. "Do I want to see her and hug her and kiss her?" he'd asked at the Applebee's, apropos of a text message from her. "Of course I do! Do I want her to hold my hand and support me? Yes!" But he waved it all away, explaining that love had been the downfall of his immunizer heroes. His mentor "fell off and got foggy" because of a woman. Bill Haast burned through two wives before he found one who accepted her role in his ecosystem. "Megan knows that tremendously well," Tim had said. "As far as what I need or don't need." What he didn't need was a woman worrying about him, about the risks he accepted voluntarily, begging him to stop. That it might be her who was consigned to the anguish he'd inoculated against had not crossed Tim's mind. "I'm not some vulnerable idiot," he went on. "I know what I'm doing. Meg is horribly special. But I guess what it comes down to is I have to cut a few people out of my life to save a million."

He slid open the water cobra tank. He withdrew both snakes without incident. They entwined his right hand in a Gordian knot, and he said to Dan, "There are always girls here." He propped his smartphone on the windowsill to record a video of the bite. One cobra, having recently shed, looked as though she was mailed in green glass. Tim put her back. He wanted a heavily venomous bite, and snakes are more temperamental when they're shedding.

The other one was skin-shabby. Tim gripped it by its neck and rubbed it around his left arm, trying to encourage a bite. It remained flaccid and pliant as he brushed it first down and then back up, muttering, "Come on," apologizing that "it's not usually like this, I swear." This was practice for his trip to Sudan, where he'd have to stand and deliver in front of strangers. He pushed the rope of the snake for two more minutes before dropping it to his side and sighing. "Performance anxiety."

It would have to be the black mamba, then. We took a beery recess while Tim mentally prepped. The black mamba is *the* snake, according to him. The fastest on the planet. Terrifically aggressive. Unwelcome in zoos. Well over ten feet long, and the gray green of guns, B-52s, all your finer life-taking instruments. The "black" comes from its mouth, which it opens when threatening, and which isn't pink but obsidian. Without antivenom, the mortality rate of a "wet" black bite is absolute. Two drops is all it takes.

"Let's, ah, let's just see," Tim said, badly missing the garbage can with his tossed empty. He watched as I started, then stopped, taking this down in my spiral ledger. I looked at him expectantly. "Brotherman, there's no black mamba on earth with venom enough to kill me." He made an expansive gesture with a new beer in hand. He embraced my spotlight. "I control them," he said. "I control death."

A freight train trundled across the far bank of windows. The sun didn't set so much as slowly back away. Tim drank his beer to foam and said, "We go." He slipped his hands inside welding gloves. He opened the tank and hooked the mamba. He threw down one and then the other glove as though starting a hockey fight. He took the snake behind her head. She vined herself up his other arm, tonguing his ardor. She unhinged her abysmal mouth. "She's opened up!" somebody went. I thought I could hear a faint but continuous B-flat.

Tim held his palm away from his hip as though reaching for another's hand. The mamba's eyes shined with an intense bigotry of purpose. Her exhalations seemed to jelly the air. Tim pursed his lips, tensed, and lowered the open mouth to his forearm. Then the snake nipped him. She nipped him twice, actually, in quick succession, fangs through skin making the same small popping noises as airholes forked in TV dinners. Tim's arm immediately petrified.

"That might've been the worst one ever," he said, carefully unwinding the mamba and dropping her into her tank. He noted the bites on a *Sports Illustrated* bikini calendar and had me take a picture of them. People cleared out of the lab. He watched Megan go feed the rats through the shed's window. "I'll never be that lucky," he said to Corey.

"Man, shut the fuck up," Corey responded. He talked thickly, as though there were a hand around his throat. "You ain't even divorced yet."

Six inches away from Tim, at eye level, a monocled cobra hammered the door of its tank, again and again, wishing to interject. "What I'm going to do is go for married chicks," he said, rotating his forearm, which was now a bloody delta.

"Oh, at Oshkosh Truck, it's mad easy," Corey said. "I've already had a couple."

Tim leaned forward and jabbed at Corey with his bitten arm. "Ay," he said, fixing his eyes. His smile unfastened his face, and for just one instant he looked ancient. "When you getting married, dog?"

They both forced laughter. "If it was gonna happen with you, it would've happened a long time ago," Corey said.

Tim's false laugh pushed Corey's out of the room. Dan came back in, unknowingly defusing the situation. He was exponentially drunker, with a giant lizard held to one shoulder. He petted it and said in mommy talk, "He's just a big baaayyy-bee," whereupon the wee dinosaur lifted its tail and sprayed a rich fecal foam across the laboratory floor.

"How about that Mojave?" I enticed. Tim was by then checking his Facebook messages on his phone. "Hey, should I bring the wife over?" he wanted to know. From downstairs Megan shouted, "Noooooo! She fuckin' hates me!" She ran up into the lab, a tottering smile on her face, and she reminded Tim to take a picture of the swelling that was pushing past his elbow.

"Nah," Tim said, eyes on his phone. "The wife isn't coming over, because she says she's baking. Bitch's baking? Bitch, you don't *bake*."

Megan sidled up to review the photo, her birdy hand alighting on his shoulder blade. She stepped on Tim's foot not accidentally but as though flooring him.

"Nine-by-nine-inch swelling," Tim said. "Now I just need a penis bite. A solid nine all around." He did not betray the awful pain he was feeling, his nerves vised tighter and tighter by his own expanding self.

A little later, good and drunk and sitting Indian-style, we watched the uncaged Mojave thread itself into a spring of stored energy, the position of last resort. Tim did some sleight of hand and collared it. "No dinner and a movie necessary with this one," he said, and plugged the Mojave into his forearm. It rattled excitedly as it drained itself. Tim's face gaped into an ecstatic rictus.

When he pulled the snake off, tartarous venom mizzled onto me. "There's the money shot," Dan went. This was Tim's fourth deadly snakebite in twenty-four hours' time. I scrawled, "To sin is to cheat with order." Tim saw me writing and said through a grimace, "All right, hold on now, we still got the diamondback tomorrow."

After that, things got convivial, if hazy. Beers were drunk at a ferocious pace. A gun was brought out? Tim and Megan went off in the dark somewhere. With the winking meekness of a moonlight vigilante, Dan explained how he forwent his usual rules and restrictions when selling cobras to undesirables. I poured up large-bore whiskey shots and rather hoped for pandemonium. When the couple returned, it was agreed that the after-party would move to Tim's place.

I stopped at a gas station to get us some Millers and Tombstone frozen pizzas. When I finally blundered into Tim's farmland shanty, I found him supine on his mattress with his inflated arms in the air. His wrists broke at right angles, and his hands hung plump. He looked as though he'd been long planted with his own wilted grave posies. Only Corey and Megan remained; they stood against the wall, looking down at him.

"Who else is impressed by this swell?" Tim asked, a lit cigarette balancing on his lower lip. His face barely chinned above his engorged neck. He was not able to turn to anyone. The holes in him had been squeezed shut.

"This is the sickest I've ever seen him," Megan said.

"That's what she said," Tim quipped in response to his own question. Megan asked him to take off his shirts before he distended too much. I put a pizza in the oven. Corey's face contracted into a pitying squinch. What was he going to do, call 911 and tell the Fond du Lac paramedics to bring three kinds of foreign antivenom?

"Shit's too soft," Tim said when I brought a slice to his mouth. After swallowing, he went, "There's room enough for you on here, sailor," and pointed to the other side of the mattress with his eyes. My face went blank. "I suppose you're too good for the floor, too?" he asked.

Corey excused himself, saying that, after all, he's got three kids and a Packers game tomorrow. Megan threw a blanket over Tim, who looked to me. The swelling was creeping still further, and the blue in his wet eyes seemed unnaturally bright. I slipped into my coat.

You can love a snake, but the snake's got no way of showing it loves you back. Selective pressures have made it so; the creature lacks the faculties. It probably never had them to begin with. Lucky thing, its existence was never a problem it had to solve—whereas a man like Tim was born a freak of nature, being within it yet transcending it. He was tasked with finding principles of action and decision-making to replace the principles of instincts. He had to develop a frame of orientation that granted him both a consistent picture of the universe and a basis for consistent living. Thus did he choose to build himself up: his Creation is one that does not care and will never cease. Seen this way, self-immunization doesn't just make sense. It's the only logical response to his world.

"I am gloved in fire," he said.

Last one out, I flicked off the light and took the beers with me.

The next day came and went. I sent Tim a couple of texts from my hotel room while four inches of snow fell. I wanted to see a fifth bite. When he didn't respond, I began to consider the legal ramifications. It'd all been his idea, I argued, freely chosen. I was just there, observing.

Late in the evening, I stopped by. I found Tim huddled over a portable electric heater, only the one light on. Inflamed under his same clothes, he appeared soft but also rigid, like something that had been stuffed and mounted. He'd been lying in bed since I left. "Just staring at the ceiling," he said. "I came close to crying, and there were a couple uncool moments when my eyes started closing on their own."

"Do you think you could still pull it off?" I asked.

"If I didn't have to work tomorrow. Or if you thought you could throw some money my way."

I patted myself down, shrugged, and said that that was against the rules. Tim's right arm had been cocked Napoleonically, but now he absentmindedly pumped it with his other hand, loosening his elbow joint. "What you have to understand," he said, "is you have to become the snake. The snake—they call it a 'recessive' step when you lose something through evolution. But the snake *improved* itself by getting rid of legs, extra lungs, everything."

He asked me to pass him the fifth of Jack Daniel's hidden among the bottles of generic painkillers on his countertop. He unscrewed the cap using only his palm. "Had you ever even *seen* a venomous snake before this?"

I had. One Christmas morning, in my overgrown backyard. I was stalking trash, shooting it with the compressed-air rifle I'd just unwrapped. I stepped softly through rusted bike frames and skirted the Braille of hamster graves. I was about to set sights on a bleach bottle when my body froze. That's a cliche, but it's absolutely true: I was arrested by the cold and tingling sensation of the familiar gone strange. I suddenly knew I was in the presence of a ghost.

Amid the litter at my feet was the candy tilde of a coral

snake. How long had it been there? Was it offering to bite *me*? I considered what that might be like, getting digested from the inside out by a creature that could never comprehend in me a full human being. I felt the urge to trust my life to it, to see just what the outcome would be. I bent to the snake in the grass.

I had no doubt that Tim would take a fifth bite if I coaxed him. But there'd be time enough for that. After all, Tim had been doing this here, alone, for quite a while, and he would be doing it for a long time to come. "To sound arrogant—and I hate to say it—but I don't think anyone'll ever be able to go through what I go through," he said. "Or want to. Not in a million years."

I looked down and ruffled through the ink-bloated pages of my pocket ledger. It was just shy of full. A self that is its own antidote—there's something to be hellaciously proud of. The cheap paper hissed with crinkly sibilance as I flipped to its cardboard backing. With that, I was gone.

In the empty apartment parking lot, Dad got out of shotgun to guide Mom.

"'MONBACK. 'MONBACK," he shouted, his head turned, his arm churning. Mom sighed, glanced from him to me in the rearview. "My husband and son," she said, smiling with her eyes.

Now that she's semiretired, or maybe freelancing is the better term, she wants to pick up where she left off with the children she barely saw while supporting the family. But when she looks at me, I can tell that she sees a tall drink of *him*, husband concentrate, and barely watered down at that. Her fat, cross-eyed baby—"Fatty from Cincinnati," she used to call me—no more; returned to her is the Manchurian Son. Occasionally, she'll ask if I remember how, before Dad's unemployment, she'd come home early and sit with me on the couch, singing the transposed lyrics, "Button up your overcoat / you belong to me!" I do not.

She compensates by buying gifts. Sometimes soap or razors, but mostly it's clothes. Idealized clothes, as though I were some large, churlish kewpie. This visit, she presented me with a pink-and-yellow checked oxford shirt, for next Easter mass. "*Très* gay," Dad pronounced it. I can already see myself sitting in the pew between them, Mom gently weeping, Dad refusing to kneel before the Host. He never could take that second step, come to believe that a power greater than himself might restore him to sanity.

"Hey, *you* married him," I said. "At least you had a choice." She narrowed her eyes in the rearview, bit a nail. I think, in some or another sense, she has washed her hands of me.

Dad got back in and huffed, "We're ten goddamn minutes late to this ballgame, people!"

Is he worse now? He's never *not* been antsy, or wary, not that I can recall. To this day, he refuses even to carry credit cards, because "they got chips for the eyes in the sky." He jokes about it, but a part of him really does believe that Japanese-made autos have in them a destruction sequence that can be flipped from Tokyo. He carries coupons, notes, receipts—all his corroborating evidence—in a wallet that cannot completely fold. When he stands after sitting, its swollen, misaligned chambers look like an infarcted heart in back of his ass.

He's an analog curmudgeon. He carries on his person a cloudy plastic newspaper sleeve full of change, which doubles as a blackjack in a pinch. He once threw the GPS out of the car because he thought its scentless British lady-voice was mocking him. When I first showed him how to use Microsoft Office, he denounced Clippy as an agent of Mom. If I point a phone at him, he thinks I'm live-streaming him to the world. If I double over and tap at one, he thinks I'm taking notes to do likewise later.

Funny how perspicacity and paranoia are the two sides of the same one fish flopping around out of water.

He believes everyone's turned against him. That we've achieved unanimity minus one. Which, in a way, he's right. *He* hasn't changed. Our attitudes toward him have. But, at the same time: we've gotten older and somewhat more mature, and *he hasn't changed.* He's arch-conservative in that sense, that he'd prefer everything to be as it was when he had equilibrium in his work/home life. When he last had a job, and also fun.

For a long time now, he's been duratively locked on *control.* A white-hot boiler with the relief valve broken off.

"You know who was right?" he asked the second we hit god-awful traffic on the 101. "Me. None of you people listen to me anymore."

"We have no goddamn choice but to listen to you," I chirped from the backseat. This, our family life—even at the thinnest, earliest moments of my stretched memory, it felt like being on a ship's crew. Being a team of persons, each with a defined role and a murky backstory, sailing together through negative space. The one imperative: buoyancy. I.e., do *not* rock the boat. And at the sound of sirens, faint or imagined—our captain jams our ears with wax.

"No. No." He squinted as though there were rocks in his shoe, scratched his chest with three fingers. "What I do—it's consideration for the other."

We lurched with the traffic. Mom skipped from lane to lane, hoping to hit on one that would carry us away from this con-versation. Thirty years, she's endured. When she sees *Dateline* reports on divorce or hookup culture, she says, "I guess virtue is dead in this world."

"None of you people takes into account the goddamn *weather,* okay?" Dad coughed, hocked, stored the phlegm under his tongue.

"The *traffic.*" He opened the door, leaned out, spit demurely. "The *dangers all around you.*"

I recalled the news story about the highway shooter on the loose and found myself fearing that he was right: there's some-one scoping us out right now. The gunshot wouldn't be the worst part.

The man contends that there's a real world out there, and the only one who's visited is him. The purest distillation of this world was Vietnam, where he got fired upon if he so much as lit a cigarette at night. But getting shot at was something of a relief—he knew VC were out there; now he knew exactly where.

He'd never dream of walking under a ladder, or acting cavalier around a mirror. Every time salt is spilled, three dashes go over his left shoulder. *Left*. Wood gets knocked on, but perfunctorily, as he has completely rid himself of any hope for good outcomes. This attitude is comforting, I think, insofar as it presumes someone or something cares enough about you to make you learn from your mistakes.

He supports the death penalty and doesn't sweat wrongful convictions because, the way he figures it, even if you didn't do *that*, you most likely did *some*thing over the course of your life that was reason enough to forfeit your gift.

If no one's on the line when he picks up the phone, he will for a full minute yell into the dead silence: "Hello? *HELL*o. Heh . . . HEY? Hell*OH*? Who's . . . HELLO? . . ."

"You think it's easy? Being me?" he asked. "Think it's fun?"

"You know what's not easy and not fun?" I countered. "Being around you when you're like this."

"Then don't behave in a way that makes me like this."

Frozen on an overpass, Dad put his nose to the window and scanned. "I didn't say it then, but—you should've stuck with baseball," he said. "Killed me how you quit. You could've been a coach." The sky here was the purple not of the crayon, but of its wrapper. The Oakland Coliseum's lights blazed just ahead.

We used to take bats and balls to the small park at the end of our street during this magic hour. I'd be the one hitting fungo, because Dad had better range than me at fifty-eight. Every so often I'd overshoot him, and balls would bounce over the seawall into Biscayne Bay. Once their wool windings dried, they hardened into gastroliths. Connect bad with one of those, and I'd be zapped into mindfulness of the skeleton I wore under my cargo shorts. One such bloop—a little Texas leaguer, a dying quail—Dad ran down so hard that a tooth fell out of his mouth. His teeth back then were always falling out. Now they're dazzlingly white and fake, but back then they were U'ed in green growth, verdure, like the wall under a window-unit A/C. Verily, the teeth dripped out of that man's mouth. During afternoon naps, even. If a tooth was gold, he'd say, "Leave it in Coke overnight. It cleans it."

"Why didn't you say that then?" I asked.

"Hey, *your* life," he said. "Which reminds me: When did you get so bookish? And when, exactly, did you start taking baths like a lady?"

I had to laugh at that. Leavened now, but still considering the honking line of cars ahead of us, Dad said, "Screw it. It's already the top of the fourth. We'll watch it at home."

"Thank God," Mom said. She yanked us onto the shoulder and floored it.

"*Fuuuuuck* you, oh, *Tennnnnn*-essee! *Yoooou* bunch of *rednecks!*"
Dad was extemporizing in time with the University of Florida
fight song. The Gators had just scored a touchdown, and he'd
laddered the volume bar unbearably high.

"Good*bye!*" Mom yelled, slamming the front door on her
way to teach catechism to middle-schoolers.

This apartment of theirs isn't in San Francisco proper, but
across the bay on a wooded hill in Marin County. I don't know
what it means that they moved from one place with no seasons
to another place with no seasons. But it was salutary, I think, the
move. They've got a good view here, and the rent's not too high.
There's a spyglass for watching ships in the bay ("That NKK
freighter's going too slow—here it comes, the dirty bomb, kiss
your ass goodbye!"), and a beautiful thrush lands daily on the
railing of their balcony. Dad calls it the Bluebird of Unhappi-
ness because it eats other birds and shits on everything. He lines
up kettle-cooked potato chips for it in the morning.

It's really just a large studio with a bathroom, a few load-
bearing walls, and a spare futon. They've decorated it with the
catalog bric-a-brac Dad orders Mom for birthdays and bank
holidays—1:4-scale ceramic Jesuses, ceramic Madonnas, crystal

saints. Karen's books are out and prominent, as is a black-and-white photo of the USS *Twining*, the destroyer on which Dad served briefly as a communications officer while living in San Fran before shipping off to Vietnam. In the picture, the *Twining* is chugging past this very spot, the Tiburon Peninsula. It was a gift; guy doesn't do photos. On the mantel next to it is another gift, this one from Karen, a carved inscription that reads "How can we miss you if you haven't left yet?"

"Who was it that said this team'd get in your blood, huh?" he shouted over the fight song. Onscreen, wide receivers hopped into the air and bumped flanks.

In the big old Miami house, Saturdays were easier to abide. Starting at 1:00 p.m., Dad would shoo us from the kitchen so he could watch college football. He had his three institutions—Navy, Vanderbilt, and the University of Florida. He's never told me how they rank in terms of his affection, but I think they go, in ascending order: Navy, UF, Vandy.

With Navy, he only cares that they beat Army. Which they *did* do when we went to the 2003 Army-Navy game in Philadelphia. Mom rode out that day's blizzard by huddling in the ladies' room with all the other moms, penguin-like. It was the first either she or I had seen of snow. I was supposed to be taking the SAT II that day, but, fuck it. Knowing no better, I wore a windbreaker and corduroy pants. I actually froze my ass off.

The Gators, Dad loves for their endearing manner of being always on the brink of falling apart. But they win more than they lose.

It's doomed Vanderbilt that has claim on his heart. When watching their games, something compelled him to stomp around the kitchen, open and close the oven a certain number of times, flick the porch light on and off. His curses got strange, absentminded. Cigarette smoke would curl alchemically from under the door. I'd look through its diamond-shaped window, but I saw only his outline. He watched the losses in darkness, backlit by the portable television's cemetery light.

He'll often brag that during his time there, the Commodores had no more than two wins in a season. This he will follow with a prideful recounting of how the Sarasota Sailors won none and tied one in the years he was on the high school football team.

And, as parents are models whether they want to be or not, I, too, have come to desperately love and need a sport—ice hockey. It's something he's never understood. Doesn't get where it came from. I've skated on ice like three times in my life. But he respects it, my fandom.

He knows that I can't bring myself to cheer for a team unless they blow irredeemably. They must play ugly, hopeless hockey. They need to lose night in, night out, like it's their job. Only then will I devote myself to them. Then, I'll watch and watch and watch, because it seems to me that *someone* has to. *Someone* has to tend to all that defeat. *Someone's* gotta cram it in there, oozing and deleterious, like spent nuclear fuel in a hollowed-out mountain.

No, I love hockey even though—precisely because—it can never threaten to love me back. *That* he gets.

When he finally ratcheted down the volume, I asked him, "What frat were you in again?"

"That was at Vanderbilt," he said. "You know, you think, 'Huh. *Animal House*. That was a funny movie.' What you *should* think is, 'Those people really existed, and they were monsters.'"

He wondered if he'd ever told me about the time he shit in a small box, hid said box inside his dorm phone booth, then laughed for weeks as the stink made young men weep while collect-calling their mothers?

He wondered if he told me about the times he and some buddies ambushed a bus at the top of an icy Nashville hill—mobbed it, stopped it, pushed against one side until it spun to the bottom?

What about the time he threaded a freshly caught gray mullet into the seat springs of his friend's new car?

"Yep," I said. "*And* the time you were coming back from Tijuana in that car. You slurred to the highway patrolman, 'I can tell by the cut of your cloth you're not a communist,' puked, and still got off scot-free. You've told me all of them. Many times."

These were our bedtime stories, back when me and my sisters had to share a mattress after Hurricane Andrew. Before hitting the lights, Dad would selectively re-create his life for us. The time he woke up to a dead British tourist in his apartment? I know it better than any fairy tale. When he fell into a canal, drunk, on his way to ask Papa for Mom's hand? Could sing it like a griot.

Usually, he cut these stories up with long, interstitial jokes. For instance, there was the one about the Chinese junk merchant who lurked around some soldiers' camp, now and then popping out at them, shouting "SUPPLIES!" There was another I can't quite piece together—something about a camel race, a laggard camel's dangling scrotum, and two bricks?

Anyway, they were all obliquely self-congratulatory, his stories. Collectively, they added up to the kind of no-show, all-tell coming-of-age that's so packed with oddballs and locales and cock-and-bull that, eventually, you can't make heads or tails of what's going on. You just tag along because you're held in the thrall of a voice.

But in rewriting his nightly bildungsroman, he left out a lot of stuff. Namely: the mimesis. Also, the *repercussions of his actions.* These got elided by fits of giggles. To hear him tell it, you'd think the man never suffered any fears, inadequacies, or shames.

. . .

Like most other wondrous things about this nation, the exalta-
tion of Daniel Boone began as a scam. An okie-doke. Boone was
on the downswing of his life, just a few choice claims of Kentucky land to his name, when a freelancer approached him with
a can't-miss opportunity. This freelancer was a former school-
teacher who had quit his job, turned his inheritance into twelve
thousand acres of same, and decided to chase his dream and
just *write*. Together, he and Boone partnered in this plan: pen a
bestselling book; boost immigration to Kentucky and drive up
land prices; profit.

The freelancer's name was John Filson. He was an easternly
dandy whose "mournful eyes bespeak a hopeless despair . . .
Stiffily bound up in a high-buttoned vest, a cravat, and a coat in
the style of pre-Revolutionary France, this melodramatic little
man bears slight resemblance to the stereotype of the American
frontiersman."

Word of Boone had reached Filson thirdhand, after having
been spread first by Boone's fellow travelers, the frontiersmen.
Frontiersmen met infrequently, clearly, but when they did, they
got up to bragging contests. And they bragged about none more
than Boone.

From their stories, Filson recognized that Boone had in him
the distillate of the frontier experience. He contained the many
faces of the new god worshipped everywhere throughout the
young country. There was a great, foundational meaning here,
Filson knew. And he believed he was just the man to release it.

So for two years, he trailed and interviewed Boone. His
problem was that he very much considered himself an artist,
so he took Boone's statements and the legends he'd heard and
repurposed them into his idea of a masterpiece: literary myth,
artfully contrived to appeal to men concerned with literature.

In Filson's hands, Boone became the Rousseauian natural man, *Emile* in buckskins, content to lounge in the shade and philosophize. Filson made no mention of the time Boone threw a dude to his death from a rope bridge, all because the dude was standing in his way. Nor the time a guy mooned Boone, whereupon Boone shot him in the ass. There was nary a peep about Boone getting cuckolded by his twinnish younger brother, and Boone shrugging at this, saying of his daughter-to-be, "She will be a Boone anyhow."

The Boone in this book had little of the man's rude grandeur. He was a projection of Filson's. An expedient. Which was fine by the man himself. The only thing that mattered to writer and subject alike was that readers believe this Boone's world existed. "Incredible as it may appear to some," their book would begin, "[this] is not published from lucrative motives. . . ."

Unfortunately for the odd couple, their book flopped. It was never reprinted in their lifetimes. Filson went on to trade in fur, found Cincinnati, and get murdered by Indians. Boone continued to hunt, trap, and tow his family from one temporary home to another. He wasn't carrying them *to* anything; rather, he was spiriting them away from everything.

In the end, Boone forswore the United States and moved to Spanish Missouri. "He had settled in [America] to end his Days," reported a grandson, "but they got up so many squabbles over land, that it annoyed him, and he Did not want to Die among them." Before he quit our country, Boone supposedly told a young acquaintance, "I have lived to learn that your boasted civilization is nothing more than improved ways to overreach your neighbor."

Unbeknownst to either Filson or Boone, their book had been pirated in Europe, where it became a minor sensation. (Lord Byron was a big fan.) Decades later, it reappeared stateside when a Connecticut printer deleted Filson's philosophical digressions and published the more audacious bits of narrative under his own name.

It was a smash hit. After that, writer upon writer felt compelled to set out and tell the story of the "real" Daniel Boone. They quickly discovered that, while the man's deeds spoke volumes, he was unreflective about the subject of himself. Luckily, there was very little about him that could be fact-checked. So, with Boone unwilling or unable to flesh out certain aspects of his own story, his tellers filled in the rest. Thus, following Filson's Boone came Hall's Boone, Brown's Boone, Peck's, Eckert's, Metcalf's, Draper's, McClung's, Farragher's, Flint's. Each was different, a synthesis of Boone and the writer who looked into him.

William Carlos Williams's Boone was "the antagonist of those of his own blood whose alien strength he felt and detested." James Fenimore Cooper's Boone-clone was a quiet, guileless hunter, one deemed by the *Cambridge History of American Literature* "the most memorable character American fiction has given to the world." In D. H. Lawrence's hands, Boone turned into "the myth of the essential white America. . . . The essential American soul is hard, isolate, stoic, and a killer. It has never yet melted."

Regarding these print treatments, one of Boone's few friends resigned himself to the fact that "they may say what they please of Daniel Boone." Boone himself said, "With me the world has taken great liberties, and yet I have been but a common man."

Depending on the time and the teller, that common man would become: an untutored republican philosophe; a white savage; a slayer of Indians; a principal agent of Manifest Destiny; a stooge for the landed elite; a paragon of racial superiority; a bumbling, garrulous family man. Most often, though, he was written up as the avatar of that particular American—practical and not theoretical, active and not contemplative. The hunter, whose acts of love and sacred affirmation don't sustain his wilderness. They destroy it in the name of something higher.

His story has endured and will endure because, like as in crystal balls and mounted trophies, whatever it is writers want to see in it, they see themselves.

"I know you're tired of my stories," Dad said from under a blanket, his gray eyes on the game. "But at least I *have* stories. Your mother ain't got no stories."

"Yeah, but you wouldn't *want* her to have stories."

"Hell no! When I met her, I'm, what, thirty-eight, hanging around with my ball-playing, shitheel friends—and here was this girl who knew nothing bad. She didn't even know bad *words*. Her favorite song was the theme to *Swamp Fox*, for Christ's sake. It was fucking *amazing*."

The Gators punched one in from the four-yard line. Dad put the fight song on blast. "Every now and again, you do get lucky," he called out.

Although, according to Mom, how it actually went down was:

It's the night of the deciding game of the '77 World Series. She neither knows this nor cares, but she's at a tavern with some colleagues regardless. There, she espies this little tomfool in Dingo boots and a three-piece suit.

Everybody knows him, or else they've got a story about him. He's convivial. Amenable to mayhem. Precipitates lots of toasts, and also grab-assing. He carries himself like he's the main character in the place—and lo, he is.

He's no braggart, but it doesn't take much begging to get him to spin yarns. A captivating rake. That's more or less his role at the small Miami law firm he's transferred to: generator of tall tales, self-mythologizer in chief. He's the guy taking clients to outlying tonks and houses of ill repute, helping them to indulge in their grodier passions. The rainmaker, who beguiles people while simultaneously trimming from them the deep fat of their money. He is the very picture of charm. A soft power, charm, but power nonetheless. A way of asking for nothing and still hearing *yessir*.

Alcohol, of course, is his go-juice. It grants him momentum, which he uses to barge through the world, announcing his place in it. (This place, one imagines, was more often than not the urinal next to another middle-aged white guy pissing with his hands on his hips.)

You might not be able to count on him, Mom's friends tell her, *but neither can you help but root for him.*

Somewhere between Reggie Jackson's second and third home runs that night, this unreformed sailor, this pickled picaresque—he gets around to Mom and starts chatting her up. She's struck by the magnanimity of his abandon. The bright, vicarious thrills. He tosses off unbelievable anecdotes like they're shiny coins; he flings them to hungry hands from his death-bound sleigh. He has hair then. He seems *fun*.

"But, seriously, never get married," he was telling me as Florida ran away with the game. He's been telling me this since the second-grade summer he started dropping me off at Red Berry's Baseball World.

"If you should choose to disregard the cautionary tale that is my life, okay, then at least do me the favor of settling for nothing less than: the only child of recently deceased parents who stands to inherit their chain of liquor stores and strip clubs."

"And watch out for the Chinese!" I added, reciting the practical addendum to *Never get married* before he could.

"Jesus, yes," he agreed. "Stay close to Ryan, Kent. Stay close to the guys with the guns. It ain't zombies you're gonna be fighting—it's the fucking Chinese."

When the final whistle trilled, Dad turned up the fight song one last time. I told him my own story of how, in honor of the Gators' 2005 victory over Tennessee, I played Edward Fortyhands—twice—and then swam naked across the campus lake without getting mauled by one of the team's namesakes.

"You idiot," he said. "The world has changed. It started when people began to *record* all this shit, okay? Used to be that you could just *pour it out*. There was nobody and nothing there to capture it.

"Now, the world has precious little room, or lenience, for dumbasses. *Especially* dumbass writers. Did you type up that little lake escapade? Make some nominal coin off it? Isn't there something else you could be doing to get rich?"

I lifted my leg, countered with a chortling fart.

"Can you teach?"

"Nope."

"Can't fall back on teaching?"

"Na uh."

"Gonna always have to slave for the Huffingtons of the world?"

"Yep."

"Create content? Be a 'content creator'?"

"We got a problem here, you and I?"

"Yeah, we got a problem. You got smarmy, somehow, is my problem. You turned into the *intelligentsia* all of a sudden. You're *ashamed* of me. And now you're going to tell the world I'm this socially unacceptable rube."

"You gotta be fucking kidding me." I gestured at my Kirkland glad rags, old gifts from Mom. I gestured at my can of Coors. I gestured at the life he'd made for us.

"All I'm seeing is Generalissimo Nibshit, rubbing his hands mentally, transcribing what I say."

Right. But what I'd add now is: It's not all betrayal. I am

doing this for reasons beyond the personal. I think. I have to unearth and drag into the light the hissing, congenital demons that are bleeding me dry. Yes. I have to stake them right in the heart. I have to, because I won't allow them to sink their teeth into one more member of this family.

4.

SHOWING UP

It having become apparent to him that his was not the brightest of futures, Bob Probert punched out another boy's upper bridge of teeth.

He didn't know what else to do. His junior-league teammates and opponents had caught up in terms of ability. For the first time in his life, he wasn't the most talented guy on the ice. He still scored okay, and professional scouts still came to his games—only now they were watching the wispy under-agers who toyed with the puck as though biding their time. Probert was getting left behind, and he knew it. He saw but one way forward: become a tough guy.

So he swallowed his pride and assumed the role of his team's enforcer. He made sure no liberties were taken; he fought when they inevitably were. And, as it turned out, he was good at it. A kind of outlaw artist, like some juke pianist, rowdy types arriving from all over to see him mash ivory. Scouts took a renewed interest. Before he could say *goon*, Bob Probert—Probie, as he was known to his teammates, enemies, and cultish fans—was launched on a sixteen-year pro career. Along the way, he collected millions of dollars and 3,467 minutes in penalties (the vast majority for fighting), and he came to be known as the most dreaded tough guy—the most indomitable man—in ice hockey's recent history.

Probert died three years ago, age forty-five, after collapsing on his boat on the Ontario side of Lake St. Clair. Surrounding him as he went were his wife and four children. Though results of his autopsy were never made public, Probert's biographer revealed that he had been taking eight OxyContin per day at the time of his death—two in the morning, two with lunch, two with dinner, two before bed. He liked to dissolve the pills' time-release coating by dipping them in Coca-Cola; then, he'd grind them into powder and inhale them in lines.

The following summer, a smallish tough guy named Rick Rypien killed himself. Rypien had hoped to earn his keep in the National Hockey League by going after opponents well above his weight class. But he lost often, and never quite secured a place in the bigs. They say he'd been suffering from clinical depression for a decade when he decided to end it.

About two weeks after Rypien's death, a hay-haired colossus of an enforcer named Wade Belak hanged himself in his Toronto condominium. He'd only just walked away from a modestly lucrative NHL career. He had a job in broadcasting awaiting him.

Two months before these suicides, Derek "the Boogeyman" Boogaard overdosed on a combination of alcohol and painkillers. Boogaard was a mantispid six-foot-seven. He caved in faces with his fists. Everyone agreed he was Probert's heir apparent. The booze and pills had been his way of self-medicating another in a long string of fight-related concussions.

Like Probert's before him, Boogaard's family donated his brain to neurological researchers at Boston University. And, like Probert's before him, Boogaard's brain showed signs of chronic traumatic encephalopathy, CTE, a degenerative disease common to boxers, hockey and football players, and combat veterans.

CTE can be diagnosed only posthumously. While alive,

though, the afflicted exhibit symptoms like memory loss, depression, anxiety, and rage. They live in a bruised fugue that used to be called dementia pugilistica, punch-drunkenness. Lately, ex-enforcers like Dave Semenko, "Missing" Link Gaetz, "Chief" Gino Odjick, Darren McCarty, Brian McGrattan, and Chris "Knuckles" Nilan have come forward with corroborating stories of post-hockey lives ruined by addiction and psychological anguish.

Concussions appear to be CTE's leading cause, but no one knows how much head trauma is needed for it to develop. One researcher said hockey enforcers "tell me that about one out of every four or five times that they fight they suffer what sounds to me like a concussion."

Hockey is, essentially, entropic. Its central drama revolves around men attempting to create, maintain, and subvert order where there is none. To begin with, the foundation of the game is *skating*, on *ice*, something that comes naturally to zero humans. On top of this balancing act, hockey asks that you: control a rubber disc; pass that rubber disc to your teammate as he, too, skates on ice; retrieve the rubber disc by jarring it loose from another man, also ice skating; all while moving at Olympic-sprinter speeds (via knives attached to your feet) throughout a circumscribed field of play where contact is not only encouraged but guaranteed, as the only things scarcer than respites are exits. Also, everybody's got bludgeons.

We're talking here about a frontier pastime, first played by sanguinary ruffians on the ice of the northern waste. Referees, when present, chose what to call and, like lawmen in the sticks, were pained to do even that. A hook might be a hook in the first period but not necessarily in the third. In overtime, or the playoffs—forget about it.

You get viciously bodied down; the game continues. Your

temper flares as infractions pile up; still, the game continues. Something begins to seep into the play, something bad and communicable. Your frustration leads you to start taking advantage of hockey's unique amnesty vis-à-vis the legal system. You slash the backs of knees with your stick, cross-check vertebrae, butt-end ribs. You, and everyone around you, commit assault.

All involved believe in the personality of the law. A foul is as much an offense against the victim as it is a violation of the rules. The cry in hockey is, "Let 'em play," which rings about the same as "Boys will be boys" and actually means "An eye for an eye."

Reprisal has always been at least one-half of the game. (One Canadian poet called it a "mix of ballet and murder.") It's the unforgiving element hockey's fugitive grace floats on: original violence tolerated, then accepted, then in time turned into custom, into spectacle, into tactic, and finally into theory.

Thusly does the game continue until, at last, your baser nature has flooded and colored your soul. You're ready to crack open an opponent's coconut—*slavering* to, like a castaway—when two men decide it's time to fucking *go*. They drop gloves. The game stops. They throw hands for retribution, or intimidation, deterrence, protection, or momentum—really, what they fight for is catharsis. The way things were going, someone might've gotten *hurt*. They do single combat, and then the game can start up afresh, purged for now like a drained wound.

That's why there's fistfights in hockey.

This willingness to drop the gloves—win or lose, for oneself or a teammate—is called "showing up." Traditionalists would have you believe that, time was, every man on the ice showed up, even immortals like "Rocket" Richard and Bobby Orr. This changed when hockey leagues expanded nationwide in the late

'60s. Suddenly, the talent pool was diluted; all these new teams in the south and west were filling up their rosters with muckers and hatchet men. (Their seats and coffers were filling up, too.) It was no longer viable for a hockey player to be some combination of skill and grit, a willing draftee in any fight. These new guys were thugs, *animals*—laboring skaters who kept getting bigger and stronger, punching harder and harder, even as their quarry's skulls changed not one bit.

The game became specialized, stratified. Now you had #1) your scorers; #2) your less-skilled players who tried to stop the scorers by any means necessary; and #3) your guy at the end of the bench who beat the bejesus out of the #2s when they got overzealous. This guy belonged to the new lowest class of player, the grunt whose sole job it was to look out for #1s: the enforcer.

"When I think of Dave Semenko now—and I often do," Wayne Gretzky wrote of his enforcer, "I don't picture the piercing glare that caused other heavyweights to look down or up or anywhere but back at David. I remember instead the little smile, the quick wink, and the words, 'Don't worry, Gretz.' And you know what? I never did."

The former head of the NHL players union once said that Gretzky would've played "several hundred" fewer games had it not been for Semenko's absorbing and meting out punishment on his behalf. It was this seeming indifference to pain that earned Semenko the nickname "Cement Head." He did things like box Muhammad Ali to a draw. He was a thoroughly terrifying enforcer—though nowhere near as terrifying as Dave Schultz, the dread warlord of the most fearsome team of all time: the late-'70s goon squad known as "the Broad Street Bullies."

Schultz today is still mentioned in hushed tones. Saying his name is unsettling, spooky; no one wants to chance it, like with "Bloody Mary." Instead, he's called "the Hammer." He threw his right fist like a man releasing a bowling ball. His single-season penalty record will never be eclipsed. But ask Schultz who *he* thought the scariest was, and he says, "John Brophy was the toughest and wildest I ever fought."

When Schultz got his clock cleaned by Brophy, he was barely out of his teens, playing in his first professional season. Brophy was at the end of his minor league rope, having spent the years between 1952 and 1973 bouncing around the now-defunct Eastern League, skating in snakepit arenas in decaying industrial cities. The violence there was so thick that Brophy went gray before he was old enough to drink. The closest he'd get to the National Hockey League was breaking an NHLer's leg during an exhibition.

Schultz wrote in his autobiography that Brophy "employed his hockey stick the way a samurai uses a sword. If he had any scruples, he must have buried them the first time he put on a pair of skates." By the time he ended his twenty-year playing career, Brophy had racked up 4,057 minutes of penalties, which comes out to three fights fewer than Rick Rypien, Wade Belak, and Derek Boogaard *combined*.

Props to Bob Probert and Theogenes—but John Brophy was the baddest. Yet the last anyone heard from him was 2007, when he quit his equally storied coaching career. (Only one head coach, the Hall-of-Famer Scotty Bowman, has won more professional hockey games.) Then he just . . . disappeared.

Did he eat a gun? Shove off and put fire to his own Viking funeral?

I had to know. Such is how I found myself one spring morning in a diner in Antigonish, Nova Scotia, Brophy's hometown, feeling stiff and brittle, having not slept well. I ordered two eggs, scrambled, and took a seat at one of the truck stop tables bolted into the linoleum. The space had the dimensions of a shoebox or budget coffin—low, rectangular. In one corner, an ancient empty Coke fridge chanted Gregorian.

Fat men in khakis tinkled the door's bell and sighed while walking past rows of empty place settings. A few elderly couples were drinking tea and scanning the paper. I went ahead and leaned across and called to one huncher gumming toast: "John Brophy, yeah?"

"Brophy?"

"John, yeah."

"Brophy's a Maritimer, sure."

"What're you saying?" asked another gent around the way.

"Brophy."

"Brophy went and he played in the States where they got down on hands and knees and marveled at the indoor ice."

"Team bus'd need a police escort to the county line," the first agreed. "Yessir."

Another old-timer, this one fox-faced, lifted his head from his breakfast and added, "I'll tell ya right fuckin' now—sorry, Ma—I saw a fan spit one on Brophy, right? He spits one on Brophy, and then later Brophy makes like he's digging the puck away from the boards in front of the guy—they didn't have glass separating you from the ice back then—and Brophy butt-ends the guy right in the teeth. Right in the kisser. And then how does he go? He goes, '*Now* spit, motherfucker!'"

"I seen him fight Don Perry. I thought it was like those Japanese monsters. The world was ending."

"When he coached, the fans would throw batteries, and the security guards had to keep him from going up after them."

"Brophy. Whatever it took to get things done, he didn't mind doing."

"Once, he got to stick-swinging with Bobby Taylor, the football player. Like somebody was gonna die. The sticks were shattered all over the place, and they were trying to spear each other with the splinters."

"I don't even know how many times he came out of the dressing room with the needle and thread still in his face, the brawl still going."

"Haw, you miss three *shifts* back then and you were out."

"Different back then."

A leathery waitress in a nurse's uniform brought a patron his milk on ice and then told me where Brophy was: an old folks' home outside of town.

I got directions and found a farmhouse awash in green pasture-land. Behind it, a flock of dingy sheep grazed in a Fibonacci spiral. The wind was tossing fistfuls of slitty rain every couple of beats, like wedding rice. I walked in—the door wasn't locked—and tried the first bedroom. A big guy, not big like tall but big like a mascot, was sliding a cable-knit sweater over his head. I waited, and then we shook hands across the threshold.

"I didn't think anybody'd come," Brophy said.

"It's an honor," I said.

Our handshake stalled. He looked at me obliquely, begin-ning to grin, as if, fine, I'd mangled the pronunciation, but he'd accept the shibboleth.

"I'm going walking today," he said. He stared until I'd retraced my steps to the front door. "Come back tomorrow." Outside there was one heckler, a crow.

The traditionalist would have you believe that enforcers took accountability out of the game. (Do *not* get the traditionalist started on what would happen if all fighting was taken out of the game.) To them, the unprecedented level of technical ability in today's hockey is a kind of decadent virtuosity. A different sport altogether; an exhibition that ought to be scored by judges. One does not simply *get to be* an engine of consequenceless will and expression in this game, according to the traditionalists. Fuck around, and you should have to answer for it. But, no, guys now are able to have their picnic and eat it, too, because enforcers are smoldering blackly at the periphery, keeping out bloodsuckers.

The way the traditionalist sees it, time was, each new crop of players had to venture into hockey's brutal element and test themselves against it, like sailors. And, like sailors, the old would tell the green how poorly they were measuring up. The toughest were dead or retired; the way they played—perfectly irretrievable. Old-time hockey, it's called. It could never exist in the present, any present, because present hockey is always too slick, sleek, knowing, and indulgent. "If some of the longhairs I see on the ice these days met Sprague Cleghorn," coach Red Dutton once remarked, "he'd shave them to the skull. Jesus, he was mean." Dutton said this a *lifetime* ago.

Old-time hockey is in perpetual retreat, never further away than at the present moment—but still it *keeps hanging around*, like a sun slow to set on the horizon. This is just how generations work, I guess. The ideal of old-time hockey lingers in rinks because so do the graybeards who lived it. Or think they did. If it's not how they played, then it's how they *wish* they played. And, with time, it has become how they *remember* themselves playing, their fuzzy past and obscure present cohering like bad binocular vision.

It is no less true now than it ever was: old-time hockey is disappearing. There are many reasons for this, most of them cultural and economic. The short of it is: in the last fifty-plus years, as hockey grew exponentially around the world, peaceable goalchiks began arriving from the Soviet Union, Scandinavia, western Europe—places where the game's revanchist grammar didn't translate. This globalized workforce sped up the pace and quality of the play to the point where tough guys have had a hard time keeping up. They still enforce, but their pressure-release methods have come to seem more and more atavistic to our otherwise sports-and-violence-saturated public.

This is why today's hockey leagues—ever after broad appeal and the casual fan's pocketbook—impose stiff penalties on the instigators of fights. They suspend players for on-ice offenses that used to be settled mano a mano. They dock their pay for overt retaliation. They are legislating violence out of the game.

Meaning that all of a sudden, and for the first time, tough guys are being put out of work. The ones lucky enough to *have* jobs have begun to fight only one another, night in and out, to contest their right to exist. Traditionalists would have you believe that this is the enforcer's just deserts for fracturing old-time hockey's unified nature. As the game is now, though, the enforcer also happens to be the last guy left embodying it.

Let's picture him in a locker room before a game in the minors. He punches into the hard sickle of his left hand, testing the give in his taped wrist. Now—and here especially, in New Haven's clammy dungeon of a rink—his body feels frangible. Flash-fossilized. Let's have him spool another half roll around his wrist.

On his and the other plywood benches, teammates touch elbows to knees and hike socks, adjust shin guards. An eighteen-year-old Albertan, so pale and thin that he appears to be both flesh and light, says, "Colder than a well digger's ass in here, eh? Just as soon start a brawl in warm-ups so as not to catch cold." Let's have our guy think, Bust a bone in your hand and it will never heal right.

He doesn't look up from his tape, which he's wrapping now

around either side of his right thumb, aligning his knuckles. Our guy should like to say that it's them he does it for, personally, his brothers. After all, they're minor league lifers, just like him. Just like him, they have mouths like tied balloons, puckered and toothless, and running tallies of scar tissue all over. Just like him, they'll never do better than seven hundred dollars a week playing ice hockey. They're just like him, except for the Albertan kid. If he can be kept alive long enough to learn how to skate with his head up, he'll be on his way to the Show.

Our guy should like to say that he's happy to intercede for them, but he can't. Long Island is his eighth professional club, and his third in five years. This is a job, same as it ever was. Shit, I've had fights with three guys in this locker room, he'll think. No hard feelings.

He remembers what precipitated them. Dutchie there braked hard in front of my goalie, sprayed ice chips into his eyes, an absolute fucking no-no. Gomer got worked up and said some unfortunate things about Rusty's wife. The Métis by the coffee urn, he was just tweaking out before a face-off, talking gibberish, making me uncomfortable. So, away we went.

His memory is elephantine. It must be; it's part of the job. He accounts for discrepancy. Every cheap shot, each subtle disrespect, any advantage unfairly taken—these have to be balanced out. This game or the next.

Take New Haven's Jackie Leclair. He clipped the Albertan kid in the face at the end of their last meeting; now, our guy has to demand satisfaction. Everyone knows it. "Don't you go get mellow on us," his teammates say with their eyes when they glance at him. "No, I haven't forgot," he says with his. "Do it to him," they conclude, as always, lowering their heads to their gear, "or we'll find someone who will."

Our guy's near done taking close care of his hands. They're

the guarantors of his self-sufficiency, the guns of a gun-for-hire. He butts them together and is satisfied with the distant crackle of pain in his bones. Because of all the chipped and poorly mended metacarpals in his right, he imagines the worst-case scenario, the one that would spell the end, where he tags some numbskull but has his skin split open like a trash bag with broken china in it.

He forces this thought to the bottom of his mind, stands, taps gloves with his teammates, and tinks down the concrete runway to the rink. *The smell's what you fall in love with, damp and raw, like a box of fresh nails.* New Haven is warming up. Their wild shots are barking against the glass. The couple thousand in attendance are already half in the bag. Our guy can hear every word they call to him, up until his right skate touches ice. Then, he is as keen as a bird dog in a field.

A cold, gnatty drizzle was riding in on the wind when I returned to Brophy's farmhouse. He lived here with four elderly women, three of whom were seated with us at the lunch table. The last one couldn't join, but the pneumatic gulping of her oxygen machine lent her a ghostly presence.

Brophy was next to me, eating a ham sandwich. He had a ruddy, swollen face that looked as though it had continued to annex space long after exceeding its bones' infrastructure. He chewed while glaring at the woman across from him.

"She says she wants the death penalty, but she doesn't want it," this woman was saying, referring to the latest development in the sensational trial of Jodi Arias, who had just been convicted of murdering her ex-boyfriend.

"It certainly wasn't self-defense," another added, dragging iceberg lettuce around her plate with her fork. Brophy turned and centered her in his good right eye, rime blue. His left one was half-closed and askance. It looked like the last digit in a broken odometer.

The first woman said, "She snuck up behind him, cut his throat, shot him, and stabbed him—what—twenty-nine times?"

"They should just hang her," a third woman concluded. She fingered a big wicker crucifix resting on her breastbone. "That's what they do? Hang them, still?"

I accepted an oatmeal cookie. The grandmother nearest me asked what on earth I could be doing out here. I told her I'd come for Mr. Brophy; he's a folk hero. She said she doesn't know about all that. "Though John sure knows how to get under your skin when he wants to, boy."

Brophy pawed across his mouth. Everyone stopped talking. "I once seen a long drop," he said. "The head comes off like a champagne cork." He crumpled his napkin, stood up with a little difficulty, and waved me into his bedroom.

He wanted to get away from the house nurse. "I wasn't feeling well a little while ago, so she gave me one of those tests, where you got a letter here and then a letter down there, *there's* a letter, who knows." She took his driver's license away.

"What would you be doing if you had it, your license?" I asked. He sat down heavily in a waffled corduroy recliner aimed at the door.

"I don't know. Probably nothing. That's not the point." He did not put his feet up.

The only hints to his past life were on top of his dresser: three Brophy bobbleheads, all emphasizing his shock of pure white hair. Three lucite stalagmites, from the halls of fame of bush league shitburgs and naval towns. A black-and-white photo of him in his playing days, hip-checking a guy. ("Ass over teakettle! He got the worst of that one!") And hanging above it all was a plaque from the double-A Wheeling Nailers, commemorating his thousandth win as a coach. "Put It in the Books!" it read.

An NHL playoff game between Detroit and Chicago was about to begin. I flipped on Brophy's bedside TV and scooted over in a chair. The walls of his small cell were painted Peep-yellow. All else he had in there was a framed photo of a chocolate Lab, two twenty-pound dumbbells, snakeskin loafers, and one pill bottle, nonprescription.

The lowing wind sent feelers through the poorly sealed window. When the puck was dropped, Brophy squeezed the end of each armrest. His hands were to other men's hands as puffed rice is to rice. A player onscreen picked his head up just in time to dodge a big hit, and Brophy went, "Whoa ho ho! He fuckin' bailed himself out there!" Then, as though a tuning fork had tinged the right resonance and shaken something loose, he inundated me with stories of what his playing days were like.

Our guy's on the bench. *Been* on the bench. He plays maybe eight minutes a night. *But look at the Albertan. Look at the time and space he's given. It's like public skating.* Without it, the kid wouldn't be able to develop the team's offense. His decisions would be rushed and his perception narrowed by anxiety; he'd play as though looking down a length of pipe. But instead he's free to create—see how he both moves through and directs the action, like the open eye that pinions a hurricane?—because it's understood that if he's touched, there'll be hell to pay.

So the kid doesn't worry. But our guy does. The fighting for him started a couple of days before. He looked at the schedule and saw New Haven and knew he'd have to go with Leclair, who ate his lunch a month back when they last fought. *Anyone who does this work and says he isn't scared is a liar.* Our guy tried going to the movies before tonight's game, to distract himself, but he couldn't follow along. He kept imagining Leclair, the way he'd made these faux-scared faces while fighting. A brassy taste flooded his mouth then, something like a kissed ring.

Their last tilt had not been a good one. Our guy was at the end of a rare shift, gassed. Leclair knew this but challenged him anyway, violating one of the game's implicit rules of conduct, known simply as "the code." Our guy obliged, though, and Leclair surprised him by pulling to the left and throwing southpaw. Tagged him bad right off the bat, and our guy wondered, *Is this it? Is this when I become obsolete?*

He was able to hang on. But Leclair had bloodied him, and then he'd done some pro-wrestling hamming for the crowd on his way to the penalty box. *Trotted like a dog just done pissing.*

Now, sitting on the bench, it's as though our guy is back in social studies, looking at the clock, knowing full well that the bully's waiting for him by the monkey bars.

He never did make it through high school. He played major-junior hockey instead, spent his teens crisscrossing the Canadian prairie on thousand-mile bus rides. That first year, he was forced to ride in back, next to the piss hole. *This gap in the floorboard that screamed freezing air and reached for my overnight bag with yellow tentacles.* He was allowed to sit away from it once he had his first fight.

It went down like this: Coach had seen just about enough of our guy—a gangling punk with feet slow as Christmas—try and fail to be "Rocket" Richard out there. So one scrimmage the old bastard sends out someone to test him. *Kim Something*, our guy's height. But whereas our guy would've had to put kettle bells in his pants pockets to come in at 175, Kim Something went 200, easy. He had a five o'clock shadow.

"Wanna go?" Kim Something asked.

This was all brand-new to our guy. He'd never been in a fight before. And not just a scrap during a hockey game—he'd never been in a fight, period. The world might not be ready for the news, but our guy had been a prolific goal-scorer in his bantam and midget leagues. *Certainly nothing of Wayne Gretzky proportions. Hockey Night in Canada never came knocking on my old man's door.* But he'd topped points columns. He'd been scouted for major-junior.

Yet here he was in practice in godforsaken Swift Current with a grown man in his face, shaking free of his gloves. Our guy just reacted. *I was too scared to be a coward.* He reached out with his left hand and grabbed Kim Something's jersey. He looked at his right hand, and there it was, pistoning back and forth, back and forth, back and forth, as though a switch'd been flipped. Before he realized he was in a fight, it was over. Kim Something was down, holding in his face. *I knew right then I was in for it.*

He'd have much rather just played hockey. Contributed with goals or assists. *It was beyond me why anyone would want to take themselves out of the game over a silly thing like a fight.* But he had a job on the team, and there were plenty of other guys lined up to fill the role if he didn't. He made sure Coach never had to say to him, "Go and fix that sonofabitch." He didn't need to be told what he had to do to get on in the game. He went out and he fought when he knew it was warranted.

Was it demeaning? Even if it was, our guy refused to let shame stop him. The way he figured it, he couldn't start to think he was a *thing* to them. *A thing draped in colors and paraded around, like some communist missile.* You start worrying that you're just a goon, and then you find yourself trying to prove you don't deserve that characterization. *You end up going from crusher to rusher to usher.* And, anyway, fighting made our guy a celebrity. *Crowd roars just as loud for a fight as they do a goal.*

When he got his first professional contract at eighteen, it occurred to our guy that he could earn a living playing the game he loved. If he did his work, if he didn't let a lot of irrelevance creep into his thinking, he could make a good life for himself and a family. He could help people he wanted to help; he could have the freedom to make choices. And the price? *If the price was getting tenderized now and again, so be it. It'd've been nice to win those freedoms the way the kid did, but that wasn't up to me.* He was just another guy whose one opportunity had come bound up with obligation, like the army ads say.

"The game now is easier to play," Brophy said, eyes on the TV. "Everybody's more skilled, and they skate better, sure, but that's because they're *allowed to.* Nobody hits anybody anymore. You can be any pretty princess you want when there's nobody out there'll take you to task."

"How would Sidney Crosby do back in the Eastern League?" I asked.

"Who could fuckin' say?" The wind and deathly metronome of the oxygen machine combined in eerie threnody. "Guys like him and Gretzky, though. Gretzky was such a little shit. A whiny little shit. When I coached against him, he goes—" Here Brophy rubbed limp-wristed hands against his eyes and said in an effeminate voice, " 'You guys don't deserve to hit me. You guys can't hit me.' "

"We can't hit you? Okay. Here's a bucket to cry in."

In his playing days, Brophy's postgame ritual sometimes included nights spent on the bathroom tile, prone and puking. His off-season regimen was manufacturing hangars in Labrador and working high steel on the Verrazano-Narrows Bridge.

Opposing teams would sign guys away from their day jobs just to have them go after Brophy on the weekends. Amateur boxing champions, barroom heroes—he beat them so badly that some nights, the riot police had to be called into the arena. Some nights were worse: after one game in Connecticut, the apocrypha goes, a fan of the rival club climbed the rink's fire escape, peered through a window that looked into the locker room, saw Brophy in the shower, aimed a Saturday night special at him, and fired. The bullet ricocheted around the room before spinning to rest at Brophy's dripping feet. Some say he laughed.

All in all, Brophy played for twenty-two years, never reaching higher than the double-A leagues two rungs below the NHL. He wound up his playing career in Cherry Hill, New Jersey, living out of a closet in an apartment he shared with teenage teammates. "I just wanted to play as long as humanly possible," he told me. "Fighting made it twice as good, and I could do it. I vowed that I'd never lose my job to another. I didn't."

When he was done playing, he started coaching. He coached his way through several minor leagues—the Southern, Central, American, North American, World—imparting his same means of survival onto his players. He taught them that fighting was about minimizing weaknesses, and hockey about never showing them. He wanted to make sure his boys were prepared for the sport as he'd known it, so he instilled in them a slow habituation to pain, a numbness to violence.

"Don't consider this a threat, boys," he used to say, "but I'm coming after each one of you." He dared them to hit back. He saved his most hateful language for anyone who refused a fight. "Look at that Charlie Bourgeois!" he'd say. "Turtling up like a pussy!"

His playing ability never got him to the NHL, but he did coach his way there for a few seasons in the late '80s. Toronto, the richest club in the league, thought its roster had become complacent, spoiled, so they brought in Brophy to straighten them out. His motivational tactics worked long enough for the team to make the division finals. Soon after that, though, they turned on him. "We'd all like to go and shoot him between the eyes," one of them said. Years later, reinterred in the minors, Brophy discovered that all of his young wards had come to feel the same way. No longer able to make himself understood, he quit the sport.

What was the greatest moment in his lifetime of hockey? "The hell kind of question is that?" What was the first thing that just came to mind? "This time in Clinton, New York, when Don Perry was beating the fuck out of this Charlie Bourgeois, and a fan jumped on the ice and ran for him. I laid as nice a hit on him as you could've asked for."

During a long commercial break, one of the other residents shuffled in, joggling a tray of hard caramels in one hand and a shot glass full of pills in the other. "Oh, please, you've got to put him in the *Casket*," she said, referring, thankfully, to the local rag.

"I said I'd get them," Brophy told the woman, pointing to the shot glass.

"I've tried to get my children to tell the editors, 'Make Brophy famous!'" she said to me. "Take his picture. Promise me you'll take his picture."

I did as she asked with my cell phone. Brophy looked from me to her with pursed purple lips.

He stirred the air with his shot glass, smiled. The TV announcer (whom Brophy once coached) interjected: "Let's watch that contact to the head!" Brophy took his medicine. Then he said to the two of us, "Oh, yes, *let's*."

Our guy's in a corner of the rink, in a one-sided fight. His hands have shed their gloves and are flying about the face of some plugger like new moths around a sodium lamp. Everyone else on the ice has found a partner to hold on to while they watch our guy get his. He's hitting mostly forearms and elbows; the plugger is hugging his face and sinking to his knees.

Moments earlier, the Albertan kid had been handling the

puck with his head down when this nobody here took a run at him. The kid sensed the hit at the last moment and sidestepped it, but the plugger stuck out his right leg and knee-on-kneed him. *It's a miracle nothing snapped.*

Our guy had just jumped onto the ice as part of a line change. He saw the kid spin down, writhing, and he didn't need to look for the puck or listen for a whistle. *Heard a piercing sound, like when regular scheduled programming's interrupted.*

"Pull that shit again, fish," he says. "Manhandle" isn't the term for what he's doing. It's something more desperate, the way he's clutching and yanking and pawing at him—our guy is *ragdoll*ing his antagonist.

He's easing up on punches to the skull because the plugger's got a helmet on. *Things're dangerous; things'll pop a knuckle.* Uppercuts, however, he's wheeling with abandon.

Did the plugger mean to do it? *Does it matter?*

Our guy keeps throwing until an official steps in. On the way to the penalty box, this official asks him no questions as to *why*. No one ever has, or will.

Shortly after, the Albertan kid does score, and his goal's a thing to behold. He glides from behind his own net, calls to the man with the puck, takes his pass in stride; then he blows past the first forechecker, cuts inside on the next, crosses the blue line and powers through a heavy slash—*he can stay upright when he wants to, the fucking gamesman;* then he gets the right-side defenseman to go fishing on a deke, then he fakes to the backhand before cutting forehand and sliding the puck between the goalie's legs—then he punctuates it all with a war whoop and a punch to the glass. Our guy is on his feet, thinking, *A little selfish, maybe.*

And watching from the box as the kid's mobbed by teammates. Given affectionate face-washes and attaboys. The child beaming, at home in his body as only one whose body is not his job can be. Our guy catches himself smiling at the thought of looking the other way, spreading the evening paper in front of his face, letting the other boys have at him.

Brophy didn't want to finish watching our game. Instead, we bundled up against the wind and went outside with Lady, the home's communal golden retriever. The late-spring landscape was vibrantly green, the tint of inexperience.

"You suffer a lot of concussions in your career?" I asked.

"I should fucking say so." He knocked a knuckle against the mantle of his skull. This was the thick head, I'd heard, that not once but *twice* was ejected through windshields (Brophy having truck with neither man nor belted seat). That was so often a weapon it was not unusual to see Brophy in the box shunking incisors out of his forehead the way Civil War soldiers used to do minié balls. He rapped this head, and if a sound was made, I didn't hear it.

We ambled along a post-and-rail fence some stallions were grazing behind. "Jesus, look at them," Brophy exclaimed. "Jesus Christ, they're beautiful. You know who's in shape? Waists like *this.*"

I wondered aloud if his thick skull was the reason he wasn't susceptible to all that scrambled-brain stuff. "I don't know." Wasn't he ever scared about what comes next? "I don't lose any sleep over it. I might not win it, but I sure won't lose."

Depression?

He chuckled, the sound of a single stone plinking down a well. "Are we in a prescription drug ad? You want me to talk to my doctor about pills for my guy?" In the daylight, I could see the faint blue webbing of burst vessels in his cheeks. He said,

"Look, you could die on the bench, but you could not die on the ice. You crawled to the bench. Your own players would shanghai you if you were out there rolling around. No, you crawled. And I made lots of 'em crawl. But they made the goddamned bench.

"They say now that they're addicted?" Brophy went on. "I coached Dave Semenko. Piece of shit. Worthless. Worthless alcohol addict. Once, he missed a home game. *A HOME GAME.* I went into his room, found him with, I don't know, bottles of wine everywhere. He said he needed help. Help. You drink—you're a hockey player, of course you drink. But then you quit when you quit."

After a moment, I said, "That sounds about as feasible as squeezing it off mid-pee."

Brophy dropped a trembling hand onto Lady's head, letting it do the petting the way an electric mixer beats an egg. Then he bowed once, twice, three times to relieve the tightness in his lower back, and added, "I never considered the fact that *anything* could keep me from doing my job."

The one day I was sure Papa couldn't lay me out was the last day I saw him alive.

He hobbled out of his bedroom with his sport shirt untucked and his face unshaven, the only instance of either that I can recall. His big blue eyes were screwed deep into his head. The doctors had only just found it, the cancer that was knotted through his intestines like a rat king, gnawing away. The pain he could no longer deny. But by then, of course, it'd *been* too late.

Throughout his life, Papa had worn the scowl of Samuel Beckett and thrown hands regardless of who was in the right. This was remarkable to me. Papa wouldn't equivocate if he suspected someone of threatening him or the people he was close to. He felt froggish, so he jumped.

One time, when we were walking down Ocean Drive on South Beach, I toed a brown scuff against the grain of a seated stranger's crispy-white Air Force 1. The left one. He stood up very quickly, asked "What the *fuck?*" With my still-breaking voice, I let out a noise like an inexpertly squeezed accordion. Papa flexed his knees, leaned back, weaved his fingers together over his stomach, and chugged this, "Oh, ho ho, ye-ow! Oh!"

By then, Papa had come to stoop under the thick back that'd stood him so well in his younger years. His traps—all his muscles, really—were broad and ill defined, labored after. I doubt there was anything he could not shoulder. And his hands were enormous, real mitts. They were hardily expert but surprisingly soft. Every Saturday, he showed up at our house and used them to fix something mechanical, eat a ham sandwich.

One of my favorite things used to be punching into them. The ol' one-two, his palms enveloping my rocky kid fists. I both loved and feared the pliable forcefulness of those hands. Every sentient creature did, I think. Animals respected his touch. Our dogs esteemed him highest. Fishing, we'd catch crabs, and Papa would invite me to watch as he tickled the underside of each until it fell asleep in his palm, discharging this gross black unguent before it got chucked in the pot.

The front of his right fist was a shambles, though. His knuckles were badly set, like the rolling letters in the HOLLY-WOOD sign. Still, he planted them just the same in the face of that large, angry man. The man scuttled in a hurry, to leak there on the ground. Papa continued to laugh. This was neither the first nor the last time he would fight for me.

All he had known was impersonal violence. Or so I was told. When he was a boy, he found his father swaying from a barn joist. His mother he had to institutionalize. After his older brother abandoned him to their decaying Pennsylvania farm, Papa survived the Depression by trapping minks. At eighteen, he went to war.

He could joke about the killing. He wouldn't talk about what it had *felt* like—depth being a suspect dimension—but he'd crack wise about the poor bastards who'd got theirs. He could spin this long yarn about the time he escorted a soldier to his execution. The guy had inadvertently murdered a fellow GI when he brained him with a full beer bottle. Papa took him and painted London red, burned through the last of the condemned man's cash. Then, he delivered him to his hanging, and stayed to watch.

He still wasn't saying much that last day I saw him. It was as though he was in another place altogether, lacing up. He wouldn't bring any dinner to his mouth; my mother fed her father like an infant. Afterward, sitting on his living room couch, cargo jets shearing the silence as they landed at Miami International across the street, I asked about his life as best I could.

What was absolute tops? He shrugged. What stuck out the most? He mentioned the afternoon he saw some guys playing baseball while riding on donkeys. Donkeys were shitting all over the diamond, he said. Bucking guys off, biting them on the hands, on the asses, on other donkeys' asses. I suppose now that that's what *was* memorable to him. Not the hard work, suffering, or violence. A fish knowing least about the water it swims through—that kind of thing.

Prior to that day, I had never thought to ask him about his past. He was a *grandfather*, you know? What's a grandfather but a grinning, declawed mascot of the man he used to be? An anthropomorphized beast. He punched a few guys out every now and again, sure. But he loved to golf and dance and steward his church. That he had once been someone other than Papa—had in fact been a clenched man named Alexei Romanchuck—had seemed impossible until then.

What I wanted to say but could not was: Your life is literally unimaginable to me. It marks the distance between *then* and *now*. Had I been slotted into it, I surely would not have been strong enough. How did you do it, survive? What can you share? Please. Am I made to guess?

Whatever it was I *did* say prompted Papa to maunder about other things: the big bands that used to play during movie-house intermissions, the free trips to China and Greece he was entitled to as an Eastern Airlines employee. He offered up more and more non sequiturs. He was like some foreign-language speaker handing me a spoon, then a pack of playing cards, then a glass of water, smiling all the while, handing me anything and hoping to hit on what would make me stop talking.

Later, Mom came up to us with melting eyes. She said it was time to say goodbye. I said, "I love you," and for the first time Papa didn't say, *Yeah*, but rather, "I love you, too." We made promises to see each other soon.

The cancer that killed him a few days later looked more like a gemstone, I was told. A geode, wetly glistening. What was it Hemingway called guts? Grace under pressure?

It's late, and our guy's team is down a goal and looking flat. He's on the bench with his elbow over the lip of the boards, effervescent with adrenaline. He knows what's coming. The couple thousand in attendance know what's coming.

New Haven changes lines on the fly—out comes Leclair. Now our guy's like a rocket about to lift off. Shaking from the inside out. He's anticipating the moment he'll be released from gravity, his body falling away like a delivery booster. He gets a pat on the back from Coach. Over the boards he goes.

The arena's ringing palpably, an expectant tinnitus. The tough guys are rounding the ice, a little behind the play. People stand and point.

Our guy glides up behind Leclair. He runs the toe of his

stick's blade overlong his head, ear to ear. "Now or never," he says. Leclair pivots into a backward skate, spits, and smiles.

He has an inch or two on our guy, as well as a shovel chin and a forehead lined deeply from squinching while punching. His hairline is in deep retreat, so he's shaved his round skull clean. He looks, like most bullies, obtuse.

He and our guy toss sticks and gloves well clear at center ice. Being both righties, they circle counterclockwise. They hold their left hands out and open in front of them, snatching at the air as if after a fly. Leclair lunges, and because of his extra reach is able to grab our guy's jersey where it rests over his right shoulder. He's bringing back his fist for a punch when our guy reaches out and takes hold of the fabric around Leclair's right elbow. Our guy tries to deflect Leclair's right, but it comes in over our guy's left arm and lands on the crown of his head. Leclair throws a few more glancing blows while our guy attempts to shake his right arm free.

Neither man is angry. They are, in fact, in an almost ecstatic state, agape, as though finally able to relieve themselves.

Our guy's trying to land rights, but whenever he throws one, Leclair pushes his own jersey-gripping hand deeper into our guy's shoulder, tethering his range. Now Leclair is popping our guy in the jaw with a few rabbit punches delivered by that jersey-gripping left hand. He rears back as if to come with another overhand right, but instead slides underneath our guy's guard and shivers him with an uppercut.

A male chorus is howling around them. Teammates, coaches, fans, fathers and sons—each of us is singing his release. We're urging or critiquing a fighter, cheering or hissing, pushing him to give more of himself or ridiculing him if we think he's holding back. We're a bizarro panopticon, thousands of guards overlooking our captive.

It's us our guy has to bend and comply to; us who hold his

life in our hot little hands. We each think meanly of ourselves and how we've shaped up in the eyes of one another, so we have our guy play the part we decided was meant for us.

We watch him, weigh him, judge him—we made him! He's a tough guy, but he's a tough guy only so long as we say he is. We conferred his status; we'll take it away if he fucks up once.

Together, we are a petulant god, as vindictive as a sewing circle. And we will cut out heart after heart until we get our perfect sacrifice.

Our guy butts his lowered head into Leclair, causing him to lose his grip on our guy's right arm. They seize each other around the collar. They open up.

They turn away their faces and reel off punch after punch as though burning through a currency about to go defunct. They hold each other upright, counterbalanced, and spin with blows. They are gusto, vigor, and virility, or else they're the recurrent problem of civilization. They beat on all the more fiercely because, in another world, they might've been friends.

With each hit, their fists bloat and soften, sponge. It's been forty-five seconds; they're almost empty. No clear winner, they try now to wrench each other off their feet, style points going to the guy landing on top. They torque. They make awful strangled noises, *hnnnghh!*'s. They're forehead to forehead, swapping respiration. Our guy watches as one and then another drop of blood blots the ice. He doesn't know if it's him or Leclair who was cut in the punch-up. They spin one last time, skate blades spraying red shavings. Then the linesman steps between them, saying, "That's it, boys! You're done."

Our guy glides arm-in-arm with the official. From behind him comes the sound of both teams drumming the boards with their sticks, thunderous recognition. He doesn't need to look to know the kid is one of them, nodding as he does so. If intoxication means going too fast from feeling worthless to worthy—*so be it. Everything else might go to shit, but this is something I can count on.* He feels relief wash over him like helicoptered water dropped on a wildfire.

And we just clap and holler, happy to have seen it played out. The official closes the door on our guy. Sealed in the box, he does whatever a rung bell does after the sound fades.

A lovely young nursing student from Uganda came and prepared meatballs, steamed vegetables, and perfect scoops of whipped potatoes for dinner.

"You get drunk again last night?" Brophy asked, a half-chewed olio in his open mouth. The student looked seriously flustered. Then he added, "Na, I'm just funning." Under everything was the absent respirator's puncture/sibilance/gasp/puncture.

A halo-bald Irishwoman in a tartan skirt, tartan blazer, and tartan bib sat next to Brophy and told indecipherable but really ribald-seeming jokes. Everyone but him guessed politely at her punch lines. ("Tea?" "Brie?" "Who took high tea?" "No, we don't have any Hi-C." *"Bees??"*)

Then the others chatted hopefully about a Jodi Arias execution while I watched Brophy struggle to feed himself. He could shovel the food just fine. But the nearer to his face he lifted his spoon, the higher the frequency of the tremors in his hand. Again and again he'd scoop some succotash; and again and again it would shake free on the way to his mouth. I could see the rage trapped in his dead eye, all pupil and a thin ring of iris, this black-and-blue Saturn. On the cheek below it was a keloidal blossom from who knows what. A bite, probably. Looked like a cauterized kiss.

"You really want to know why those guys offed themselves?" Brophy asked, putting down his spoon. "It's because of now. They came up one way. They were told that they were great scorers; they got trophies and mentions in the newspaper. All that bullshit. Maybe it was true, to some extent. But then it turns out that to get to the next level they had to change. Lower expectations. Play their part. They had to stop with the Gretzky shit and fight. They thought they'd make it as Charlie Bourgeois!

"So they do it, but they don't like it. But they still have to do it. And they try to cope. Tell you the truth, they'd be better off if they'd grown up with it, instead of having to change. Nobody plans for being a fighter anymore."

After dinner, we watched a horse race on TV. I was slow in leaving, but when I did say goodbye, I said, "Mr. Brophy, you're a legend." What I meant was, It's a shame you'll disappear from life before you can see yourself become a myth.

He said, "How I saw it, I fought, or I disappeared. And if I wasn't playing hockey, I knew I was going to die." Then he smiled with his whole face, leading with his chin.

The Bay Area is *nice*. Mom and Dad's apartment is *nice*. Nice in the way that any place that is not your home—that you will be leaving directly, and are not responsible for—can be *nice*. The new technocrati hovering above us in app-chartered helicopters—I'm sure that if the capability is extant within their slouched physiques and posthuman, delphine psyches—they, too, think it's *nice*.

But it would be incorrect to say that I miss the big old house. You couldn't pay me to spend a night there alone. Even (especially!) if it somehow reassembled itself like the House of Usher in reverse. I wouldn't so much as lay my head on the now-empty lot. You know, take away the headstones—it's still burial ground underneath.

We called it "Russellhaus." I have no idea why. We liked the musty, ancestral connotation, I think. Vaguely mead hall-y. A warm place to hunker down, wait for Grendel.

It stood in a hammock, which is an environment where things live and die so quickly and often that they create solid land out of swamp. At points in its history, our neighborhood—the Grove—was favored by key deer, Bahamian laborers, hippies, and drug lords. The roads aren't straight, they knot neuronally, and the place is forever shagged with fronds, ferns, and noose-less braided vines. A golden grout of sunlight makes it through the fretwork, but you can't see the ground for the crushed berries. There are no sidewalks.

The last time I visited, I saw that our street had only four listing old-Grove houses left. I went around and counted. The rest were now-typical Miami homes, gated and garishly painted. Their yards were defoliated, as if to keep clear the owners' lines of sight. Aside from leased luxury sedans, these homes are the smallest units of what the city's made up of, its atoms. If public life depends on sympathy, and if sympathy means being able to say *Your issues are not my issues, but I want to understand what they are, and respect them*, then I cannot say there's a lot of public life, or sympathy, in Miami.

At the end of our street was a small park that fronted the water. This was where Dad and I would play ball, sometimes for an audience of Miccosukee who had come to the park's free-standing chickee hut to get lit. After October, migrated midwestern vultures would roost in the trees, like committees of bald scholars blackly hunched. Every other month, we'd find a beached, makeshift raft there. These inspired Karen and me to attempt our own escape. Amid some spousal tiff one day, the two of us inflated a pool lounge and took covered tennis rackets for oars. We made it as far as the channel marker a hundred yards offshore before our craft sprung a leak. A single gull was sitting on the marker's piling, and a skipjack flashed out of the water, chased by some predator. The waves pushed us back.

When the sea returns for Miami, that park is where it'll start. The end of our street also happened to be where, through some quirk of meteorology, people's celebratory New Year's bullets rained down. I'd find the flattened shells in the soft earth next to crab holes. I kept an old cigar box full of them, would scoop and tinkle them through my fingers like doubloons.

To grow up there was to confront vitality and spontaneity, with all that that entailed. Every dead thing a sacrifice. Such a beautiful place.

What was *not* beautiful, however, was Russellhaus. Structurally, she was a single, narrow story that rambled down a hill (or what passed for a hill in Miami) like an architectural landslide. Quite the heap. There were three bedrooms, three baths, several small staircases of two or three steps. A pool full of dead leaves and water bugs. Tile *and* carpet. Wet bar in the master bedroom.

The façade was poured concrete, bunker thick, surrounded by a six-foot wall of same. Aerating it were a lot of poorly sealed plastic windows and French doors. There once stood tall iron gates at the end of the driveway, but these rusted off their hinges and were left to blanch in our trash-strewn backyard. We had no garage, but we *did* have the shed and the canopy. The shed was originally conceived and built by Papa as a seven-by-six playhouse for Karen and Lauren. They got to use it three times before Dad turned it into a dog food, lacquer, and scrap lumber repository, shot through with spiders the size of baby hands. The canopy was a tent designed to keep a van out of the elements. It was filled with tools and curios; then, over time, snakes; finally, a family of feral cats.

She was not watertight, Russellhaus. Rot caused the kitchen ceiling to sag to head height. Tree roots grew through walls, becoming structurally integral. When it rained, which was almost every afternoon, ochre water dripped into buckets at the rate of bagged saline.

"Character," Dad reiterated whenever a newer house went up on the empty lots around ours. They were Mediterranean-revival compounds, neo-eclectic superstructures, art deco mansions. Each bigger and more expensive than the last. "Whereas your home, it's lived a life," he'd say, roping down the American flag that flew on a tall pole within our walls from sunrise to sunset. On the bus home, classmates would see this flag sopping limply in the humidity, and they'd wish me and my sisters *Adiós, Americanos.*

Inside, the overwhelming sensory impression was: fungal. Russellhaus smelled like damp transmigration. Thinking back, I wonder—Is that why we took so many naps? Why we all staggered through adolescence, logy as fuck? *Black mold?*

Whatever it was, it made me . . . imperceptive. With my close neighborhood bud Ricky, for instance. Ricky was a well-fed Panamanian with a mushroom cut and the eyes of a ruminant. We'd been fast friends since his family moved in up the block. We played in the same baseball league, shared a third-base coach who'd sing "Let Me Ride That Donkey" if you tripled. After school, we'd kill hissing invasive lizards with sticks. He seemed to have a million different uncles, these sallow-eyed, lipless men who'd take us deep-sea fishing.

But one warm December day in '93, I found out he was moving. A thing he did often, apparently. He invited me to a combination housewarming/New Year's party his family was having.

His new place had high walls topped with sharp fleurs-de-lis, and first-floor windows decoratively barred. Cocked quizzically above a steel door were two security cameras looking like air quotes: "Welcome." Dozens of guests had already arrived. Everybody was in finery, kids included, in excellent gaucho boots and gowns that swooshed and riffled. The action was around the pool, fifty feet long with a swim-up bar at one end and a fake rock cliff at the other.

Normally, Ricky's mother floated about the house in what now seems to have been a heavily narcotized state, bathrobe unbelted, ponderous fake breasts hard to ignore. Here, though, she was chastising the Incan-looking help in moneyed Spanish.

Ricky's dad I'd never actually spoken to. I was told he worked as a salmon fisherman in Alaska. Now, though, he was across the pool in teak-colored lenses, laughing among a murder of brickish dudes in suits. He was beaming like the newly convalescent.

All the guests were smiling like that, like they'd just beat something. They seemed to have done it together, or at least were complicit. Everyone knew everyone and was toasting something—what it was, they weren't saying. A DJ spun Grupo Niche salsa. The mood was such that people were jumping into the pool, shoes and all, and swimming up to the bar.

Later, Ricky's dad smashed one of the caterers' faces on that pool bar. Something about weak drinks, and not keeping up with demand. He swung over and started pouring generously. He clinked glasses with another of my friends' dads, Roberto's, a contractor who built all or part of the new house, I'm not sure. He was a real jocular guy, Roberto's dad. Practically every time I stayed the night at his house, he'd have his associates and friends over, electricians and landscapers he slipped jobs to. They'd go into the den to drink and smoke cigars, fuck around, talk a little business—things I imagined I'd do as a grown man in Miami.

He's in prison now, Roberto's dad, for fraud. Just the other year, I learned that Ricky's dad was a Noriega coke lieutenant. He lessened his sentence by becoming a federal informant. He and his family were in the witness protection program. My own father found out but never mentioned it. His suspicions were confirmed after a sleepover, when he called Ricky's dad and told him, "I have your son here—how do you want to do this?" One gravid pause later, Ricky's dad said, ". . . What is it that you want?" "To . . . get rid of . . . your son . . . ?" Dad said, suddenly wide-eyed and cognizant. Asked later why he didn't say anything—"God*damn*it, Dad, I could've been blown up with their Chevy Venture!"—he responded: "Shit, everyone was getting well back then, myself included. Who do you think built this place?"

When the New Year ticked over, the male guests at Ricky's new house fired rounds skyward. I jumped into the pool, too, drank cups of fountain Coke and ruined my rented tuxedo.

Russellhaus was herself purchased out of bankruptcy from an associate several degrees removed from Ricky's dad, an "international coffee importer." Strange shit was certainly abrew in there. For instance, there were *waaaaaay* too many phone jacks. Phone jacks where there should be no phone jacks—in the attic, under the carpet, deep inside closets. Add to that the several false walls, and rooms with non-Euclidian geometries. The angles in my bedroom did not add up. It was painted a jaunty teal, but still it felt like some Lovecraftian gateway chamber. Not least because a bricked-over door to nowhere stood at one end, occasionally seeping this oxidized ooze. I would not be surprised to find that, in its blueprint design, Russellhaus was less an architecture than the diagram of a psychic event.

All of us but Mom were absolutely *certain* that something was hidden in there with us. Treasure, or maybe worse. Periodically, a hive of bees would appear in the living room chimney; the next morning, they'd be littering the floor in their death throes. Violent midnight thundershowers often caused the electricity to cut out; when the lights came back up, there'd be a dozen blue crabs slowly suffocating in the shallow end of our pool, their pincers up like dukes. After Hurricane Andrew, when that pool was drained of detritus and storm-surged bay water, a dorsal fin, then a caudal fin, and finally a shark's lifeless snout dawned at the bottom like the worst realization.

We were broken into and (ostensibly) ransacked three times. Only once was anything taken.

Karen and Lauren: "Of course that dump was haunted." Karen: "The worst juju was in your closet." Lauren: "Oh, fuck, yeah—your closet." Dad: "When we were cleaning out the house before selling it, I went up into the crawl space above your closet. Eerie shit, man. I was not comfortable. All the wood up there—it was like brand-new. Blond, firm wood. Remember, that was underwater during Andrew."

The thing about a haunted house is it's narcissism's friendly confines. A place where time passes slowly, if at all. Where you grow more and more obsessed with your own sordid past or problems. The past *itself* becomes the specter darkening your present.

There, you screw inward instead of growing outward. You're caught in an endless repetition of neurosis-driven thought and action. There, you have setting as psychological pathetic fallacy. A palpable disease you drink in, unconsciously.

Strangest of all at Russellhaus was an outdoor bust of Bacchus. Not the cherubic Bacchus you usually see—we're talking aged Bacchus, leathery in the face, his grape-leaf wreath come undone. Bacchus through the wringer. His eyes looked skyward, and his chin was tucked into his neck. His hair was matted, and his thick lower lip hung ajar, grouper-like. He looked indescribably pained, or else about to barf.

His bust was affixed to a back wall, on top of a hollow, coffin-shaped plinth. Our meter reader thought he was the Devil. Another guy refused to clean our pool because he feared we were LaVeyan Satanists. To combat this, young Karen X'ed out Bacchus's eyes and scrawled "I LOVE THE LORD" across his base.

The only thing that for sure ghosted around that place was Dad. Russellhaus's animating spirit. He was there when we woke up, there when we got back from school, there when we went to the kitchen to fix a midnight snack. (Though by then he was usually passed out in the recliner with the lights off, the TV on, and the shadows of muted snow flurrying across his face.) From the day after he lost his job to the day I went off to UF—a closed loop of character who was not exactly *pleased* with his new plane of existence, but who was resigned to existing intransitively now.

Although, unlike most ghosts, he did not want anyone to uncover the crime that had created him. Jesus, no. He does not want a proper burial for his bones.

5.

SAY GOOD MORNING
TO THE ADVERSARY

What it was I felt was the fist of my heart in my chest. I felt this every night, unless I happened to be spectacularly drunk. The feeling gripped me at least forty-five minutes after I'd fallen asleep but never more than sixty. It jolted me awake with the full understanding that some *thing* was in the room with me.

The feeling often coincided with noiselessness: the thermostat shut off, or the traffic vanished, and I was roused by the scream of the silence. Sometimes I'd come to but wouldn't move. I'd think, I'll be okay, so long as I don't budge. Sometimes I threw the cover two feet above me, where it briefly caught air, me-shaped, like skin jumped out of. I'd be down the hall by the time it came to rest.

Usually, though, I sat up and just stared at what I took to be a person. He smeared the air around him, made it go viscid like preignition shimmer, so it was hard to tell. I wished he'd have the decency to announce his coming, maybe groan a little outside my locked bedroom door. At least then I could've girded myself. That was the worst part—not knowing how long he'd been in there with me, with nothing between us.

This particular time, I was in a hotel room in Pittsburgh. I stared and stared at a sort of mirage with a face. My heart clenched, but the rest of me shook at an awful frequency. The only thing I can think to liken it to is the wobbly singe you feel when you make bad contact with a baseball bat. The man or his ghost evanesced eventually. But I did not get back to sleep, and I lurched through the next day, my first at the program.

I was eight the last time I slept soundly, and for this I thank one man: Tom Savini.

Tom Savini is a sixty-seven-year-old special-effects artist, a sometime director, and an actor on the up-and-up. Distinct geeks revere him for his effects work in horror films from the 1970s and '80s, stuff like *Dawn of the Dead* and *Friday the 13th*. But it's not like he was the best effects guy back then. Back then, Rick Baker was winning the first of his seven special-effects Oscars. Tom Savini was never so much as nominated.

What he was, though, was the pioneer of hyperrealistic blood and guts, what the film historians call "splatter." "The Sultan of Splatter," they christened him. "The Godfather of Gore." He was the first and best at making bodies reveal themselves onscreen. His work also happened to be the literal embodiment of the shift in horror movies from fright to terror, from beatable alien monsters (*The Creature from the Black Lagoon*) to the abominations within (practically every serious horror film since *Night of the Living Dead*). *Film Comment* wrote of him, "It can be argued that Savini, through his effects work, offers us a distinctly modern view of an alienated human existence. The assaulted bodies he creates are all flesh, and no spirit." His death scenes are glorious, and his creatures dense and unctuous. His stuff cuts deep.

When I caught my first glimpse of it, eight-year-old me inched as near as possible to the screen, the better to gawk at the fonts of blood and stomachs pulled agape. I laughed; I was enlivened by it. How'd they manage to do this, I wondered, make it seem so real? I couldn't look away from the man's handiwork then—and I still can't. Neither can a lot of maladjusted dudes come of age: Quentin Tarantino recently put Savini in *Django Unchained.* He was just featured in Robert Rodriguez's *Machete Kills.* J. J. Abrams loves him, as do Matt Groening, Oliver Stone, and Stephen King, whose head Savini has exploded on camera. Darren Aronofsky wants him for his upcoming Noah's Ark project. He's been on *Letterman* five times. Less famous devotees have hand carved or tattooed countless homages to his creations: Jason, Lizzie, Fluffy, Bub, Dr. Tongue, Helicopter Zombie—the whole silicone gang poured directly from the dark matter of childhood subconsciousness. His engagements at horror conventions are rumored to earn him as much as ten thousand dollars a pop.

During one of my interrupted nights the other summer, with nothing else to do but futz around online, I discovered that Savini has an academy. An atelier, more like. Tom Savini's Special Make-Up Effects Program, in Monessen, Pennsylvania. It's the first of its kind, a sixteen-month curriculum in which students learn sculpture, makeup, molding, and casting from guys (and it's all guys) who're either done with Hollywood or taking a break from it. The instructors have each worked with Savini, apprenticed under him, or been inspired into the craft by the man. I signed up for the summer session and flew to Pittsburgh. The idea, I suppose, was to learn how to reverse engineer the things that haunted me.

Monessen was a corpse of a place. Steel supports jutted at fractured angles from abandoned buildings downtown. Ribby grills were pulled across spiderwebbed shop windows displaying dusty nothing. I counted a dozen houses of worship, about ten more than I did pedestrians. The Savini School was the only thing astir. It's a four-story bloodred brick building backed up against a Catholic church. It used to be a nunnery. Across the street was the decommissioned steel mill where they shot part of *Robocop*, the scene where a bad guy gets melted by toxic waste.

Inside was a narrow honeycomb of workshops, makeup stations, sculpture banks, and coves of power tools. Some rooms were done up to look like reanimation laboratories; others, torture chambers. Along the walls were old murder implements, monsters under glass, the severed heads of celebrities. Altogether, the place was like some imaginarium of the id.

My first class was Beginning Animatronics. The assignment: vampire fangs. My dozen classmates in the chalky workshop were the same energetic young people you can find in community colleges across the country, just more heavily tatted with pop hieroglyphs and attired almost exclusively in the grays, blacks, and blues of floater bloat.

Our teacher was a serene hulk of a man in a too-small baseball cap, a Savini alum and, prior to computers, the best tooth-and-claw guy in Hollywood. He had shown us how to create casts of our mouths; now we were working to roll our fangs out of clay before painting them with acrylic and buffing them to a sheen. I tried to use a wood-handled dentist's hook to detail my tooth, but I succeeded only in shaping it into a scale-model Uluru.

Most of the students here had enrolled with a high school diploma and no background in art. For them, an eighty-thousand-dollar degree from the Art Institute of Pittsburgh or some digital-animation lab was out of the question. I took my stumpy cuspid and followed them into a studio where the more competent were using rotary tools to file the efficacy of their effects to an edge.

At the station next to mine was a dude with muscles in a

beater. He was especially capable. I asked what brought him to the program. "Heard about it from an ad in the back of *Fangoria* magazine," he said.

This, I'd discover, was how many first heard about the school. If forced to sketch a brief ethnographic portrait, I'd say this institution attracts mostly white males who dislike any reliance other than self-, who hate crowds, waiting, and the feeling of being a small piece of something greater, and who would refuse the steep and perpetuating cost of modern convenience if they could. Oh, and who still read print media. Simpatico, to say the least.

My neighbor's own teeth were brown and furrowed and pushed this way and that, like old, crowded headstones. His name was Andrew. He fought mixed martial arts on the side. "I didn't know there was a home for what I always wanted to do," he said, polishing his fang into a pearlescent scimitar.

There hadn't been one for Tom Savini, the only boy who shined shoes around '60s Pittsburgh for makeup money. Coming-of-age, for him, had been about fashioning disguises and inventing monsters. He spent his days sculpting in the garage and curing wounds in the kitchen. By his late adolescence, Savini knew effects were what he most wanted to create. He practiced on himself.

Savini joined the army rather than wait to get drafted, because enlisted men got to pick their jobs. He served as a combat photographer in Vietnam. After the war, he moved to North Carolina and started acting in a repertory theater. He was still playing around with makeups, still using them to scare the holy shit out of people. (In Vietnam, he had been all, "Mama-san, take...a...look...at...*THIS!*") In fact, that's what earned him his early notoriety: the verisimilitude of his wounds. "There's something about seeing the real thing that sets me apart from, let's say, some other makeup artists who have never experienced that," he said in a post-Vietnam interview. "When I'm creating an effect, if it doesn't look good to me—real—doesn't give me that feeling I used to get when I'd see the real stuff, then it's just not real enough for me."

In North Carolina, he received a telegram from George Romero, whose *Night of the Living Dead* Savini had been set to do effects for when he got called overseas. The telegram read: "Start thinking of new ways to kill people, we've got a new gig—George." That new gig—the zombie magnum opus *Dawn of the Dead*—Roger Ebert would call "one of the best horror films ever made."

Dawn of the Dead didn't aim to scare audiences, not explicitly. The film is a biting satire of consumer culture as told through scene after scene of hashed gore. In place of *Night*'s black-and-white slow burn, *Dawn* has Technicolor brain splurk, and human skin rent by zippy teeth like the thin offal prophylactic that it is. Romero would go on to say that "if it wasn't for Tom, we wouldn't have been able to do ninety percent of what we did."

What they did was beget the germ of our current zombie-pocalypse. The film's critical and commercial success ensured that decayed but insatiable automatons would become *the* monsters for a postindustrial, postrational America. And it was Tom Savini who created them, with his bare hands.

In Savini's studio, Andrew explained to me that three-quarters of the students who come to Savini's school come as fanboys. They account for most of the washouts, too. "They think it's play, then they come and see it's real-ass work," Andrew said. "That this takes art and manual labor and makes a dirty baby."

Off my other shoulder, a bovine young man in a sleeveless red tank top leaned over a buffing wheel. He was watching his fang intently, right up close, curly blond hair a-dangle.

"The problem is that the fans can sometimes see Savini as

almost like a living comic book character," Andrew continued. "Fans think he's going to ride off with them on zombie-killing adventures. When he doesn't, they get resentful."

With one false twitch of my wrist, the rotary tool wore my tooth to a nub and ruined hours of work. "What I want to know," I said, thrusting the butt of my tooth at Andrew as if it was his cigarette I'd been holding, "is, like, can you really master fears here?"

He laughed. "Bro, you know where most of us go on to work? It isn't Hollywood. They've outsourced *that* to computer nerds. For us, now, it's dental labs, the haunted house industry, sex toys. Prosthetics for vets. They've got four or five of us making RealDolls."

The high whine to my right stopped. There was an affectless "Ooch. Please help." I turned and saw the buffer had shimmied up the bovine guy's forelock and blown a fuse.

Andrew slipped his finished fang over his left canine. In his best Count von Count voice, he went, "One! Tooth! Ah ha ha!"

In subsequent classes, they showed us how castor oil keeps a demon from chapping. How syringes and condoms and squeeze balls combine for the most realistic panting apparatus for your yeti. How, if you want to sell a wicked bite, you have to paint red liquid latex on a flat surface, dry it with a hair blower, powder it, then do X and Y and Z until it bunches into a web-like structure that will stretch and tear like tissue.

Most of the time, though, our instructors stressed the many variations of one theme: this ain't about just flesh and blood.

The Savini School's core curriculum centers on anatomy and abnormal psychology, art history and technique. The thinking is that first, an apprentice has to know his own self. His bone structure, his theory of mind, his being a really shitty craftsman. He has to know what is human before he can put it through its about-face. Which is what we were really apprentice to: the convincing transformation. Man to wolf, young actor to old, mossy bones brought back to life—we were working toward the effect that looked so believable it might just step out of the frame with a life of its own.

This was also, I realized, what it was about Tom Savini's movies that filled me with such delicious anxiety when I was younger.

Though later it would become more of a nuisance, the nighttime was something I dreaded very much as a kid. As soon as I saw the sun start dropping down the sky like a dynamite plunger, I raced to screw shut the bedroom windows, turn the dead bolt on my closet door, and remove all mirrored surfaces. Chance—or anything else—was not getting invited in. I double-checked all drapery and crannies before I laid me down.

Then, when it was just me and my brain in the dark, I'd begin to consider the creeping horror that lurked everywhere under everything. The great disparity between what I beheld and what was potentially visible. The monsters were real, I knew, and they were coming. Sure as a clock ticks.

"Night terror" has no verb form, but I can assure you it's a transitive activity, something that involves kicking holes into the drywall or alligator-death-rolling off the top bunk. (I demanded bunk beds for myself, because only a fool would sleep that near to what lies beneath.) Many mornings I came to on the tile, pedaling against nonexistent sheets, hearing the magnetic resonance of thirty TVs on but muted, and tasting a sharpness like green pennies. My dad's voice would reach me through thickness. No words, but I could make out the amplitude and the frequency, a short-long-short-short that I'd heard enough to know was "For *Christ's* sake, son."

So, so often did I hit my head on the nightstand or the floor on my way down. Consciousness then felt like knee-walking on gravel. And burned into my mind's eye were the after-images of horrible dreams. They came in many flavors, but vanilla was zombies pouring in, and there's me, a decent caliber deep-throated, waiting till the last possible moment to pull the trigger.

I took enough of these night-terror-induced gainers (and resultant CAT scans) that the Florida Department of Children and Families felt it necessary to have a sit-down with my father. He was the one who'd bring me to the hospital; he was the one who'd find me.

My father took it upon himself to wake me each morning. Gently, usually. But every now and again he'd kick open the door, and if I wasn't concussed on the ground, he'd clutch at his chest and scream, "Heart attack! Embolism, right this minute!" I'd ratchet upright, hyperventilating. Then he'd ask, casually, "Did you say good morning to the adversary?"

My old man had lost both his brothers at tragic ages in separate, horrific accidents. Then he'd served in Vietnam. He thought it was important that I greet Death as part of my morning routine.

Our sculpture teacher carried himself with the quiet easiness born of manual competence, but his reedy voice splintered when he yelled at a student—"Donald, Jesus, that looks tremendously unsound!"—as Donnie took practice cuts with a baseball bat he'd sawed off and glued a sledgehammer head to.

"Did you hear about the guy they claimed was on bath salts when he ate his dog?" Donnie wanted to know, pivoting, following through. "I think he was a carrier! I think it's about to go down!" Donnie, unable to modulate his pitch or volume, talked as though he was impersonating a poststroke Edward G. Robinson.

The sculpture room was narrow, with stools pulled up to a ledge that ran around its perimeter. On the wall above each was a fiendish head sculpted and painted by a student. I picked a stool near Donnie; the head canted down at me was a mean ape in a Brodie helmet. Today I would start work on a self-portrait formed out of umber Chavant.

Unfortunately, I had joined the school a couple of weeks into the summer semester and missed the lesson about what makes a face. So, rather than make one of those, I spent the morning forcing crests of clay around a hydrocephalic head. Donnie glanced my way with increasing regularity, and concern, until he scraped back his stool, stepped over, and pointed out where my replica came to a point. "See this?" he asked. Then he slapped his palm onto the crown of my actual head, drawing out one long *Booooop!* I looked at him, and he looked at me, and still he *Booooop!*ed like a quiz-show buzzer. We were maintaining eye contact when he did likewise to my clay dome. I added my own plaintive *Booooop!* Finally Donnie unhanded me, and then the little me, and I saw he'd made him better.

After that, Donnie let on and on about the time he'd spent in psychiatric care, all while thumbing a better-than-faithful bust of Robin Williams. His own face, acne-knurled, was curtained behind black hair. This made his hands appear to be working of their own accord. They scrambled around the ledge, one of them crumbling a brick of clay while the other pinched Robin's earlobe tenderly. Their capacity for both power and dexterity had me thinking of sea creatures evolved to eat soft things hidden in shells.

Donnie got close and told me he wanted to make toys, figurines. "An indie like me would get the Stephen King licenses, see?

"It started when I met Tom Savini at my mall in South

Pennsyltucky." He stopped sculpting to pick up his hammer bat. "Now, where I'm from, by now, I should've been killed three times over. But here I am standing before you today." He hinted at some kind of boonie meth predicament, choked up on the hammer bat. "Because I'm from a lower-middle-class family, see, I believe meeting him was an act of God."

When I checked the clock, the six hours of class had flown by. It was pretty remarkable. The inside of my own head had fallen eerily still while I shaped its doppelganger. Laying hands on clay—who knew?

But things about my analog were off. Cheeks sagged. Lids drooped. Skin flaked. It didn't seem at rest, but rather ill at ease, its grimace curling inward. Frankly, it looked like a poorly embalmed face halfway awake in the grave. So much work remained to be done.

In my hotel room that evening, after having taken my fright, I nodded off in the small hours. I dreamed of something I've been dreaming of since:

My dad's in a cramped bathysphere, dropping gently into perpetual night. Deeper and deeper he goes, the pressure mounting, the warm side of the spectrum squeezed out until all that's left is blue-black water and the white of his craft's spotlight. Through the one porthole he sees nightmare creatures, wraiths with shiny lures built in. Leaks are springing, the hull crumpling, but he's plugging holes and digging in his heels, pushing back. I don't know that there's a bottom, but whatever he's on his way to, he won't reach it alive. He's holding out for as long as he can, even though—*in spite of the fact that*—he knows his vessel will be crushed like a beer can between invisible hands.

. . .

At the start of my penultimate day, we few students placed our sculpted heads on the chest-high workbench in the animatronics shop. It was almost time to plant servos, animate them. My hours and hours (and hours and hours and *hours*) of careful handling had yielded an inhuman likeness, this rictus-faced gremlin that belonged floating in a jar. I'd had it with the thing.

To ward off classmates who might try to help, I'd taken to raising my notebook and flipping through it as if searching for the protective spell. Still, a classmate named David started speaking at me and would not stop. "I can talk to people, is what this made me realize," he said as I nodded hollowly. He was putting the finishing touches on his rendition of Two-Face. "This is me," he said, pointing to the human side of the monster.

David had muttonchops and a pushy chin. He was a veteran of the 82nd Airborne, but he was unacquainted with Ryan. How he got into this was he would scare his squadmates by faking razorblade suicide. "I made those bitches be*lieve* that shit," he said.

The sclerotic, tendony half of his sculpture was intricate, the focal point being a lidless eyeball mapped with veins. David crosshatched the clay flesh with a dog brush and rubbed baby powder into the corrugations. "This is the thing that keeps you up at night," he said. "And it's never going to go away."

The power tools in the shop screeched to life. David said that when his face was operational, "the eye will wink, the head will turn forty-five degrees to obscure the fucked-up side, and the smile will peel back." It took hundreds of hours for him to achieve this.

As he worked, I noticed that his hands had the same expression as his face. They held out his nature like an offering, and they added themselves to what they touched. "There's never been a time when I haven't been trying—avidly trying—to figure. Out. How. That. Worked," he said. "I watched horror movies still by still to see how they accomplished the effect. You got scared? Break down why." I looked at my own small and soft hands and thought of benthic mollusks.

"Isn't that what gets us in trouble in horror movies to begin with?" I asked. "Isn't presumption what gets us overrun by dead things when the end comes?"

"You talking about the Shit?" he asked. "The *Shit* shit? Because when that Shit goes down, I'm going to be, fucking . . ." David made an AOK sign, and then he took off his shirt to point to a tattoo over his heart, his name formatted into a UPC bar code. "I've got my bugout bag ready. How about you?"

Even after all my friends got girlfriends and grew out of the habit, I would stay in weekends and watch horror movies. Zombie flicks mostly, D-grade, and these with my father. We'd sit staring out of our faces and judge the characters' awareness, discuss what we'd do differently. Foremost: we'd *never* open the door to our boarded-up farmhouse/fortress/keep. Not a goddamned crack. All that work at becoming impregnable, undone.

Though not quite on the level of bugout bags, my dad and I *did* have a pseudoserious Z-Day Plan. (It just also happened to be his Impending Race War Plan, his Aftermath of a Mondo Hurricane Plan, his North Korean Invasion Plan, et cetera.) First, we'd grab his service weapon from the crawl space, along with the hundreds of rounds of surplus Chinese ammunition he kept therein. Then we'd take stock of the canned goods in the pantry, supplementing these when necessary with fish caught from the bay down the street. Onto our flat rooftop would go plastic buckets, for the constant South Florida rain. Onto our many windows would go plywood from storm seasons past. Our doors we'd reinforce; behind them, we'd make nary a peep. Hell, we couldn't *wait*! The dead would punish the living for us, and we'd be left alone at the center of creation. There, within the structure we'd built to keep out what terrorized us, we'd defend ourselves unto death.

What's interesting is my sisters had them, too. The night terrors. I know because some nights, when we were young, I'd jog awake, and from the bedroom next to mine would come the sound of two feet slapping tile, concurrently—a sister having gone from supine to athletic crouch—and then a pause for bearings, and then the Bronx applause of those same feet booking it down our tile hallway.

And of course we *knew* our old man had them. Were we to hear some bump in the night and then go to get him to investigate, we'd often find him wandering in a fugue, opening closet doors with one hand, stabbing into the void with a fillet knife in the other.

Again, my dad is like a secular Puritan vis-à-vis his devotion to vigilance. A man who is troubled by nothing so much as peace of mind. Who believes above all in Death's acquisitiveness, and that the surest sign his cold hand has caged your heart is if you *feel no danger.* Does that make sense? Who believes that safety is found in the very dread of ever feeling safe enough to rest your eyes.

Parentally, he practiced admonitory judo. A black belt, that guy. He would intercept the force of your amenability and joie de vivre, and he'd flip and twist it until you, too, were immobilized by fear. Going for a walk in the woods, eldest daughter? *The horned deer are in rut, extra stampy, plus there's rapists.* You would like to earn a few more dollars working the graveyard shift at the all-night pizzeria, son of mine? *You'll get shot in the face with the quickness.* In all his ponds were alligators, and only psychos rang his bell. The first thing he made my mother do on their honeymoon cruise? Crawl the route to the lifeboats, blindfolded.

Any attempts we made at psychic intervention were met with a shrug and the phrase "I'd be scared of nothing if I was alone." The implication here was that we, his family, had summoned all these demons simply by existing. We were objects to be loved, meaning we were objects to be protected. His empathic wall had expanded to accommodate us, but all that meant was he had more to lose. As long as either he or we were alive, the best to be hoped for was a kind of padded equanimity.

Thus, when any one of us knocked on his bedroom door and tried that old chestnut "I'm a little scared," the response from inside was always "You damn well should be!"

I met Tom Savini in a conference room full of filing cabinets and blank diplomas. He was about five-foot-eight, knottily muscled, and dark like stained wood. His partially unbuttoned linen shirt, midthigh blue shorts, bushy beard, and grayly threaded ponytail had him looking not like a dad but like a man who could beat up a dad; a lion tamer, maybe.

He spoke to me for four hours about horror and his place in its history, and it was pure romance. We ordered in—minestrone—and talked shop re: how he managed to dredge fear from me, and people like me, and shape it into golems, and breathe life into them. We lamented computer graphics, the tools become our masters. We agreed that when watching all these modern blockbusting CGI fests, we felt as though we were the only ones left who still preferred the squish and crunch of a real, live monster up there on the screen.

Eventually, though, we got down to existential tacks.

"People think I'm this goremonger," he said, shaking his head. "It's the writers who write the stuff into the script. The last thing I'm trying to do is desensitize people. Me, I cry when I see someone being indiscriminately, unnecessarily good." With age, his sharp Mediterranean features have spiked downward, as if from the steady drip of something erosive.

"I'm done with effects, for the most part. I give what work there is to the students. Now it's about becoming someone else." He put his hands to his temples, tinkling them with his middle and ring fingers.

Across the table, I beckoned strangely with both hands, an unconvincing coax. How could he abandon horror? Horror, I pleaded, is about the perception of the truth of our condition. What does it mean to be a self-conscious animal? "It means to know that you're fucking food for worms!" I clawed at the space between us. "Your work, zombies, all of it—it's the ruthless chaos of existence made flesh."

He parachuted his thick eyebrows. "It took me sixty-five years and a few amateurish, embarrassingly bad movies to get here, but now I understand that it's about us. *Us* as in the audience, *us* as in you and me. Fears and projections. All that. *The monster* . . ."—here he grimaced and held out a palsied, pointing finger—"*is* YOUUUUU!"

Taken aback, I fumbled through my notebook. To give myself time, I asked which of his effects was his favorite.

He spidered a hand inside his beard and said picking a favorite was like choosing among his kids, but that he was partial to one from a movie called *Maniac*. He called it "the closest I've ever come to the feeling of having committed cold-blooded murder."

What he did was make a cast of his head and shoulders, and from that a thin latex mask of himself with a plaster lining on the inside. He filled the cast with apple cores, corn chips, ten blood-filled condoms, and calf brains from a slaughterhouse. This he placed on a urethane-foam-and-chickenwire chest. Then, with the film rolling and him dressed up as the Maniac, he emptied both barrels of a shotgun into his material counterpart.

It was at this moment that I had an idea. "Mr. Savini?" I asked. "Tom? Could you shoot me in the head? Like a zombie in *Dawn*? Doesn't have to be a blowout. Just a nice pop shot. A blurty little coup de grâce."

He said in a soft voice that skipped along in dactyls: "Okay. That's called a *squib*. A squib is simply a *det*onator. I'd place the *det*onator in a *tube* that's filled with *gun*powder. And that would be placed *in*side a prophylactic which's filled with *blood*, so when the blast goes off the concussion *blows* the prophylactic *and* the blood from be*neath* you."

But then he shook his head. "I'm not licensed for that anymore."

He watched my enthusiasm deflate. Then he said, "It still amazes me, the zombie thing. I never would have guessed they'd strike this chord."

Tom Savini walked me out, wished me well, and got into a blue BMW with the vanity plate "SHAZAMM." And that night, locked into a hotel room with my clay self gaping on the nightstand, I considered why horror in general and zombies in particular should be striking this chord.

We—or at least I—love horror and zombies and gore because it's all apocalyptic, necessarily so. I mean this in the original sense of the word, *of the nature of a revelation or disclosure*. This stuff effects a revelation, but it's not the revelation I used to think it was. It's not that when we feel in our bones how contingent we are, we become afraid. That watching a horror flick is a reality check, an affirmation that my sight still clearly registers the universe.

What resonates, I think, is the suggestion that I'm haunted by a force majeure. The idea that there's this entity—be it collective like zombies or individual like Jason or even insubstantial like a damn ghost—and this entity is relentlessly after me. Besieging. It resonates because it's homologous with this other gut feeling. And that's that whatever it is that's out there—it's going to get in. No matter what. It's going to get *me*, in the end. Relieve me of my life.

Contemplating this, I fell through to a sound sleep.

"Totally fine to drive," I was telling Dad. "Just gonna run in and grab me and Mom some more, you know, aperitifs."

From the kitchen, he went, "Oh *no*, Kent, you can't leave your car idling in the CVS parking lot for even a *second*. You do that? And someone comes and steals it? And they kill a pedestrian? Then that shit's on *you*, my man, in the eyes of the law. Everything you worked for, gone like *that*."

I redlined, said, "That's goddamned absurd. Who does that happen to? *Who*?"

"I'm a lawyer. It's my job."

"*Were* a lawyer."

"Let me drive you to the CVS."

"It's down the fucking hill."

"C'mon, man."

"You talk a big game with all this personal responsibility hoo-ha, but you're, like, *the* childproofer. You're a human outlet cover."

"Whoa, hey"—he came around the load-bearing wall drying his hands on a dishrag—"who's the guy who managed to fall out of his *stroller*, okay, and nearly get himself killed?"

According to Mom, how it transpired was: He and Papa are

blotto, and I'm in an umbrella stroller, unsecured. Also, I'm a toddler, and so have about as much control over my bulk as does a sack of meal. Some quick acceleration/deceleration on Dad's part—he's using the stroller as a prop in the tortuous retelling of a DUI near miss—starts me pitching forward. Slowly, slowly, I topple, slicing my neck open on the jagged nub of a STOP sign broken off at the root.

He and Papa turn, yelp *"Shit!"* into each other's face. Vents of hot blood arc in time with my heartbeat. Later, in their fond remembrances, they'll tell me that this, foremost, made them really have to pee.

And yet Dad's litmus test for granting a sick day was barf. Barf had to be present if I was to be absent. And he'd inspect it, too. He could tell when I'd watered down tomato paste and spangled it with Cheerios.

"Three-fourths of life," he'd say, crouching, picking up and popping a few soggy Os, "is showing up, and showing up on time."

The last fourth? "Never, ever volunteering."

Thus did he not volunteer to drive me to the ER when a water beetle lodged itself deep in my ear canal while I was swimming in our pool late one afternoon.

"Calm it down," he said. I barked and spasmed on a wicker chair in the sun. The bug was inching angrily. Dad stood, Sherlockian, with his magnifying glass to my ear. "It's just wax."

He jabbed at it with a Q-tip. I yowled and made a move for his larynx.

He said, "Okay, have it your way. Pinch your nose and blow. It'll shoot right out."

Following the loss of consciousness, and once I'd pulled myself back onto the chair, a string of blood began to leak out of my ear and run down my neck. He handed me a turkey baster and said, "Flood it out."

After that, he blew cigarette smoke into the opening, saying, "Like in Westerns."

Of course, if you asked *him*, he'd say that the real tragedy here was a father's having to care for a son whose one true skill lay in improvising injury out of any situation, scat-like. To which there's more than a little truth.

I emerged from the womb cross-eyed to the point of functional blindness. Only post-(expensive)-op was I able to see straight. Sort of. Not long after, I toddled off and filled my diaper with handfuls of what I believed was sand but turned out to be ant pile. Karen and Lauren considered me a fun plaything; they liked to drag me about by my arms, till the day they dislocated both of my shoulders. The one home video we submitted to *America's Funniest* involved the two of them convincing Dad that they'd taught me how to walk down the stairs. I've needed to close my left eye in bright sunlight ever since Lauren thought it was a good idea to tie a length of rope between our bicycles before racing downhill. I shattered my ankle within five minutes of attempting soccer. I forwent the chocolate bunny and instead ate a toxic box of egg-dye pellets one Easter. I broke and swallowed a sprinkling of teeth on *Christmas Eve*. (The bright side, I thought, was I might have occasioned a dalliance between the Tooth Fairy and Santa.) I got a hernia in the *sixth grade*. When the attractive female doctor had me go pantsless on the diagnostic table, I knew then from mortification. Dad looked on; I plucked at my baseball jersey while shaving tears with blinks; the doctor poked around my bald, prawnish sex, explaining that my guts had breached my nutsack.

I think the guy might still be paying off the Mercy Hospital CAT scan I ruined by way of vom, gasping concussedly as I did so, "Now! [*blegh*] You! [*blegh*] Believe! [*blegh*] Me!"

So, when he said while buckling his seatbelt: "I'm telling you, a bug is natural, biodegradable"—I didn't fault him.

"Its bodily fluids are full of nutrients and shit." He looked at me, tapped the key near but not in the ignition slit. Pity, fear, and anger were eddying around his face.

"Probably do you some good," he said.

Then he delivered this lead-footed soliloquy on the way to the hospital: "Look. A guy's courageous who, when he knows what his kid's up against, the kind of shit that's in store, he still lets life bear down on his child. Because that child, as soon as you have him, your heart belongs to him. It isn't holed up inside you anymore. It's him. Your biggest vulnerability's up there at the plate getting beaned, so to speak, in the game of life—and it hurts like hell. You want to pinch-hit."

Though I'd always hoped that the sum total of pain I sponged up—or one spectacular instance of it—would put me through. Would find the right frequency. Say I get a fastball thrown down my throat, and then when I whistle through splintered teeth, "What're you looking at, asshole?"—open sesame. The secret passageway into Dad's respect, unsealed at last.

Anyway. I let him captain the beer run.

6.

ARTISANAL BALL

We all crowded against the right-side windows as our tour bus crept on the Amish. There were three of them—brothers by the color and cut of their hair—and they sat in descending order on the driving bench of a horse-drawn cart. As they rolled on, some rusty contraption plucked cornstalks out of the ground and fanned them on the cart's bed.

"Do *not* take pictures, y'all!" begged our driver and guide, Gail. "They're huge on the Second Commandment, which means no graven images, which means no pictures. Please. Every time. No pictures." We were a baker's dozen, a couple of families and some seniors, and we'd only just begun this three-hour, handicapped-accessible tour of Amish farmsteads.

"These boys don't need a license to drive that baby," Gail informed us in his southerly lisp. "Y'all know the buggies, but here's one for you: eight percent of the Old Order Amish here are millionaires." He explained that nowadays, most supplement farm income by selling furniture and handicrafts to tourists. Some even operate small-scale workshops that fill orders for retailers like KMart. They keep overhead low and won't expand past what's prudent. "And more people come to see them now than go on out to Ellis Island. Ten million a year. Who'd've thought?" Gail checked us in the rearview. "The Amish, rivaling the Statue of Liberty."

We pulled neck and neck with the cart. Some sound buzzed around the horses' fibrillated clop. The middle brother stood with the reins.

Our bus went amurmur with something like relief, the adults glad that the Amish were out there, reaping, and they and the children both gladder still that it was not them out there, reaping. I myself found them stirring. Strapping, blue-eyed brothers, harvesting corn in 2012! No incessant Instagramming, no real-time Twitter updates: *Jacob's got the reins, FML.*

A dozen camera phones captured the boys with fake mandibular clicks, and Gail sighed, "Goddamnit." As my window came level with them and I framed a picture, I realized that the sound underneath the clopping was Kris Kross's "Jump" issuing from a hidden stereo.

I made eye contact with the oldest, inches away. He looked back with this mirthless inner grin. Then he faked a lunge, to see if I'd balk, and totally flinch-flexed me, prison or high school style. He laughed as he passed from my window to the one behind.

I'd come back to Lancaster County, in the southeast of Pennsylvania, because years ago, when I was driving back from the Gathering of the Juggalos, I took a detour through Amish country and happened upon something that I've thought a lot about since.

That day, I stopped at a one-room schoolhouse. It was barely visible from the macadam lane, brick and vinyl-sided behind a woodworking shop and a house selling brown eggs. I would've never found it had I not typed "New Hope School" into my GPS.

Simple wood fencing ran along the lot's perimeter and kept me far from the Amish kids enjoying recess. Some preteens huddled around back. Others hung linens on a line to dry. A chain of downy-headed toddlers pedaled Big Wheels across a field where, in 2006, a milk truck driver walked into the old schoolhouse, barricaded the door, and shot five Amish girls to death.

A hard breeze soughed the surrounding cornfields, a shush I spun around to appreciate. Then I noticed the backstop. Not just saw it, but realized that all the other Amish schoolhouses I'd driven by—they didn't have hoops or goals or uprights in their playfields—they had backstops and baseball diamonds. One boy ran barefoot across the grass and positioned his shoes as bases. Then several more joined him, and they sidearmed a ball around the horn with terrible mechanics but unflinching competence. A lefty took up a bat, and I took a few steps back, understanding now that the fence I stood behind doubled as the right-field wall.

He was a new teen whose taut physique and knobby joints had him looking like a system of ropes and pulleys. He stroked a ball over my head, laces hissing. I made like I had somewhere else to be. When I sneaked back a few minutes later, he was fielding impassively, scooping and throwing with kinesthetic tics I remember having once, when I was little and in love with the game, before coaches smoothed all that out. The tics made him seem more authentic, more faithful to the form, like warps and bubbles in handblown glass.

The Amish play baseball! I thought. *Of course they do.*

What's become of baseball? We don't seem to want to play it or even watch it anymore. Participation in Little League has been dropping steadily for the past two decades. The nationwide player pool for slow-pitch softball has shrunk by a third since 2000, mostly in the twenty-five-to-thirty-four-year-old age bracket, the biggest decline of any team sport other than wrestling. Meanwhile, this past year, as *Sunday Night Football* repeated as our number-one-rated primetime program, fewer people watched *Fox Saturday Baseball* than ever before. And the World Series—a quarter century ago, more than half of our nation's televisions were locked into the deciding game of the 1986 Fall Classic. In 2012, barely 12 percent tuned in.

I used to play in leagues year-round, and watch the parade of home-run highlights on *Baseball Tonight* after prayers but before bed. My dad was my assistant coach then. In my youth leagues, he acted like he didn't at home. At home, he was some-one else's dad, a dad at a sleepover who cares only that nobody gets hurt too bad under his supervision. At home, my dad would sometimes poke his head into the living room and just watch me play video games. When I'd pause the game and look back, he disappeared like a TV nature guide who didn't want to upset the specimen. But in the dugout, my dad paced up and down and got angry, or excited, or happy. He kicked the cooler and yelled, "Be a hitter!" or "Let me blow the sand out of it for you, Chesco." He spoke a foreign language, one you only learned through immersion. He slapped asses. He held me by my shoul-ders and whispered instructions. He hit extra flies for me after practice, because he knew that nothing back then made me feel as good as that immaculate moment when the ball went from white reticule hovering on blue sky—*pock*—to unseen kernel seeding a glove.

The game is so freaking interminable, though! Tune in to the afternoon half of a Tuesday doubleheader held in Colorado, say, and you will start to taste your own mouth, displeasedly, as though you've just bitten into a mealy leathered apple. One of Colorado's guys takes *thirty seconds* to throw a *single pitch*.

What baseball is is anachronistic. (Important, yes. Hugely, fundamentally so. But so are the *Federalist Papers*, and no normal person reads the *Federalist Papers* more than once.) This is what's most celebrated about it, the single narrative sweep of a game that's changed little if at all over the course of a dozen generations. How me and a farmer sent forward in time from 1860 could sit down and enjoy nine innings with few or no expository leanings-over necessary.

But this is also what makes baseball so oppressive, so dense with numbers and precepts and bones. If you want to get into it, you have to be okay with yoking yourself to the game's considerable weight. It's like an inheritance, a gift old people want you to accept, maintain, and someday pass on. Which, really, is the last thing any one of us wants when he's young.

Before heading back to Lancaster, I looked up Amish baseball online and got a lot of hearsay. There were never-updated web pages listing Amish teams as the eighteen-and-under Ohio state champions, as the winners of a Texas "world" softball tournament. Depending on your blogger, they belted dingers and rounded the bases full bore, in silence, without moving their arms; or else they were dirty as all hell, flapping elbows on the base paths, coming in spikes-high on slides, their dogged consciences not extending to sport.

I did find one trustworthy story reporting that in the late '40s and early '50s, Amish ballplayers in Lancaster were recruited onto semipro teams. They played under assumed names so no neighbors would spot them in newspaper box scores. One of the last of them, a late pitcher whose deception was never found out, had a nephew living in the area, a prominent business owner.

"LANK-uster County," Jim Smucker corrected me when we shook hands in the gift shop of his Bird-in-Hand Family

Restaurant & Smorgasbord. Smucker has long acted as a sort of docent to Lancaster's tourists, holding weekly Q&As for the guests of his restaurant and his inn next door. His parents were apostate Amish. They raised him a practicing Mennonite, which makes him like a Reformed Jew compared with the Amish ultra-orthodoxy. Most of his friends and neighbors and employees, though, are Old Order.

He seated us in one of the roped-off wings of his recently expanded restaurant, laying his cell phone on the tabletop, where it would chitter between us throughout our conversation. "Amish contractors built the original," Smucker said, and gestured to the huge, rectangular, irregularly windowed place. "And they've built each addition."

Smucker then launched into a brief history of the Amish, explaining that what began three centuries ago as a handful of families escaping persecution in Europe by sailing for the nascent Pennsylvania colony is today 273,700 adults and children spread across thirty states and the Canadian province of Ontario. (Though two-thirds of them have remained in Pennsylvania, Ohio, and Indiana.)

Amish belief then as now is completely grounded in the New Testament, which they hold to be the sole and final authority on all things. From it, they take their impetus to remain separate ("and be not conformed to this world"—Romans 12:2), as well as their orders to renounce violence in all spheres of human life, to refuse to swear oaths, and to obey literally the teachings of Jesus Christ. Still, they shun their undisciplined and wayward, to make it a little easier to keep the community of faith intact.

And the Amish *are* a true community, in every sense of the word. They believe that what we call "individualism" is actually pride. Or, more bluntly, selfishness, which opposes God's will, which should be yielded to with a dedicated heart. This communal spirit is regulated by an unwritten code of conduct, the Ordnung, which prescribes clothing and grooming and language, and prohibits things like divorce, military service, owning or operating automobiles, taking electricity from public power lines, and installing wall-to-wall carpet.

Basically, the Amish way of living argues implicitly that tradition is sacred, that preservation is as important as or perhaps more important than progress, that obeying and yielding are virtuous, that the personal reality might not be the supreme. And in this way, above all else, they take the integrity of individual choice really, really seriously.

Or, as Smucker summed it up: "The Amish are very intentional. Whereas we just take on everything we're offered without even thinking about it."

They're Anabaptists, which means they do not baptize babies but only those who can understand and accept responsibility for what they're getting themselves into. They don't cotton to the evangelicals and the born-agains. Declaring oneself "saved" is presumptuous, prideful; the Amish simply live faithful lives and hope for salvation.

And, contrary to popular belief, they're not Luddites. They'll use technology so long as it isn't "worldly," doesn't connect to the outside or pull one's mind away from the task at hand. Solid-state gas engines are okay, as are battery-operated calculators. If a machine can be retrofitted to run off oil or hydraulics, it's allowed. Appliances may run off battery power. Cars may be ridden in if driven by an Englisher. (Anyone who isn't Amish is "English," because they don't speak Pennsylvania Dutch.) Rollerblades are fine, and wood scooters, but not bicycles, because they, like cars, take you too far too fast too easily. Newspapers, trampolines, and gas grills: all kosher. Central heating systems are not.

Therein lies the problem they have with a lot of modernity: it's fragmentary. And insidious. You allow central heat, and next thing you know, everyone in the family leaves the fireside after dinner to go off to their own warm rooms. This is why the Amish live apart from us. So that they might remain whole.

Smucker himself has lived in Lancaster his whole life, save four years at college. When he came back, he played ball against the Amish in local park leagues and at the field he built into his brother's corn.

"Are they good defensively?" I wanted to know. "It seems like they'd be good defensively."

"*MMM*mmm . . ." he said, pushing all of his mouth to one side of his face. "It can be sandlot stuff. Cow-handed batting stances, Bob Tolan swings. Just terrible mechanics. But they're so good despite that."

Baseball, he went on, was forbidden by church elders around 1995. Baptized men had been wearing uniforms, and traveling to play league matches, and neglecting their duties at home. So, now, the game is strictly for the unbaptized. What I saw in the schoolyard was the noncompetitive stuff all kids play until the eighth grade, when their formal education ends. ("Knowledge puffeth up"—1 Corinthians.) The only ones who can ball for real are the boys who have entered Rumspringa, the few free years of "running around" in the secular world that the Amish allow their youth (and about which we make feature-length documentaries and National Geographic Channel reality shows).

Rumspringa—ostensibly a time for finding a mate—is a kind of inoculation. A manageable dosage of culture is introduced to unbaptized Amish, the hope being that this exposure will keep them from succumbing to the whole pathology later on. From their sixteenth birthday till their mid-twenties, they sample what they've been missing—cars, hip-hop, food courts, double plays. Then they make the biggest decision of their lives: get baptized and get married, or forsake their world for ours.

"The unbaptized, if they play competitively in uniforms,

that means they're from a faster, more liberal district," Smucker told me. "But you can still tell they're Amish by how they carry themselves."

"What should I scout for?" I asked.

"You'll just know. But it's getting less and less apparent. How are you gonna keep 'em down on the farm after they've got the MLB app on their iPhone?"

"The ballplayers are losing their religion," I said, pleased with the joke.

"Not quite," Smucker replied, suggesting that I look up Amish retention rates at the Mennonite Information Center a few miles around the way. About 85 percent of today's Amish choose the church, I'd learn—far more than when there were semipro ballplayers about. More, in fact, than at any point in their history.

Officially, the Amish spurn private telephones, but an Anabaptist academic I contacted snuck me a number. He told me I'd need to first leave a voice mail—the Amish have voice mail on their communal outdoor telephones, and they check it once a day—and then I'd get a call back.

And so, at the close of regular business hours one Friday, an Amish butcher rang my cell from the phone he hides in his basement. "All Amish kids are baseball fans," he confessed. "My sons follow the Phillies very much. Avidly."

He spoke a bottlenecked English, this brogue through which "do" became "dew" and "ill" squeezed into "eel." "They watch *SportsCenter* on their cell phones," he admitted. "What can I say? They're in Rumspringa. I did the same. Or similar."

He used to love baseball, he said, used to play all the time before it was banned. "It's fine for kids to play. But as Paul says, 'When I was a child, I spake as a child, I understood as a child, I

thought as a child: but when I became a man, I put away childish things.' "

I said I had it on good authority that the Amish play ball
in uniform or in civvies all over Lancaster. He claimed not
to know. I badgered. I had to see them in their element, I told
him.

After some time, he relented. "All right," he said. "Now.
You don't know who told you. And please don't use my name.
We're not allowed to have our names printed. And you have to
be careful, now. The Amish don't want no reporters." Then he
asked if I had GPS and gave me coordinates.

I waited two full days at the coordinates he gave me. Empty
clasps clanged against a flagpole. I found out that mooing cows
sound incredibly frustrated. To do *something, anything*, I started
and stopped e-reading *Ball Four* and *The Natural* and Roger
Angell's baseball compendiums. I flipped between *Bull Durham*
and *Moneyball* and *Field of Dreams* on my iPad in the shade.
Nothing.

Some weeks later, after a couple more trips spent staking out
diamonds around Lancaster, I settled on one behind a century-
old general store. It had a hitching post, sheds for dugouts, and a
two-story chain link fence about three hundred feet from home.
I installed myself on a bench beyond the fence in left field. I
waited. The late-morning air was thick with oily wafts of mown
grass. The heat loitered. At some point, I fell asleep.

When I heard a *thud* and opened my eyes, I saw a small boy
riding by atop a miniature buggy pulled by a Shetland pony. I
figured I was dreaming. Then came another *thud*, closer, and I
turned my head in time to dodge a yellow softball one-hopping
directly at my face.

Ballplayers, at last. Ten of them. They wore athletic shorts
and cleats, but I knew they were Amish because they chattered
misaligned English in elfin accents.

"Attaway, Amo!" shouted the guy nearest to me in left. "That's how you Tootsie Roll!"

This was practice. They were a competitive slow-pitch team. I tossed the softball back over the fence. The fielder said, "Sorry, sir."

These boys were from liberal families. They had filled the parking lot with forty-thousand-dollar trucks and big white Escalades bought with the money they earned working trades or construction right after middle school. (Should they decide to join the church, their vehicles will wind up in fields full of near-new cars with FOR SALE signs in their windshields.)

The kid at bat launched one on a directly proportional incline. It cleared the fence and burst the treetop above me, the ball then falling into my hands ahead of flittering leaves. I asked if I could shag flies with them. They waved me over. I ran to get my glove from the trunk of my rental car.

I would prefer to keep with genre standards and describe these boys as a dugout's worth of motley *isolatos*. But I can't. They were as chippily uniform as a litter of golden retriever puppies: long limbs, tanned bodies, unstylish haircuts. The sons of farmers and craftsmen. They used Pennsylvania Dutch for jokes they didn't want me to hear; for everything else, musty English learned in school.

They were eighteen, nineteen, but clearly had never been coached. Some stood in the batter's box with their feet touching. One lefty pinced his right knee and elbow together crab-wise before swinging. Another held the bat above his head as if preparing to kill a snake. Categorically, they creamed the ball.

In the field, their every throw sizzled. They jumped into the path of hit balls as though playing through a memory. They dropped to one knee, two knees, laid out horizontally—whatever it took to block grounders. A freak hop bloodied the shortstop's nose, and the cheer from right field was "Ya, looks like ya need another Red *BOOL*, Morty!" Everybody laughed but me; Morty's smile was wishboned by blood. "Ya, buy it with your credit card, Credit Card!" went the pitcher.

I've played enough to feel okay saying: never before had I seen a team of young men be so good without also being repulsively cocksure. These guys had a prelapsarian sweetness about them. This straight *joy* that I last knew as an adolescent dicking around with my friends Friday afternoons on a pebbly field behind a RadioShack.

I was never great or even very good. I couldn't hit a bear in the ass with a banjo. (Or, as Papa Lou put it, I "couldn't buy myself a hit in a Chinese opium den.") At the plate, I was confounded by pitches that rode too fast, broke too hard, popped in the catcher's mitt behind me like a paper bag full of air. My game was defense. I could play most anywhere, but I begged off from center field and second base. Center because of the spotlighted solitude of in-game fly balls. Second because the throw to first was so short. Both because there was so much time to *think*.

My dad videotaped what ended up being my last Colt League game. In it, I expertly snare a two-hopper several steps to my backhand side. Then I just *stare* at the first baseman with the smiley grimace of a guy waiting to get punched in the face. When I finally force the throw from second, it scatters the upper bleachers. This was the first of *four* such throws. That was it for me.

Lots of people walk away from a beloved sport once they come of age. They tire of the game. Develop new interests. Maybe they finally refuse to be a parent's proxy, wearing a uniform in a man's stead like a Civil War substitute. That's not why I dropped baseball. Baseball, I think, is different.

What makes it such a great children's pastime is also what makes it so goddamned difficult for even proto-adults to play well. As major league pitcher Ron Darling famously said: "Most people have the physical ability to play this game. To excel in it, I think it's in your head." What he meant is: if you are conscious of yourself—like, at all—baseball will eat you alive. It measures you against an absolute standard—1.000 batting average, 1.000 fielding average, 0.00 earned-run average—and it reminds you every step of the way that you are falling short. If you can't handle that, if you get interrupted by the infinite regression of anxiety and doubt (. . . *I made* that *throw, which excuses me for striking out last inning, but I'm still 0-for-11 lately, and I double-clutched on that fielder's choice, which Ross'll remember but not mention because he stockpiles my errors like they're his own critical deterrents, and SON OF A BITCH, back up the bag* . . .), you are fucked.

To be good, you have to be either so self-assured as to be nigh catatonic, or you have to choose to pay attention in the most literal way. That is, you have to realize that your attention is a valuable, finite resource, and how you choose to spend it the one skill—not speed, not power—that separates the wheat from the chaff.

"Control your thoughts before they control you," I triple-underlined years ago in my dog-eared copy of *The Mental Game of Baseball*, the big-leaguer's Bible. "If there's no future, there's no distraction."

According to the book, the easiest way to achieve this stillness was to vacate yourself and enter the mind of the pitcher or the batter. To be forever considering: What's the pitcher's best stuff, and what's his best today? What sequence of pitches has he gotten this guy out with in the past? What's the situation in the game, and what does the hitter want to accomplish? Is there something about this ballpark and this day—short porch in left, wind blowing out, his last embarrassing at bat—that could affect that desire? Which base would I cover or throw to if he got his way? Or if he didn't? What would be the permutation of all our failed intentions?

If not this empathy, then the book said your only other choice was to keep a lid on your brain. Force your conscious world to fit inside every next pitch. Abridge yourself. Play in a gnomic present. And labor to maintain this link to your surroundings, always, if you're to have a snowball's chance.

I managed neither. And the more I matured, the more self-consciousness snuck into the cracks of my play and pulled me apart like weeds taking ruins back to nature. I couldn't help it. Weak grounders skipping toward me took on the aspect of pebbles leading a rockslide. I'd flub one, then another, and another—and each error would feel like one more stone stacked on my chest, death by crushing. I'd look to my dad in the dugout. Where he stood, the sun reflected off his aviator lenses in a single molten beam, focused on me. If I tried to maintain eye contact with him while jogging back to the bench, his stare would burn a blue hole in the center of my vision that got bigger the closer to him I got. I was not a ballplayer, I knew. I was a head case.

The Amish, though. They didn't seem to care who was watching. One after another, they stropped pitches over the fence. "Hyume run!" they said. "Holy smokes!"

Four Amish girls in heart-shaped bonnets stopped walking dogs to curl their fingers around the chain links. They had light eyes and sheer cheeks. "You girls runnin' around, are ya now?" asked Aaron, the left fielder. He nodded to the boy at the plate, who then knocked one deep into the gap. I took a few perfunctory strides. Aaron ran hard enough to lose his hat. Then he dove, snagged the liner backhanded, and rolled into a somersault before springing to his feet. The ball was sticking half out of the top of his glove—a snow cone, you call it—and he feigned a lick. The girls tittered.

As Aaron and I trotted in from the outfield, I asked how his Rumspringa'd been.

"Na, ya know. Other than ball, running around makes me feel restless."

He told me they had a playoff game that evening at a different park. I made him type the address directly into my phone.

Along the old Philadelphia Pike, between Lancaster City and Intercourse, traffic coagulated. Tourist vehicles braked to take in each buggy that jangled down the extra-wide shoulders. So many signs were crowded at the road's edge—signs for clocks, jams, buggy rides, pretzels, Old Amish apples, Old Amish peaches, Old Amish furniture, country knives, a stay at the Old Amish motel, the Amish Experience—and they all were angled and a little desperate, like raised hands eager to answer a question. This was something I'd read about, how acres of farmland were going for $17,500-per at auction, so only half of the Amish in Lancaster could still afford to farm. The rest were moving to other states, or adjusting to nine-to-five workdays punctuated with leisure time. At a red light, I watched a family of six hit the Susquehanna Bank branch, barefoot.

Stopping and going, I snapped photos of sprawling Amish estates, their roofs flanneled with solar cells. When I looked through the shots on the digital viewfinder, I noticed that surrounding the farms were English homes on artificial rises. They were stone houses of an imagined rusticity, built by well-off retirees who had push-pinned American flags on sticks all over the property. These houses managed to seem both really invasive and really conscious of not seeming invasive, looky-loos with hands folded behind their backs.

This is the attraction, this *idea* of the Amish. That we might come to Lancaster and encounter what appears to be our past, the simple, rich, idyllic existence back when our freedom *from* had yet to develop into our freedom *to*. Here's what we could have been had we stayed the inevitable.

It's both condescending and a self-deception, of course, this idea. But in my car, I had to admit: it's hard to lay off of. When I saw Amish in buggies waving across two lanes of traffic, it cheered me up. Their homogeneous presence was a merry sight, like nuns in habits at the airport. It's a relief to know that people still live this way, because as these sorts of Jeffersonian fundamentals shrink further from our world, I find it more necessary than ever that someone harvest summer corn, cultivate virtue, play baseball. Abandoning that would mean something about us was dead, or at the very least outgrown.

I took a seat on the bleachers next to a stout Amish man with a salt-and-pepper beard. He'd taken off his clodhoppers so he could fan his toes on the row in front. Our view past the outfield fence was a darkening one of barns riding the corduroy swells of corn like arks. The floodlights switched on.

"Looks like rain," said the man next to me, whom let's call "Dan" because, were his real name to appear in print, he'd be censured by the faithful. "What's your phone say?"

This was the semifinal of a local league championship, the fifth game of a best-of-five series. The Amish boys had won the first two; the English men the last. About eighty or so Amish had come to watch. They outnumbered the English four to one.

Many were families, but most were young men from fast districts. They looked just like middle-American teens on television, all swooped bangs and skinny jeans tucked into fat-tongued sneakers. The few girls wore dresses and bonnets. The prettiest one sat in a truck that idled while "Call Me Maybe" spritzed through the cracked windows.

I told Dan that my weather app was saying all clear. In the dugout, the Amish boys brought it in and chanted, "One, two, three—KICK ASS!" before flowering their hands. I cringed and waited for the communal reprimand, but none came. A cloth-freckling rain began to fall.

The English team was sponsored by a construction company. They looked to be men of a mean utility, ornamented with sun-blued tattoos. "I know it's tough, but if he's throwing that short shit," their burly coach instructed them, "take all the pitches."

The Amish boys conducted themselves through warm-up drills. They wore gray jerseys and white pants, some belted and some held up with suspenders. I asked Dan if he was cool with these kids wearing uniforms instead of their Ordnung-prescribed trousers. "For now," he said. "When they're married, their clothes will be their uniforms. In terms of God, I mean."

The first couple innings were tight. The Amish turned a smart 6-4-3 double play. The English retired them 1-2-3. They accepted umps' close calls with nodded equanimity.

The rain picked up, sprouting umbrellas. In the field, the boys tensed and attended to the ball. The English cracked two home runs that left the park trailing tails of sound. "Sit! Sit! Sit!" Dan called out to the Amish boy who'd just swung and missed so hard he spun off his feet. The boy then looped a double. "There you go, that's what happens when you sit."

Dan turned to me. "So, you're a tourist?" The ease with which I lied and said I was visiting family startled me.

"Some think tourism is a new kind of persecution," he said. "On account of we don't want our souls marketed." We commented on the irony of this, the disguise of plainness they adopted way back when now making them glaringly obvious and strange.

"I don't know," Dan said. "We could never have stopped it. Now, we need it."

The boys fell behind by a few runs after succumbing to

impulse in the field. They forced throws, overran balls, bypassed cutoff men. "Bah," Dan went. "Playing young. In a hurry."

I told him about this Rumspringa documentary I'd seen? Where, like, all the kids went to these huge parties? And had unprotected sex? And did, like, meth and stuff? And did that happen out here?

"We got problems just like anybody. Drugs, pregnancy. Some of that stuff'll probably go on after this game is over. It's being a child. But then that stops. Or it's supposed to stop, if you make the right decision.

"You just feel silly after a while, running around. 'Where am I going?' Ya know?"

Giving no notice, I touched his shirt. I rubbed it between my thumb and forefinger, as though pantomiming the universal gesture for "very costly."

He cocked his head and curled his lower lip under his upper. "You like it? My wife buys them in the store in town. She don't wash by hand, just so you know. We're not, what do you call—"

"Noble savages?" I offered.

"At the shop, I have a Gmail. Washes 'em in the pneumatic washer, my wife."

When Aaron the left fielder walked to the plate with the score tied six all, the guys in the dugout hummed a ragged facsimile of "Here Comes the Bride." The men in the bleachers stamped and hooted. One young lady in attendance put her face in her hands, wracked with either laughter or sobs. This, it turned out, was Aaron's final at-bat before marriage, the last pitch he'd swing at.

I decided that I could not watch this. This was like sneaking into a bar mitzvah, or trying to peek through the fogged window of a car parked on an escarpment. This was a turning point I should not be privy to.

On the unlit diamond to the east, four Amish boys in slacks

and suspenders were playing pepper, a game where fielders crowd around a batter who slaps quick grounders into the array. I mumbled a hasty goodbye, fetched my glove, and joined them.

I gobbled up the first dozen balls hit my way. After each one bellied my pocket, I felt good, great, like a coin had been slotted and I could play myself a little longer. I whipped the ball back to the batter, who chopped it at someone else.

Then that good feeling vanished. It always vanishes, because it's always contingent upon the next ball.

The boy off my forehand side fielded by reaching down with his one hand while raising the other straight over his head. When the ball popped in his mitt, he slapped his hands together in front of his grinning face. He was gawkily storkish, and very consistent.

I thought: This boy knows nothing of the yips. He will be forever in the world's childhood. If only I could play as purely and single-mindedly as he does.

But doubt nagged: Does he really play unknowingly? And even if he does—did he really ever have a choice?

I could've asked. He was right there.

But what if an Amish boy also felt turned around, overwhelmed, scared, like he was trapped in a place many times too big for him, where his only recourse was to run from person to person and place to place to see if anything bore any relation to him, or if it might not help him get to where he thought he should be, wanting to cry but trying hard not to, wishing most of all he was in a warm, small, familiar place?

We played pepper in silence. On the other diamond, the roars of the Amish were less frequent but more intense, the sound of faith unstoppered. I tried hard not to fuck up. I thought of not throwing behind the batter, and then did, more times than I'd like. I envisioned my dad's face, and remembered a time when each muffed ball would inflate my anxiety a little bit further, like breaths into a blown gum bubble. The other boys handled the field with an uneventfulness that resembled meditation.

Right down the street from the Amtrak station, in the husked industrial half of Lancaster City, there was a minor league baseball stadium with GAME DAY signs in the parking lot. I decided to catch a few innings while I waited for my train.

I got a seat behind home plate for twelve bucks. A team from Long Island was visiting the Lancaster Barnstormers, whose logo is a cock-topped weather vane. Around the stadium, there was all this stuff to do other than watch baseball—merry-go-round, inflatable slide, pit barbecue, dunk tank—and all these families doing it. Maybe people will always at least *go* to the games. They can be like a historical farm, a nice-day alternative to taking your family to the Air and Space Museum and not reading any of the placards.

A small-bore sun setting in the west made the clouds glow along their margins. At the end of the first, I spotted three traditionally dressed Amish teens in my section and decamped for the seats behind them.

The boys were in Rumspringa. We talked about the schoolhouse shooting, how the Amish set up a charitable fund for the killer's family, attended his funeral, and comforted his widow and parents, one man holding the killer's sobbing father in his arms for an hour. The boys quieted down whenever the pitcher began to toe his rubber. The fielders held up as many fingers as outs, the repetition to make sure that the appropriate thought was firmly in mind at the appropriate moment. "His name was Charles Carl Roberts IV," one of them said during a time-out.

The Barnstormers' in-house MC trawled the rows around us for between-innings tricycle-race volunteers. The Amish kid sitting in the middle wanted to know if I'd been to college. I told him I had. He stared at the alluvial veins on the backs of his hands. I blurted out: "No, but you're lucky, though. School till eighth grade, then labor?" I got a little agitated, actually. Restricted consciousness? Making a *choice* to be protected from the burden of *choice*? Did they not know how blessed they were?

The one on the left said, "You could join, y'know."

I daydreamed on it for a whole inning: sweatily carpentering, whispering to horses, sniffing handfuls of crumbly manure late in the day—whatever it is you do on a farm. And never knowing what else I might have become. How does that sound? Choosing to live a life buffered by a freedom found not in options but in the diminution of self? Having faith that peace of mind will become one day possible and then effortless after that? I lost track of balls and strikes. The clouds burned out on the last day of summer.

I said no. I said no, and I relished it. I relished it almost as much as I relish getting obstreperously bent around new people, or declining second dates.

All the time I was in Lancaster, I couldn't help but be reminded of this other group of votaries I'd come across in my research. They, too, cherished their separateness. They, however, took up arms against the world to maintain it.

In A.D. 72, fifteen thousand Romans laid siege to the Jewish city of Masada, a lofty, isolated, and seemingly impregnable citadel built atop a table mountain. For a year, 960 men, women, and children manned its defense. Stymied at first, the Roman legion moved thousands of tons of earth and stone in constructing a monumental ramp and battering ram. When they finally breached Masada, they discovered that the fortress was uninhabited. Desolate.

Littering its streets were the cutthroat bodies of every man, woman, and child. Their religion forbade suicide, so the defenders had drawn lots and killed one another in turn. The last man standing was the only one condemned. But before taking his life, he set fire to the city, burning every last thing to the ground. Everything but the granaries, the storerooms. He wanted the Romans to understand—they had chosen death over surrender.

That man. I imagine the Romans finding him slumped against a rear ruin, the brim of his helmet tipped back, as if the last thing he decided to do before damning himself with his own hand was wipe it across his forehead.

I asked the teens, "Hey, you guys didn't happen to be at this softball game the other night?" They nodded at one another. I told them I left a little early and wanted to know who came out on top.

"Oh," said the middle Amish. "The English went on a tear. They mercy-ruled our boys in the seventh."

9/27/13

For years, Dad has made allusions to some mythical family tree. A Russell Codex, bound maybe in skin, that was compiled by his own father over the course of his life.

Dad went through it once and declared it off-limits. "Reparations, man," was his reasoning. Yesterday, I asked to see it.

"This is not any attempt to research your Great American Novel, is it?" Dad wondered. "Spoiler alert: a group of shitbirds merged with a newer group of shitbirds."

"Look," I said. "Even if they *were* fieldmasters, and even if we *remain* peckerwood, I'd still like to know the stock whence I sprang."

"Little did you know, I've already ordered and received your DNA analysis. You are: sixteen percent deported criminals, seventy-nine percent carnival workers, two percent defrocked priests, one percent female midget wrestlers, and, as you suspected, two percent circus animals. And that's not even counting your mother's side of the family. Don't you listen to them when they say they're Italian and Russian. They're some escaped, unprosecuted Nazi prison guards, is what they are."

"Nice math. Just gimme the fucking thing."

"You're gonna make fun of it."

"Why? Why would I make fun of it?"

"Because you make fun of shit. That's what you do. These were regular, hard-working Americans. Ignorant though they may have been."

"I'm not gonna."

"If you make fun of them, I will give them permission to haunt you. *I* will haunt you. On you like white on rice, my ghost."

The Codex, it turned out, was in an accordioned file folder. Dad took a sheaf of onionskins out of it, held on to them several beats too long, risked a tear before finally letting go.

According to the documents, the first of us came to Maryland from Yorkshire in 1650. He started several tobacco plantations, adopted the motto *Patientia et Perseverentia*. Many years later, his great-great-grandson, "a strong-minded man, unmovable when he had formed his opinions," "a devout Methodist in religion" who had "no fear of anything or anyone"—this man fought for American independence. Then he went home and freed his slaves.

After that, he ventured with the family into Ohio, back when the place was a hinterland full of pissed-off Indians. Russells built the first schoolhouse and church in a town called St. Clairsville. There they settled, and multiplied.

At first, our men did one of three things: they preached, taught school, or soldiered. As time passed, they did only things two and three. Then mostly three. Pasty white Americans, the lot of them. Men with broad faces and sharp thoughts. Chawbrowned teeth, reliable sidearms, baaaad dispositions. They were involved in most minor and all major military conflicts. Fought on both sides of the Mason-Dixon. Did harm for country and kin.

Reading about them, I felt . . . what? Not pride, exactly. Eh, pride.

But actually: more like a felt lack. Like something should be in me, but isn't. Has been lopped off, in fact, and tingles like a phantom limb.

This phantom-limb feeling haunts my body *and* my mind. In my body, it's diffuse, like the dark applause of bats leaving a cave. In my mind, it's this Cheshire grin floating in a void. Altogether, it's me wishing, *wishing* a motherfucker would.

As to whether this feeling causes me to fantasize about justifiable homicide—or vice versa, that it's fantasizing about justifiable homicide that dredges the feeling: I don't know. I *do* know that I do a lot of brooding. Mostly about the day when I can finally put some loved ones behind me like so many eggs in one basket. When I can absorb all the blows meant for them, or else distribute some on their behalf. When I can finally, thank *God*, expend myself in a violence of kindness.

Late at night, when I'm in bed or watching a West Coast hockey game, I think about what that must feel like. Taking the shortcut between flesh and spirit. Regifting my unwanted self like a breadmaker. I bet it feels good. The way a log in a fire looks like it feels good.

It has given over to its physical fact. It has learned that there is indeed a best way to go out.

I know I should be pleased if not proud of how I have handled myself of late. Despite a strong youthful predisposition, I haven't had a fistfight in more than a decade, when me and my opponent were built like uncooked hot dogs. I should be fine with the fact that I let my battles slide, or else let someone else fight them for me. When confronted, I use my words. It's enlightened! I know that the principles of white American masculinity are atavistic. Invidious. Really, they enforce a paring down, a closing off—not a reaching for but a turning in. A kind of spiritual fist-making.

I know all of this, and should be fine with it, but I absolutely am not. Such is why a boy is infinitely more dangerous than a man. He's so sensitive about the perception of his courage.

Those later Russells who felt likewise had four choices, according to the Codex. They could learn a trade, join the army, go to sea, or take advantage of the land and labor opportunities out west. A goodly number of them left St. Clairsville to chase the vanishing frontier. Dad's dad stayed. Papa Lou went to Ohio University but worked as a flagman during the Depression. He taught school after that, and then he fought in the Pacific Theater. He came back with a respiratory condition.

This being the era in which doctors thought there was something to recommend about Florida's fartgas atmosphere, Papa Lou took his two boys and started a breakaway sect of Russells on the Gulf Coast. Baby boy Kent did not make the trip. He had by then been lost to a routine tonsillectomy. The anesthesiologist gave him too much ether, fever-dreamed him to death. Dad's aunt Didi was supposed to be the attending specialist, but she couldn't work the surgery because of the conflict of interest. Kent was put in the care of a stranger, and he died.

Didi was the one person in whom Dad had confided his *other* boyhood dream—that of becoming a song-and-dance man. He used to ride his bike over to Didi's place to sing and bake cookies. "She was a little weird. A little lonely. I had to take the back way to see her," he has said, as always talking about or asking after other people's problems when, really, he means his own.

Papa Lou broke the news this way: "Your brother's not coming home. He's dead." Kent was five. One year younger than Dad. The two of them had shared a bed. "They murdered him," is how Dad puts it.

The rest, as they say, is history.

7.

ISLAND MAN

WHERE I LIVED, AND WHAT I LIVED FOR

And when Dave swung the dinghy wide around the cape, his customer at last caught sight of the island, a shark's tooth of sand and grass jutting from a small mountain of impenetrable bush. *Heaven!* Dave said to himself.

Heavy seas shouldered the tin boat sideways. *Up front, mate!* Dave shouted over the bee-loud motor. His customer clambered forward and sat himself backward on the bow, twisting at the waist to keep his eyes on the islet. The evening sky behind it was striped orange to purple.

The customer was thinking about how a guy can't get himself shipwrecked anymore. Can't one day discover that his storm-tossed ass has been beached upon a refuge, where he's free to wile away life, alone with the Alone. It's impossible now. All the deserted but potentially habitable islands are privately owned, or secret naval bases, or satellite tracking stations. Among other reasons.

Head on a swivel! Crocs! Dave sang out, his hair a white pennant behind him. Soon to be seventy, Dave Glasheen was the smooth sienna of well-oiled and -kept things. He had been living on this outlying island for more than fifteen years. *We wouldn't want to swim this at night, no we wouldn't,* he said. The water leaking into the bow rose above his customer's ankles.

Hours earlier, Dave had picked him up from a World War II–era airstrip many miles distant in the mainland's thick jungle. This intra-Australian airfare, as well as all sea transport, had been included in the $3,100 Dave charged for his two-week desert-island experience. The customer had wired the money directly into Dave's bank account, as instructed. Also as instructed, he'd brought salamis, two loaves of good bread, coffee, and little else.

This was like a vacation but not. The impulse was the same, maybe. Long had the customer been shopping around for a space that was remote from the world. A spot where, he hoped, everything had been got rid of except for whatever couldn't be done without. What the smart set's always wanted from their getaways.

The customer had inquired after fire towers and bathyspheres, deep caves and sensory-deprivation chambers. Idaho. The Arctic. He even looked into elective lobotomies and self-trepanation, just to see. Then—of *course*. The desert island came to him one winter Saturday. He had been in the bathtub, apocalyptically hung over. He was paddling warm water against his face and wondering, *Just what the fuck is it I'm doing here?*

The question was not new. It was what his mind reset to whenever he stilled himself, stopped diverting. For instance, he would close the browser on other people's Twitter feeds and Instagrams, finally put down the book, or, yes, wake up cottonmouthed in a spinning chamber of shame—and then it would begin to materialize: *WTF, man?* The question wavered in his mind's eye before tightening into painful clarity, as vision tends to do after hard blows to the head.

The truth was that most things for him had turned into giant, squawking question marks. He was living far from home in an unfashionable part of New York City, uninsured and friendless (but for the roaches). He was a relatively young man, yet even a young man's bliss had not been his. He'd loved little but had his fill of a hell of a lot. Had indulged himself, in fact, to the point where he made himself sick. Now he hid from the everyday melee of competing agents and material forces whenever he wasn't scheduled to work. Should he have to take the subway somewhere, he found himself blinking back tears. What attempts he made at meeting new people were prewritten and floated into online ether, like bottled messages. He almost *wished* he'd knocked somebody up.

Instead, he decided to venture to a desert island off the edge of northeastern Australia. It was at least the first step, he figured. If a boat is foundering, you dry-dock it for repairs. If you suspect your heart has a hole in it—take yourself out of the world.

DAY 1 (CONT.)

WRECKED ON A DESERT ISLAND

While Dave anchored his dinghy in the wave wash, the customer waded ashore, where he was immediately leapt upon by two dogs, Quasimodo and Locky. Quassi was caramel-colored and hulking, part dingo but mostly pit bull. Down his trunkish right foreleg was a rune of a scar tissue like lightning along an elm—at night, Quassi guarded the island against saltwater crocodiles. Locky was a spry dun mutt, three months new to the place. He had belonged to Dave's youngest daughter, but he wound up here after she killed herself.

Clouds had gathered, and all four walked the path to Dave's shanty manor as hot rain began to fall. His place was just as the customer had imagined: tentatively walled, cantilevered under scabby sheet metal, and cozy with things scavenged. There were glass jars of all hues; rough furniture and rusted pots; canned goods, batteries, and salt-curled paperbacks; skeletons and snakeskins in overhanging netting; buckets under every leak; and blades, nippers, pliers, tweezers, scrapers, wrenches, wedges—too many tools to name. The lot of it reminded the customer of how a nonnative speaker will hoard nouns while trying to recall the verb that animates them.

He had dreamed of such a place since early childhood, when he devoured any and all books about a man improvising survival from the limited resources at hand: *Robinson Crusoe*, *The Swiss Family Robinson*, *The Cay*, *Lord of the Flies*, *The Mysterious Island*, *Island of the Blue Dolphins*, *Hatchet*. *The Boxcar Children*, even. He'd take them to the end of his street, where he had cleared his own hutch in a dark thicket of needle palms. When things went on at home that he didn't want to be around, he crawled into this sanctuary and read, the wind fanning him with fronds.

Dave's own clean-swept main area included a gas-powered freezer, an antenna for solar-powered phone and Internet, and an L-shaped desk, at the front of which sat an eyeless woman, unpolitely, her sundress canopied by her knees. *My girlfriend, Miranda*, Dave said, winking, patting the mannequin's red hair. He showed off the adjoining patio, which sheltered a full-size mattress looking out on the sea. He made it abundantly clear that as near a man could find himself to self-sufficiency, to a world of his own making—here he was.

This thrilled his customer. This was what he came for. He felt in his bones that there was such a thing as Real Life; it was just—not only could he not get to its entrance, he couldn't even *see* it, on account of the ocean of assholes thronging the door.

Thus did he not think twice when Dave offered him several already opened bottles of home-brewed beer. He accepted them and joined his host at a driftwood table in the outdoor kitchen, intent on what he had to tell him.

Dave first set foot on the island in November 1993, having been wrecked financially six years earlier by the Australian securities crash. A marketer by trade, he'd tried to dabble in mineral exploration in Papua New Guinea. He lost all of his wealth, about ten million dollars, when his private venture went tits up. He thought the episode absurd—on paper he's worth big bickies, then suddenly he's not. But getting whacked was also the best thing that ever happened to him. A great release, it was.

He'd been a corporate bloke. He'd consulted on marketing strategies for British Tobacco, for the sport of cricket and the drink of milk. He'd been in the ice-cream game; he sold Drumsticks to Australia but failed to get TCBY into Asia. He foresaw the bottled-water craze and helped reinvent the juice box. Packaging was a very real concern for him.

Until his house was foreclosed upon, he'd lived in the most exclusive beachside neighborhood in Sydney. He'd owned two yachts, *Black Erik* and *Erik the Red*, the latter the namesake of his newly late daughter, poor ginger Erika. He adored everything about skiing, especially the exclusive lodges at his favorite American slopes. (He expected to need his skis again soon and so kept them on the island.) He came to despise banks, big financial institutions—any of the parties he deemed responsible for making him feel right minuscule and tossed about for the first time. Wasn't his fault the market crashed, he knew. Prior to the money poofing, he and his family had never rented a thing in their lives.

Naturally, the crash led to their having some pretty heavy ding-dongs, but Dave and his wife never formally divorced. Rather, he took up with a new woman, a white Zimbabwean named Denise. Dave talked her into changing her name to Denika—she ran a small business that sold jerky made from

African game, and Dave explained to her that no one wanted to buy *Denise*'s African jerky. After that, he helped her manage a spa—managed the bloody thing himself—until one day she decided she wanted to get away. An *island*, she told him in bed, in a fit of postcoital quixotism. *Our own.* So, Dave called up a friend in real estate and said, *I got this new bird, and I need an island.*

The asking price for Restoration Island was $1.2 million. Unable to buy it outright, Dave and two partners subleased the habitable third of the island from a company that owned its rights until 2039. The agreement was contingent upon Dave and his partners developing an eco-resort worth at least two hundred thousand dollars, and doing so within five years. They got the requisite permits; they drew up plans for a boutique hotel. Then the KuukuYa'u people of nearby Lockhart River, rights holders of the other two-thirds of the island, launched a title claim against them.

Though nothing came of the aboriginals' claim, Dave learned that he couldn't just waltz into blackfella country and have the run of the place. The KuukuYa'u hated him, fiercely, but still he moved onto Restoration and began readying it for development. Once he'd gotten set up, Denika visited for a rip-roaring couple of weeks. Certainly no family planning going on then! They conceived a son, Kye, who would spend six of his earliest months on the island. Talk about a Garden of Eden. It was a fantastic time. But Denika quickly tired of island life. Couldn't hack it, if Dave was being perfectly honest. It got rather nasty. She demanded Dave drive her off the island but never asked him to join her. She and Kye just piked out of his world.

Alone thereafter, Dave's days turned into weeks into years into decades. Occasionally, he left the island to visit Lockhart River; once a year, he went to buy supplies in faraway Cairns.

Development never progressed, and the KuukuYa'u came to accept the presence of this strange white man.

The lease-holding company wanted him gone, however; they had buyers lined up but couldn't sell their third until Restoration was uninhabited. The police wouldn't intervene because Dave's breach of contract was a civil matter. The resultant litigation went all the way to the Supreme Court of Queensland, where Dave, virtually penniless, represented himself. He spun a one-day hearing into six by presenting strange and grammatically incorrect evidence to a justice who ultimately ruled that he had "wrongly deprived the plaintiff of its asset for over a decade" while having "enjoyed its benefits."

Dave could be put off the island with five minutes' notice. He was at the enforced end of his marooning.

I need a white knight to kick in, you see, he told his customer as they sat under an LED lantern. *Just a little seed money. Five hundred thousand. What's that, relatively? Bugger-all. A very small amount of help, so I can buy out the majority shareholder.*

Dave got up and put a pot of fresh crabs on the boil. The customer had known Dave was in some legal trouble, but to hear that the man who had finally found a place worth mooring after floating through limitless possibility—to hear that he was getting *evicted*—this disheartened him to no end. Where did a guy go if mooks in suits could reach you *here*?

After dinner, Dave escorted his customer a few hundred yards into the blackness, to a vaulted fiberglass hut. Inside was an undulating tile floor, two rusted bed frames topped with foam rubber, and a plastic toilet that flushed rainwater. Green lizards scampered along all surfaces, scooping mouthfuls of translucent ants as if playing jacks with their tongues. The structure was wide open at its front; from the outside, it resembled nothing so much as a shell abandoned by a giant hermit crab.

Got nothing poisonous, mate, don't worry, Dave lied, at this time choosing not to mention his first dog, Kato, whom he found dead from a spider bite one morning at the foot of his mattress.

Dave *did* warn about Boxhead, however, a crocodile the size of a Buick Skylark that haunted the island. He warned that Boxhead had been stabbed once by a KuukuYa'u hunter and so hated mankind with the intensity of a thousand suns. Then he said, *G'night!*

The wind had picked up by several dozen knots, occasionally lashing rain. It seized trees with ecstatic fury and lifted boards away from their nails, honkingly. The customer sought out Quassi and insisted he join him in the twin bed. His heart fluttered so fast that, like a propeller up to speed, it seemed to be going in two directions at once.

DAY 2

FORMER INHABITANTS;

AND WINTER VISITORS

Dawn broke, and the customer reached for his glasses, which were gone. He bungled out onto what appeared to be a large clearing sandwiched between beach and mountainous jungle. It was covered in itchy grass and cocos palms.

Restoration Island is a speck, a seventh of a square mile sitting only a few hundred yards offshore of Cape York Peninsula. But the island is far removed, closer to Papua New Guinea than it is to any Australian city.

It got its name from William Bligh, the commanding lieutenant of the HMS *Bounty*. In 1789, Bligh's crew mutinied after he refused to grant them a return to Tahiti, to the idyllic life (and easy natives) they imagined to be waiting for them there. The mutineers set him adrift in an open boat with a handful of loyal men. Left for dead, Bligh nonetheless managed to navigate to this island, where he and his crew scrounged food and recuperation. "Restoration Island," they called it. They found a couple of huts, but no people.

The customer made for the northern tip of its habitable third, where the clearing, beach, and jungle met. Immediately, he tripped over something. He picked himself up and bent near the impediment and realized with a start that it was a goddamned *gravestone*, forty years old and belonging to no one Dave knew. "The Sea is so vast and my ship is so small," it read. The customer found his glasses nearby, partially eaten, in a roped-off square of scrubgrass that was, he'd learn, an aboriginal mass grave. Such had been Restoration's local *raison:* The KuukuYa'u and passing sailors considered it a dump.

Now the customer could see that the island was littered with detritus. Lengths of rope, chunks of rotted wood, cashed canisters of natural gas, dead engines and fridges. He kicked aside the rinds of the salamis he'd brought—ravaged in the night—as he walked through the shadow of a derelict sailboat keeled to port. Altogether, there were a dozen boats and skiffs abandoned above the tideline. Out past the breakers: a couple of scuttled trawlers, now artificial reefs. It took the customer a moment to realize what it was that was off—*no seagulls.*

A decade ago, this island was kempt, civilized. The grass was mown and the buildings had doors. But now it abided nothing man-made. This disrepair embarrassed Dave. It made it seem as though he, too, was deteriorating. Past retirement age he might be, but he was just *starting* his life. He saw it all so much clearer now.

The tiki bar on the south shore, for instance. Now it had crumbled into the surf. But in 2003, he had used that tiki bar to entertain Fred Turner. Fred *Turner*, the McDonald's chairman. In the midst of a fishing trip, Fred flew in on a helicopter to see the island and have a beer—and he had such a lovely time that he came back to camp on Resto with his executives and their families. Fred sat Dave at his right hand during dinners; once, he asked him to give a speech. *Fred's a hero*, Dave made sure to mention in his address. Fred's the college dropout who put the Golden Arches in 118 countries, the visionary who thought up the Chicken McNugget and the drive-thru and the whole standardized dining experience.

Oh, Dave hated the product, dearly. But no great man was more forward-thinking than Fred. He got his millions, and then what did he do? He founded the Ronald McDonald House charity. Dave admired Fred's class of corporate don best of all, the altruistic blokes who make it their business to help even after they've gathered their brass. He bet most of them were good people. How else could they have become so successful?

He explained this to his customer as they breakfasted on Cheerios and kiwis. Then Dave took him on a tour of the bush. *Do you know the Google guys?* he asked as they entered the jungle behind the clearing. *What kind of blokes do you reckon they are?*

They stopped in Dave's garden, which stank of wild rosemary. Quassi and Locky rollicked through a sinkhole where yams, gooseberries, and bananas once grew. *I hear their cafeteria gives them the healthy food for free, but you have to pay for the burgers*, he said. *This is the new wave of people, the I.T. blokes. They recognize that we should be better than we are.*

Dave did not cultivate this garden. Normally, about a dozen backpackers would arrive throughout the year as part of the Willing Workers on Organic Farms (WWOOF) program. They'd care for the vegetables, landscape the island, repair Dave's buildings, cook his meals—all in exchange for room and board on Resto. A fair trade, Dave thought, his only rule being: no camping on the beach, because of Boxhead. Some stayed a week; others, more than a year. Dave fell in love with practically every female WWOOFer who shot through. Some of those birds were bloody mature! They'd go around topless, they'd gussy up for dinner. But none had come in the last six months.

He led his customer farther up the sloping interior. He scrambled over fallen trees, naked except for board shorts, his wild white hair and cloudy beard jouncing with the effort. *You can massage your internal organs through your feet*, Dave advised. *Tremendously important.* His was a vigorous physicality, the kind often found in sinewy men of a certain age and outlook.

Dave had learned the out-of-doors from his father. Before sending him off to elite boarding schools, Dave's old man was always taking him camping, fishing, even though he was an esteemed attorney with his own busy firm in Sydney. Dave cherished the stories he heard family friends tell about how his father steered clients away from the courts, tried to get them to settle things bloke to bloke. Saved them a load of codswallop, he did.

He'd been this big bloody Irishman, his old man. A stereotypical one of theirs, you might say—touchy paterfamilias who was keen on things like driving the family to Sunday Mass while full as a boot. Dave took up the practice himself when in his teens; the whole clan'd have a laugh when he hiccupped while breaking a pound note in the collection plate.

He hadn't been able to share those kinds of moments with his own son. *You know, my Kye, he's in his Jesus phase now*, Dave said, pulling aside creeping vines. *He was an OK bloke, that Jesus. Also a healer.* A teen now, Kye rarely visited the island. But he'll be back in his twenties, Dave thought. When he wants to bring out his own sheila.

Otherwise, Dave would never force the island on him. That'd push Kye away, just as *his* father had pushed him away from law school. Lately, Dave had begun to see just how profoundly disappointing that must've been for his dad, to have neither Dave nor his rellies take up the firm. It was like him here. If your children don't come to your island, you start to wonder: What's this for, then? His eldest, Sam, turned down his offer to have her wedding out here. She had never even come for a lob. If Kye said no, well, he reckoned he'd just have to find someone outside the company, as it were.

Erika wasn't an option, of course, which was a shame because she was the one who visited most. Dave bloody fucking missed her. He figured that she killed herself because she had all these complications in her life. It right pissed him off. First of all, she was a gay lady. And trying to live as a gay lady even today in this society ain't no picture painting. Second, she could drink too much. Third, she had some psychological problems, the kind you need lithium for and never used to hear about.

Dave blamed the culture. We've been mollycoddled. Bit by bit, we've become marshmallows. But he also blamed himself. At least a little. Because of the separation and all that.

I'm from the wrong country, mate, Dave said, looking over his shoulder as his customer minced over a crevice. *Australians don't take risks like Americans. We're all a bunch of bloody soft cocks. The average ones whinge and moan. Scared of their potential, I reckon.*

After another half hour of tramping, they emerged onto a promontory. Dave jogged in place atop a sharp rock. The water far below him was the bluish slate of fancy cats. *This island's healed me*, he said. *And I can see how it could help others in a big sense.* A salesman at heart, Dave rarely spoke without making and sustaining eye contact. His own were a shallow aqua, and they seemed almost to shimmer with refracted light whenever he talked business. *I don't know what it is*, he said. *I don't pretend to understand it. But I feel energy here.*

He'd felt it the moment he walked ashore. It was as though he'd been lost in the bush and finally heard his *Cooee!* call. *This* was good fortune. *This* was the genuine article. None of that other dribbleshit, the God bothering and the money chasing.

Here, he had recovered his lost unity, his wholeness and harmony. Why couldn't the power of this place be used to restore others?

NIGHT IN THE SHELL

ILL AND CONSCIENCE-STRICKEN,

HE SURVEYS HIS POSITION

Our most enduring love story, if we go by the numbers, is man + island. We in the West adore us a maroon's tale, *Robinson Crusoe* being of course the urtext. Since its publication in 1719, Daniel Defoe's novel about an enterprising castaway and his courtship of solitude has produced about two hundred English and six hundred foreign-language editions. To say nothing of the adaptations, imitations, and homages it continues to inspire.

Crusoe himself was based on the true-life account of a Scottish sailor, yes. Maybe. No one's sure to what extent. Anyhow, over the centuries, Crusoe's place in our cultural consciousness has continued to shift. We've sort of willed ourselves into forgetting that he's a character rendered whole by an author. He has come now to exist in a kind of limbo: we don't believe he was a historical person—but we don't believe he's entirely fictional, either.

One thing he was, though, was our first realistic portrayal of the radical individualist. In Defoe's story, Crusoe gets shipwrecked on a desert island with only a pocketknife and a little tobacco in his pipe. Things look grim until he pulls himself together and works to make a heaven of this hell. Via rational thought and elbow grease, Crusoe discovers that his unfathomable depths contain: an architect, an astronomer, a baker, a carpenter, a potter, a farmer, a tailor, and an umbrella maker. He builds a fenced-in redoubt, plants crops and a privacy hedge. He glazes pots, bakes bread, stitches clothes from animal skins. He wrights a ship with a sail and a parasol. And, most incessantly, he accounts for and makes use of every single thing he comes across, people included.

Robinson Crusoe values people not as human beings, but as objects that might be of some utility to him now or down the line. For example, the Moorish boy who helps him escape from a pre-island bit of slavery? Crusoe turns around and sells *him* into slavery. He comes to regret the sale, but only because it would've been nice to have an extra set of hands around. ("Now I wished for my boy Xury, and the long-boat with shoulder-of-mutton sail . . .") The first word he teaches to Friday, the native companion he recruits? "Master."

Crusoe is free and accountable to no one, preferring his hard new liberty to the easy yoke of society. He claims to find God on the island—but, just in case, he takes care to learn how to wrest his own good from himself. "I was lord of the whole manor," he says, "or if I pleased I could call my self king or emperor over the whole country which I had possession of. There were no rivals; I had no competitor." Depending on your mien, that might sound like paradise. Or, on the other hand, the wet-dream somniloquy of a tyrant or monopolist.

Regardless, Robinson Crusoe remains one of our most influential dead white men. For better and for worse. As James Joyce said of him, "The whole Anglo-Saxon spirit is in Crusoe: the manly independence; the unconscious cruelty; the persistence; the slow yet efficient intelligence; the sexual apathy; the practical, well-balanced religiousness; the calculating taciturnity." He's who's behind the Boy Scouts, libertarianism, and three hundred years' worth of solitary, self-reliant heroes. He was wise to our condition, this *isolato*, and the story he invented for himself out of his freedom still reads like a survival guide, a crash course in modern existence.

DAY 5

A BOAT;

ECONOMY

My dream is to create a healing center here, Dave said to his customer as he turned the dinghy up a muddy creek. *For corporate people. The time-poor; not the mob.* He angled the motor out of the shallow water, and the two of them slid underneath an arch of mangroves threaded together like prayerful hands. *I think the mob's just looking for a quick fix. Do* you *think those people are equipped to heal themselves?*

A wince rippled across the customer's face. He threw out a line weighted with wire leader and a realistic six-inch lure, holding it loosely in his right hand while it trailed behind the boat. Dave went on: *It all starts with the individual, you see. People need to restore themselves. But they need to have the infrastructure to do so. That's where I come in. I'll have 'em come here, and then I'll give 'em an umbrella and an esky of champagne before buggering off. A club atmosphere, hey? Have the Google blokes visit. I'm thinking four thousand—Australian—per day.*

Dave made little slashing gestures over the jungle to show his customer where he intended to level trails for the elderly and less-abled. *This'll be private, word-of-mouth,* he said. *Right now I'm building a network of therapists and wellness birds who'll refer patients. A nice way to cop a flow.* Here, a funicular would run. There, a meditation pavilion. Up higher: wind turbines. Dave pointed out six tree house units that only he could see. *It'll be on a ninety-nine-year sublease, with some of the KuukuYa'u as employees,* he said. *That's what the guests'll want, anyway. After ninety-nine years, they should be ready to take over.*

The wind blew in regular glugs, as if somewhere someone had unbunged the day. *I just need five hundred thousand dollars to deal myself back into the game. Shit, I used to pump that in a fucking day, mate.*

The customer sat there nodding and emoting, and puppe-teering the fishing line so that it kept clear of mangrove roots. But really, he was considering how, the week before he left for Resto, he went five consecutive days without talking to another human being. Times like that, he could get to feeling like he was one of those mystery boxes at the science museum. The ones you stick your blind hand into and wonder, nervously, What's in here—a luxurious pelt? A motherloving *scorpion*? Except even he wasn't sure what was in his box; he couldn't or wouldn't feel around. Much of what he knew about himself, he knew from watching others reach in, which happened rarely. When it did, when he let them, he saw their faces go from excited, to curious, to distressed, to straight-up repulsed. Wasn't a turtle shell in there, apparently.

A few drops of rain began to pop against the tin hull. The customer wondered if he would ever find a companion as com-panionable as detachment.

What we need first, though, is girls, Dave continued, punting the dinghy out of the creek and into deep water. *Some nice sheilas would be good. Some nice female partners who aren't bitches. Though I figure that's hard to find.* He tugged the engine's pull cord.

Dave had been thinking a lot about Oriental birds. They'd probably do right-o on the island. *I'm so far out of the loop, mate,* he shouted. *I need to go to love school!* He'd tried online dating. Five years ago, a female WWOOFer set up a profile for him. There was a tremendous response—but from depressives and alcoholics. He tried all those damn websites.

Something hit the line, hard, yanking the customer's right arm behind him. Then it went slack again.

I got this TV bird coming, Dave said. *She's rather prominent, I reckon. Knows a lot about the wellness industry. And she just split up from her hubby! She has kids, which I'm not certain how that will work out.*

He circled the reefs that had grown around the scuttled

trawlers. *No*, he said, *there's nothing wrong with a bird coming and trying before she buys. Have a nice seafood dinner. Who would you invite to dinner if you could? I would take the Dalai Lama and Obama, for the peace, love, and understanding, and then I'd have Osama, for the opposite. Not including the bird, obviously.*

They fished for another hour, unaware that they were towing empty monofilament. The wire leader and the whole lure had been bit off a ways back.

DAY 7

FIRST WEEK ON THE ISLAND

All desert-island stories are in some sense about waiting. Waiting for rescue; waiting for madness; waiting day in, day out for time to be transcended. By this point in his stay, the customer was waiting for Dave to shut the fuck up.

Dave's babbling was impersonal and often senseless. It was always going and just loud enough to hear, like an Orwellian radio, or self-consciousness. Tense-wise, it was never simply present but always progressive. The customer's eyes were going a little cross from so much sustained contact. And all that polite smiling and contorted pseudo-concern—his *face* was exhausted. Sometimes he brought an empty coffee cup to his lips and pretended to tip back the dregs, just to give himself a moment's relief.

While oystering, while gathering palm fronds, stacking coconuts, spinning fishing lines—while siphoning gas—Dave kept on keeping on. He'd lecture about Australia's 10 percent goods-and-services tax. The relative value of Canadian economic geologists. Laser nuclear power. Corn subsidies. The prices of: Kenyan cattle, land in California's Central Valley, the water necessary to grow rice. He speculated on the fortunes to be made in table compressors, stone cutting, olive oil, ski lodges based out of ancient castles (of which there were many for sale, don't worry), opal.

At first, his customer had tried to redirect the monologic torrent. But Dave was inexorable; he just steady beat on like the sun. His ceaseless reasoning debilitated. It melted whatever steering queries or transitional declaratives the customer had in mind. Over time, he became stupefied, able to answer only *Yeah* or *Right*, the conversational equivalent of rubbing away eye floaters.

One afternoon, he thought to get away by taking a rusty pitching wedge and sneaking off to a patch of fallen plums at the edge of the clearing. Violet pulp splacked his face and bare chest each time he teed off; the rain washed him clean. After a dozen strokes, he looked up, and there was Dave, his logorrheic caddy, yippy-yapping about: trickle-down economics and the importance of job creators (*There being nothing wrong with making money!*). Carlos Slim and the state of the Australian telecom industry (*A bloody fucking monopoly!*). How one gets only two or three opportunities in one's life to make serious money (*The idea being a hop-on, hop-off bus, like Ken Kesey's, but for backpackers in America*).

The customer waited less and less hopefully for a connection to develop between himself and the man. He was beginning to feel stronger swirls of dread—a bad case of déjà vu—as though in meeting Dave he had skipped forward along one possible branch of his own *Choose Your Own Adventure* and needed to work out how he got there. So, he went on the offensive. He asked Dave about the first time he confronted the deep water of real, prolonged silence. He wondered whether what happened inside Dave's headspace was anything like the unpacking of luggage. He wanted to know: In renouncing the world, did Dave discover a pure and gentle sympathy with all other men? Did the island lead him to understand that true solitude is not mere separateness, but rather a discipline that tends only toward uni—

Right, no. You don't come here to reconnect with no hoo-doo. I want to point you in the direction of fixing yourself. Get you to look inside, get down to the nitty-gritty. With both hands, Dave pantomimed an hourglass figure around his customer. *You know, I could never understand song lyrics until I came out here? I like myself way more now than I ever did.*

DAY 8
THE VILLAGE

Dave had wanted to come ashore because a package was waiting for him at the inn. Getting to it took several hours, as first he and his customer had to borrow a truck from a bush family, and then they had to fix the tire that blew out on the rutted way there. When Dave had finally retrieved the padded mailer, he pulled it open slowly, with his fingertips. Inside were discs containing an hourlong television special the BBC had filmed about him some months back. Dave was going into Lockhart River to give copies to everyone he knew.

About eight hundred KuukuYa'u lived there, though that number fluctuated seasonally. They made up one of the most isolated and economically disadvantaged communities in Australia. Lockhart River is a twelve-hour dirt-road drive from Cairns, the nearest city, and a four-hour drive from Weipa, the nearest town. The unemployment rate there hovered around 20 percent, three times the national average. The community was almost entirely dependent upon government aid. They had gone so far as to ban alcohol six years earlier, an emergency measure, because their life expectancy had fallen to an age two decades younger than that of white Australia.

It took a decade for them to trust me, to stop calling me "white cunt," Dave said, pulling the loaner truck onto the gray beach outside of town. The sky there was like a lint trap, the sea rough and opaque. *Now I see myself as an agent of the KuukuYa'u.*

He and his customer tore into prepackaged meat pies purchased from Lockhart's exorbitant general store. The pies and occasionally some fresh veg were all that Dave allowed himself there; his real supplies—canned goods, flour, cooking oil, natural gas—he bought in Cairns during his annual trip. He had to have that tucker shipped to the island via barge, a great drain on the ten-thousand-dollar pension he made do on.

We've got to get these government blokes out of here, Dave said, his mustache baubled with gravy. *There's ten saviors for every one they're trying to save. Lockhart River'll save themselves when they're ready.*

Erika had put in five years working for the government in Lockhart, and what had that got her? Government was always tossing this money about, building new facilities. But the people? Erika had been a literacy aide, and a *volunteer* culinary instructor, and still they made her live in a back room at the employment bureau. She didn't even have her own fucking bathroom! A sheila without a bathroom. What a bloody waste of potential. Dave wouldn't have treated his employees that way thirty damn years ago.

All these yobbos, but did you know government don't have a full-time drug and alcohol counselor here in Lockhart? Dave asked. He was going to use the money from Erika's estate to fund one.

He put the loaner into gear and showed off Lockhart's sole restaurant and then its arts center, where two English bird-watchers recognized him from the BBC program. The town proper reminded the customer of the depressed agricultural villages ringing Lake Okeechobee, only much direr: there were brightly colored shotgun homes, hit-or-miss lawn care, a lot of stripped-down cars, and too many feral dogs fighting in the street over bones that were three feet long.

They left the truck and walked into an open-air pavilion behind the church, where a well-attended shire council meeting was just concluding. Adults milled; kids and dogs schooled like fish. Dave had working knowledge of everyone present and a rapport with most. A few locals answered his personal questions cheerlessly; a few others tolerated him like pupils do a hammy administrator. Still more begged for home brew. But many were plain happy to see him, calling him "old fella," a sign of respect. They were so accustomed to white men coming and going, implementing things and then flying away, that Dave's continued presence proved him to be true blue, *dinky di*.

Dave grabbed a couple of complimentary plates of sausages and buttered bread and took a seat at the long councilmen's table next to his good friend Paul Piva, a genial South Sea Islander fit to bursting with muscle.

How we met was Paul'd come to the island to sneak a beer and have some fishing, Dave said. They hit it off immediately, owing to Paul's latent entrepreneurial instincts. He followed Dave's advice, and now he ran a small business renting salvaged cars to the myriad government employees who flew into Lockhart every week.

I tried to get him to run for mayor once, Dave said. *Now I'm trying to teach him whitefella law. I don't want any whitefella thinking he can come in here and take advantage of Paul just because he's a blackfella.*

Years ago, Dave had made sure Paul was there on the island the one time its leaseholders tried and failed to evict him in person. *The fucking wankers*, Paul said of them, flashing a wide smile of kerneled teeth. *The fucking ding-a-lings.* Damn right Paul would dong anyone who tried to get rid of his friend. But he didn't think he'd need to; he was convinced Dave would be coming up with the money to buy back his share. *The climate's no bloody good*, Paul said, *so alls Dave has to do is hand them five hundred thousand dollars, and they'll fucking jump.*

That fucking island, Paul continued, rolling up the hem of his polo shirt to rub the oak dome of his stomach. *Fuck, it's a gold mine for us! The jobs! If I thought Dave's plan was bullshit, mate, I'd tell you straight up.*

After the meeting, having distributed copies of the BBC documentary around Lockhart, Dave and his customer snuck into a KuukuYa'u ceremony put on for white benefactors and executive out-of-towners. Along the dreary beachfront, children danced in grass skirts while singing a sad hymn about the Devil disguising himself as a crocodile and stealing a baby in the night.

With his tongue, Dave joggled the edge of his loose left canine while eyeing the business types. No doubt it was terrible how the KuukuYa'u got addicted to things, he explained. Grog, government money. Smoke-o, even. They had been a nomadic people, you see, not accustomed to surplus. More than your regular yob, the KuukuYa'u were going to eat or drink or take whatever was on hand until it—or they—were gone.

But if there was one thing that had carried over from Dave's days on the mainland, it was finding a niche and filling it first. Business abhors a vacuum, after all. He leaned in to his customer, whispering, *Don't you reckon these blokes would love to have a shout and a session? But they can't here in Lockhart. That ain't civilization. It just ain't. No, I plan on rebuilding the canteen. Have it be a club-type atmosphere, but strict. Anybody who comes in to crack the shits will be tossed. Paul's against it. But she'll be right, mate.*

NIGHT IN THE SHELL
A DREAM REALIZED

Robinson Crusoe is no longer required reading, but that's only because it doesn't need to be. The desert-island story has so permeated our culture that it has become its own meta-genre: the Robinsonade. There's *Cast Away* and *Survivor* and *Lost*, obviously, but also *Life of Pi*, *The Hunger Games*, and any one of the seven hundred movies that came out this summer that had to do with what comes after Armageddon. If it touches on isolation, tabulae rasae, or close encounters of a new kind, or if it has a character commenting on society from without—it's a Robinsonade. The island need only be metaphorical. It's all about the lone protagonist ad-libbing his life.

So, no, we don't make kids read *Robinson Crusoe*. Instead we've got them reading the domestic version, *Walden*.

Unlike Crusoe, Henry David Thoreau did the American thing and *chose* to live apart from the world. He erranded into the wilderness voluntarily, hoping there to find a purer, more deliberate way of being.

He was a huge admirer of Crusoe. There are allusions to the man everywhere in his writing—from the notched stick Thoreau measures time by, to the umbrella he sometimes carries, to his long, addled digression in *Walden* on hats made out of skin. In his letters, Thoreau compared himself with Crusoe a lot, and unfavorably. Crusoe had "the callous palms of the laborer," which were "conversant with the finer tissues of self-respect and heroism, whose touch thrills the heart." Crusoe could philosophize *and* carpenter a coffin for the dudes he shot. Thoreau wanted to be a hero in that mold.

Thus did he borrow an ax, go into his pal Emerson's backyard, and clear a space for the repurposed cabin he bought from an Irish laborer. He detailed in a journal how he dug his cellar, maintained his hearth, and struggled with weeds and poor soil in his garden. Just like his man Robinson, Thoreau kept track of himself via credentialing lists, commonsense routines, and economic pursuits. He walked in the woods and went for some swims. He labored after a conspicuous authenticity.

But he certainly was no recluse. The road from Concord to Lincoln was a field away from him. He could hear the Fitchburg Railroad when it steamed on by. Almost every day, he went into town. On weekends, the children of Concord picnicked around his pond. Sundays, his mom dropped off goodie baskets.

And after two years in the woods, Thoreau wrote a really strange book about it. *Walden* is many things: diary, sermon, nature travelogue, proto-boho fantasy about dropping out. But what ties it all together is the man himself. Thoreau is the book's true subject. If *Robinson Crusoe* is the manual of rugged individualism, *Walden* then is the apotheosis of the wannabe rugged individual.

"The mass of men lead lives of quiet desperation," Thoreau wrote at his book's beginning. He would know—he was having a midlife crisis 125 years before the Baby Boomers made it a thing. Via *Walden*, he became the early popularizer of that most American of notions, the one which proclaims that, to be happy, we need to be someplace other than where we are. A place more substantial, where we'll finally be free to turn into ourselves, use our innate powers to create. Create not a new Eden, mind you, but a new and better Adam.

"Let him step to the music which he hears," Thoreau wrote, "however measured or far away." This isn't an advocacy for solitude. More like the warm dream of a private religion.

DAY 10

A CAVE RETREAT;

FINDS PRINT OF MAN'S FOOT ON THE SAND

The customer left the red cave of his closed eyes, reluctantly. It was morning, and he had yet to sleep well. Each night, the wind played the island like a bad one-man band. Every few hours Quassi went tear-assing into the darkness, barking like mad.

He could not wait to wake up in a place that was not this place. Which was exactly how he wound up here.

Dave was seated at his desk, Miranda splayed in front of it. He was calling friends and business partners, former and potential, talking up the BBC program, among other things. His customer sat apart and watched Dave work. He saw that, whether in person or on the phone, Dave's aspect never changed. His eyes locked on, but to some middle distance, neither here nor there. He seemed to be projecting something, like a camera obscura.

Mate, I'm telling you, he said into the receiver, *you can't rob from the rich to pay for the poor. All that does is make more poor! . . . Well, the potential is in the untapped market of Chinese WWOOFers. . . . No, America loves to help people. But they're not helping themselves.*

Each call restarted his spiel, Dave like a human infomercial on the hour. When he got good and humming, he had the cadence and sly humor of a carnival barker–cum–revivalist. *Our utter financial collapse is like the pregnant schoolgirl*, he said. *Eventually that baby's gonna come!* After a few hours of such inveigling, he grabbed his iPad and joined his customer at the driftwood table.

What's my current password? Dave asked, poking at a commodities report he'd ordered online. *You know, precious-metal market psychology has been absolutely smashed by the banks. . . .*

The customer heard a crunching noise. He looked to Quassi, who was lying at his feet. Quassi was eyeing Locky, who was sprawled a ways off. Between his paws writhed a blue and yellow songbird. He nosed it once, twice, and then bit off its broken right wing. The good left one flapped erratically, to the rhythm of the bird's heartbeat.

. . . The smart corporates recognize the value of that, Dave was saying. Something about optimism and Google. I don't know. I was through the looking glass here.

This time, when I came to, I made some snide comments about data mining and the NSA. I made up even more egregious privacy breaches for Google to perpetrate, just to shake Dave's faith in corporate futurism. I was done with biding my time, with hoping—like some son at the home with his demented father—for a flicker of cognizance.

But, anyway, do you think they'd like to come here? The Google blokes? he asked, exaggeratedly flipping between financial forecasts on his iPad. *Do you think they'd come to an island to get restored?* Onto the table in front of my folded hands dropped two mosquitoes, flushed and coupling. *Well, of course, they would have to do the restoring themselves,* Dave added.

Here's one way I often find myself passing the time in my apartment: I turn on the Home Shopping Network, I lie supine on the carpet, and I listen as people try to sell me on stuff. It's like my everyday, only a screen removed. I close my eyes and let the song and dance wash over me. I feel tickled; feel this wriggling, duodenal bliss that's kin to having unscratched bug bites all over. The pleasure is anticipatory. I know that, when I'm good and ready, I can do here what I cannot outside—I can shut it all off.

That and a drink in the tub are my consolations. But they're also symptomatic of a larger issue: after four hours anywhere, with anyone, I get mortified. I become obsessed with a perpetual elsewhere. If I can't duck out—I dissociate. Not like a guy with a mental disorder. I know I'm in here. But the persona doing the shit-eating is just that, a front. A decoy. The real me is watching from without. Gauging. The me who thinks and feels and *is* remains elsewhere.

Of course, to my mind, this decoy's doing a bang-up job of advertising how I wish I felt. Mr. Golem B. Kool, all revivifying smiles and conspiratorial winks. But the reality of it, I'm sure, is different. To others, I must appear as frightened, condemnatory, and doomed as a plague nurse in one of those birdy masks.

. . . *A classic give-and-take*, Dave was saying, rain plunking into overflowing jugs. *I'm in a situation where I need the media to help me. It's a fair trade: I give you a story, you give me publicity. At this point, I wouldn't even mind a reality TV show if they brought some nice girls with them.*

I will admit I hadn't counted on Dave being such a dratted social butterfly. Alone on an island was where I figured a man would have found peace. Meaning, he'd be happy, but he'd never have a good time. That, or he'd be a crazy person anxious to brain me with a conch in the night. But Dave's guestbook offered proof to the contrary in both cases. It was fat with the signatures of hundreds of visitors. And not just the WWOOFers or the KuukuYa'u, but French luxury yachters, recreational divers, sport fishermen—Russell goddamn Crowe stopped by on his honeymoon, apparently. Almost every one of their entries reads the same, something like: "Utopia at last!" "A piece of heaven." "NO REASON FOR THE STRESS!!" "It was the perfect remedy to life!"

Was it, though? You might not be able to be a castaway in the original sense anymore, but neither can you half-ass the experience. You don't just buy a round-trip ticket to peace of mind and post pictures to Facebook later, another consumptive merit badge. If only.

I returned my attention to Dave. He was saying: *I feel safe here on the island if it all goes down. Which I think it will. It's that I'm off the drug of money. Some blokes think gold's the answer, but gold . . . it's as safe as houses. Whereas silver, old sixpences and shit— it's a byproduct. Useful in electronics. Sometimes, you know, there's more value in the byproduct than the product. The sheilas understand it, silver.* I nodded as absently as the palms in the gale. *Who runs the family budget? The sheilas. And they hide silver around the house, don't they? I knew this one old bird who filled half a dozen forty-four-gallon drums with the stuff and buried them in the yard. I admire her immensely, I do.*

Ain't a damned thing therapeutic about this place. Womb-like it was not—far more purgatorial than that. And Dave, bless him, the more he droned on and on about the enlightened man's need for a spot to sit still and wand a metal detector over his soul, the more certain I became that no matter where I go to find myself—be it a South Pacific hovel isle; a teak-floored villa with curtains a-billow; or the stained carpet in my uptown cesshole—I'll keep unearthing this gem: I am shipwrecked with a self I both fear for and loathe.

So. How did those guys escape Alcatraz, again?

Is it that I say nuts to the faux-biblical jargon of authenticity, with its consumerist undertow and accessorized cant of separation and lost harmony? Instead I should just try to wrap my head around the infinite extent of my relations and thank God I am like other men? Then I could allow myself to be swallowed by this seemingly commonplace epiphany, so much so that I become borderless, like a fish swimming at night?

Seriously. I'm asking. Which, Jesus, do you know how hard that is?

Is it that I'm not allowed off this rock until *something* has died?

Nobody's gonna restore themselves, I told Dave. *But I doubt they had it in them in the first place.*

NIGHT

SLAVERY & ESCAPE

During the darkest hour before sunrise, the customer turned on his flashlight and left his bed, having yet to explore the island at night. Quassi took up after him with the weary compassion of all bedside attendants. The wind sounded like fire, like *whoosh*, flames chasing oxygen.

Mosquitoes were landing on his bare arms and legs, but the customer waited a couple of beats before waving them off. He considered how the life span of a bug bite is exactly like that of a star: first they're big, warm, and nebulous; then they collapse into hot little pinpricks. He swept his path to the beach with the beam of his flashlight.

When he reached the top of a dune leading down to the water, he heard Quassi's growl go gnarly. The dog shot past him, running for the surf. The customer scribbled his mote of light over fizzy spume, trying frantically to locate what had spooked them both.

Two eyes shined greenly. Then they extinguished themselves. Next there came a snort, and some thing sliding sliding sliding into the breakers. At this point, I think, I began to appreciate that whatever it is I would like to find, it lies beyond or under all my attempts to find it. I said, *Holy shit.*

Forty-five minutes before our blowup, Dad was paring every last marbled ounce of fat from a roast. Now, I've taped him the cooking shows. I've tried to get Paula Deen to learn him. "The fat's what gives it flavor!" I've implored, gaveling an empty saucepan on the kitchen island. Never have I myself offered to cook, of course. Which is why he's kept on with his excision, cutting away what he thinks we might choke on.

The meat prepped, he began to dice carrots, cucumbers, and avocados, painstakingly tessellating them atop a bed of romaine. This has been his afternoon rite ever since his experiments in small-cap stock trading flamed out rather spectacularly in the late '90s. He used to record and then pore over the day's CNBC broadcasts with Talmudic scrutiny. At one point, our house held more tapes of Maria Bartiromo than any one of us babes. He'd often ask my take on, say, Electronic Arts video games, squintily parsing my response just the same as when listening to what I thought of *these* numbers, which were sometimes jotted down, sometimes not, en route to the Circle K.

Then, regrettably, he one day dumped a truckload of money into that outfit that sold those healthful potato crisps, the ones that caused "anal leakage," doubling down after that on the deadly weight-loss supplement fen-phen. I think they're almost done paying out that class-action.

"A salad, you understand, is by definition tossed," I said. "Heterogeneous. You're doing your own make-work."

Mom surfaced from the back room, done for the day with her freelance real-estate work. "Let's make hamburger helper!" she said, meaning not the boxed kind, with its sinister glove-homunculus. *Her* version, which is just mac and cheese, taco meat, and tomato sauce mixed up in a bowl. Those early years spent in a breeze-blocked central Florida trailer—they granted her many a culinary knack.

"We don't have ground beef," Dad said.

"I'll go get some," Mom said.

"Oh *shit*, Janice, don't go to Woodlands. They charge an arm and a fucking leg! Six bucks per!"

"I don't care."

"*I* care! You want to help? Help me make a roast beef hash. He didn't come all the way out here to eat hamburger helper."

From the other side of the wall, I said: "*I* want hamburger helper." No I didn't. Not really.

Mom left to go get the fixings. Dad remained in the kitchen. Snorting, slamming things, hocking loogies into the sink.

The man's made a good 90 percent of all the home-cooked meals I've ever had, but has himself eaten none of them. He's never tasted what he's prepared. (He might take a bite or two of the main protein, so that he can declaim it *the worst goddamn thing I've ever cooked*.)

Instead, he feeds himself this way: He opens the fridge and sticks both arms deep into its bottom shelf. He hugs rank condiments and bearded leftovers to his chest, rakes them in like a botulistic jackpot. With these he concocts a true ghoulash, hot brown wallow, which he eats over the sink. He neither sits nor protests. He devours this slop with the ritual gusto of a sin eater.

Suddenly, Dad was emergent, his little fists like claw-feet at the end of his forearms. Now he was pointing: "Fuck you. You want to go to Ohio? I'm not going anywhere with you."

Dad stomping around. The upstairs neighbors stomping back. Dad eyeing my hands on the keyboard.

"If I read one fucking word about this, this or anything I've said in the past eight days—that's it. Don't bother coming back home. You really will shut me up."

"Don't flatter yourself. Who the fuck would want to read about this?"

"Who wants to read about your dumb ass trying to get killed on an island?" His voice was getting progressively louder, as though straining to be heard over steam picking up belowdecks. "Or trying to get bit by a goddamn mamba? Or beat to death by grease-painted human garbage?"

"That's *my* prerogative."

"That's some *Jackass* shit, is what it is."

"*I* get to choose how to make a life. I choose this."

"How is what you're doing mature?"

"How're *you* mature? The time has long since come and fucking gone, okay, when you should've been like, 'Shit, my seed's grown. He is no longer one of the eggs in my basket. He has in fact hatched into a bird? A bird that will occasionally return to the basket, but to curl up, feign egginess, all for the sake of the basketholder?'"

"Just wait till you have your own."

"Be free, man. War's over."

"This shit ends only when I'm plotted in the ground."

There was a campaigner's red in his face when he marched out the door.

8.

LET'S GET THIS TUB
OF SHIT UP TO SPEED

9/29/13

He did not tell me where he went or what he did for all those hours. But he *did* come back with an offer: no Ohio, but a one-day road trip. He agreed to my agreement only after I promised I wouldn't write about it.

The chariot awaiting us was a 1997 Ford Taurus, dull silver. Low-slung she is, and wide, with the oblong headlights and slack little grill-slot mouth that all domestic buckets came outfitted with at the millennium. She looks sluggish, like the sort of thing that would live in the mud in a tropical river and make for your anus the second you dove in. Except plastic, of course, and a car.

Do you know her? You do. She is what you will see if you mishear your GPS and turn off the interstate midtrip, having then to drive through an eerie methtown shambles before finding a spot to U-ey. There, on a blasted side street, acreep at idling speed and driverless, somehow, is a 1997 Ford Taurus, dull silver.

"I did the research, and I told your mother not to buy this rusted-out shitbox," Dad called through the open front door. "*Especially* not used. Thing's got the worst gas mileage I've ever seen."

He spritzed off-brand cleaning fluid onto the windshield, ragged it in with the heel of his hand. Next, he tested the tensile strength of the zip ties tied to what used to be door handles. He never trusted the Taurus's one amenity, automatic locks, so, after many years of strenuous handle checking in parking lots, all but one have come off in his hands. "No good deed goes unpunished, I guess," he said.

We saddled up. Farther along the wooded hill's incline, a fawn watched us from a stand of cedars. Its face and snout were crusted with red spider mites. After three tries, Dad got the engine to turn over. "I can't take you anywhere because of *her*, you know," he said. When we pulled away, I could see that the mites were teeming, a living death mask. "I don't want to hear her bitch for months or years because we went to Ohio without her."

"Totally why," I sneered, checking the center console. The mouthwash was in there, as always.

"I really wanted to do it, but I also didn't want to get my ass chewed out."

In high school, when the Taurus was passed on to me my senior year, the center console came stocked with holy water from Mom and a small, unopened bottle of Listerine from Dad. For emergencies, both.

"I just don't want anybody bitching at me anymore," he said. "Like the trip to the fucking ballpark the other night. She didn't want to go, but if we'd left her out of it—hell to pay."

We crossed the Golden Gate Bridge going southbound. Dad hunched in his seat and Indian-burned the wheel while weaving between lanes, straddling them occasionally. He projects his anger and fear into the minds of those who make him angry and fearful. Below us, the dark shapes of container ships glided across the water like cloud shadow.

"That's what people fear most, you know," he said. "The total loss of control."

He took his eyes off of the road to mad-dog me. He glanced down at my hands, which were instinctively tapping at my phone. "People fear that more than death," he said. "Being trapped, in a kind of a prison, like. Nowhere to run, and people are poking at you, judging you." The most unpardonable offense in his world is to lay oneself dumbly on the outcome of forces. To trust in anything but yourself. "I swear to . . . If you so much as fucking—" he started and then stopped.

His antipathy smoldered. It seemed almost to give off an acrid vapor that I wished to lean into and inhale.

"I'm e-mailing Yeshiva," I lied.

"Stories like yours and worse than yours are all around," he said. "If you think you've suffered anything—you ain't."

We rode on, missile-crisis tense. When we were speeding past the headstone-knurled fields of Golden Gate National Cemetery, Dad offered, "Chester Nimitz is in there. Just one of the outlying graves. There should be a shrine to him, for Christ's sake. Guy won us the war in the Pacific."

I nodded. He continued: "Lauren should've joined the navy. I'm still pissed about not pressing her on that front. She would've been well on her way to a fourth star by now. A real ass-kicker."

"Not so conflicted about my not joining the navy?"

"You have . . . a poet's soul."

"Saying I'm gay?"

"A little."

We've allowed ourselves to come to blows only once, in line for the *Jaws* ride at Universal Studios. I was tired then, and a little sun-mad, and had had enough of his chirping—so I suckered him. And though I have grown to where I can look down upon the crown of his skull, he had the height, weight, and reach advantages that day. He dropped me with a single jab to the solar plexus. He felt bad, I think, because the moment after I received my college diploma, we drove from Gainesville to that same theme park and had a blast.

Meanwhile, Lauren—she can and does talk shit for days, and all the guy'll do is pillow his hands and bat his lashes. She is loved most because, as a child, she was so pale and blond and demure that his eyes could barely hold her. But she never was childish, Lord no; she moved through the world like a Victorian death portrait brought back to life. Dad pretends to fear her, but what it is he's scared of is his own oceanic devotion. He calls her "the Clone," after Mom.

"Big Sur Point!" he was saying sometime later. "Point Sur Naval Facility used to be right over there." With his crippled right pinkie he pointed out every object of interest as we switch-backed along coastal SR 1. "And McWay Falls is back in there a little.

"Kent? Not looking? Don't give a shit?" he asked, waggling his pinkie in front of my face.

"Thataway's the Esalen Institute," he went on. "They do a bunch of New Agey stuff. Peer into crystals, wax their scrotes. I don't know."

"It's funny that you moved out to this part of the country," I said. "Since, you know, historically, everything you detest has come from this coast."

A thin railing was all that separated us from a long drop into combed sea. On the driver's side, it was sheer cliffs, redwood groves, headlands pinned with blue flowers. Country that only an asteroid could plow.

"I bet those hippies would pay buku bucks to visit my old survival school, spend a week in triple-canopy jungle with the Negritos. I got your ecotourism right here," he said, joggling his crotch.

"No, but I've always been fascinated with the hippies," he continued. "They were arriving in full force just as I was getting ready to ship out of San Francisco. *What might have been*, you know?"

"A great many bouquets of flowers shoved up asses, is my guess."

"A solid prognostication."

Dad wanted me to see William Randolph Hearst's castle. Something about the faded glory of print, I guess. In theory, the newspaper magnate's estate was modeled after a Spanish Renaissance village. In actuality, it's a bastioned pastiche of architectures on top of a tall, narrow hill in San Simeon.

The crowd was retirees. The last generation of Americans who'll go in for this kind of thing. Women with hard, dry updos, like carefully arranged beach wrack. Husbands in hats that aphorized: *I'm not aging—I'm fermenting!*

"If there is a God," Dad said as our tour bus careened up the steep hillside, "He will not let you die amongst these people."

The estate was constructed piece by piece, seemingly on a whim. Hearst mail-ordered lots of mustily priceless bric-a-brac from Europe—portraiture, statuary, tapestries. An entire ceiling from an Italian church. None of it cohered, but as an example of that American dream of creating pedigree ex nihilo—it was neat. Fifty-eight bedrooms, and Hearst was still adding to it when he died.

"You will not, in all likelihood, be living out your days in a house like this," Dad said. We were trailing behind the crowd, cracking wise in the slipstream of their normalcy.

Hearst's estate was the place to be in the '20s, '30s. Hollywood and political elites flew into the private airfield to spend long weekends engaging in whichever depravities were clever then. Charlie Chaplin, the Marx Brothers, FDR, Winston Churchill. Cary Grant came like fifty times.

"I think Cary was sweet on ol' Willie here," I said.

"You mean to tell me he preferred the company of men?" Dad teased. "Who *doesn't*?!"

A couple of honeymooning Euros began to take selfies with iPads, holding the tablets at arms' length with two hands. "There should be a number from one to ten on back of them," Dad suggested, unquietly. "A scorecard, for how big a dildo you are."

Normally, we parley via jokey semaphore and signal lamp, communicating as candidly as warships across a gulf. But now seemed a time for directness.

"How come, do you think, we have in our hearts such contempt for others?" I asked, falling in line behind him as we climbed a back staircase.

"I'm a bit of an expert on anger, as you know," he said over his shoulder. "Suffered from it all through my youth."

". . . youth?"

"It's a pretty miserable state to be in, but it's also really gratifying. Rage is gratifying. And it's a good substitute. Indulging in your desire, okay, to fuck up everything new or beautiful? It's a hell of a lot more fun than trying to make shit more tolerable for yourself."

Atop the landing, Dad rewound his loose limb of hair. He turned to me. "We all know when to deploy our quills. All of us but your mother. Meeting her, thirty minutes in, I knew I'd found the perfect one. I just had to plan out how not to blow it. There's no woman like your mother. But don't tell her I said that. I don't want her to get a big head."

"Remember my temper tantrums?" I asked, wresting the conversation back on course.

"Christ, you were a terror. Punched out teeth. Pulled out hair."

"Slammed heads into the blacktop by their stupid jug ears. I know. Remember how you used to march me to my room and lock me in there? Till I was ready to act civilized?"

"Bucking. Snarling."

"Crying and screaming till I lost my voice. I know. And when's the last time I had one? Eighteen years ago?"

We were led back outside. The sky here was cloudless, illimitably blue, like it had no atmosphere. I looked up at it and thought, If I tried to jump, I'd keep rising.

"You know how I spend most of my waking moments now?" I asked. "Daydreaming about killing myself. Well, blowing myself up. Metaphorically. I'm sitting there at dinner with a woman—a nice dinner, bread in a basket—and I'm trying very hard to listen, and to respond to her comments about what she looks for in an endocrinologist—but really what my mind's coming back to, again and again, unless I've doused it with booze, is the moment when, at last, I can detonate my stockpiled separateness."

"Terrorist."

"*Dad.* I don't want to *be* like this anymore."

"Well, you *should.* Feel that way. People are stupid assholes. People are stupid assholes precisely because they believe they are anything *but* stupid assholes. I used to think it was just me— that *I* was the bad guy. And I was. When I was a young man, I was a bad guy who had convinced himself he was good. The United States Navy needed my ass real bad.

"So, okay, fine. We're stupid assholes. Bad guys. But, look. You shouldn't blame yourself. Your natural inclination is to condemn yourself first. I know you. And what's your second? To condemn everyone else, too. Without exception. To thin that self-hate out a little. Water it down."

"I feel like I've got a ton of empathy in reserve, though," I countered. "Stores of it. A motherfucking *cache.* In fact, I would argue that I am the most empathetic man a woman I have yet to meet has ever met."

Dad snorted several times in quick succession, bullishly. It sounded as though he was trying to hold in laughter, which would not have surprised me. The man laughs easily, but never really *at* a joke. He laughs when something strikes a personal chord, when it rhymes with his salad days. He did a quick spot check, and then he gobbed an oyster against a tree trunk.

"Shit, son. I'm not gonna be around forever, okay. And you're gonna have to learn how to watch out for yourself. If you don't watch out, you'll let the wrong ones in, and they'll siphon everything they want out of you. Take and take and take, until you're left high and dry.

"You can't let anyone buffalo you. *They* want what *you* got. And as soon as they got it, they have no more use for you. Believe me."

We wandered back inside. "Right. Okay," I appeased. We walked through dry swimming pools. We walked through nefarious-seeming sculleries. "But what I'm saying is: It's not that I'm afraid of letting the wrong one in when I lower that drawbridge. It's worse than that. I can't even bring myself to send out the negotiating party. I don't want to sue for peace."

"What do you want me to tell you?" he said, stopping. "That it's easy? It's not. It's *hard*. Every day, it's hard." He was not looking at me. He was standing close, uncomfortably close, and pointing his ear at my chest as though calling through a door. "Every day, even still, I want to say, *Fuck it!* and hail ruination like a cab after last call."

I made the mistake of mentioning that in Australia I had some fish and chips and enjoyed them, so, back on the road, we stopped for fish and chips.

Dad grabbed several of his own cutlets and dropped them into my basket. "Stop that," I said. "Don't do that. Snack on your own tray, bro."

"Eat it. Eat what you can. It makes me happy when you eat."

Moments like this one call to mind his "reluctant" adoption of Zuzu. Zuzu was a tuxedo cat, possibly retarded, who sat outside our front door for an entire week, pink tongue jutting from the side of his mouth, after he had been kicked out of the canopy by his mother. One day, Dad finally went, "C'mon, cat, beat it," while laying down a bowl of microwaved half-and-half. Then he went, "Get the hell outta here, cat!" as he made a bed of rags for Zuzu in the dining room. Went, "I despise this stupid, stupid beast," as Zuzu purred on his chest in the recliner, Dad responsible now for the thing he'd tamed.

He ate crumbs of fried errata from the bottom of my basket by licking his fingers, pressing said fingers into the wax paper, and then sucking the bits into his mouth with sharp intakes of breath. Each one sounded like an airlock hissing shut. He wiped at the greasy nimbus around his lips, said: "Text your mother and tell her we're going down to Pismo, and that we'll probably have to stop in a motel for the night. Tell her we'll be back later tomorrow. But make it sound like we're not having a good time."

We drove farther inland. The dry hill-and-vale landscape resembled the face of a cheap basketball left too long in the sun. Farming towns here and there.

"The future, you understand, is going to be roving gangs, raping and pillaging this countryside," Dad opined. "Hell, one of those Asian gangs could take over an entire town right now."

"*Mad Max*, you're describing."

"*Mad Ming*. Everybody's gonna have to be on the same page. One out of every three people is gonna have to be police, or a friend of police."

"You know, actively clinging to an outmoded view of reality is, like, *the* basis for mental illness."

"Fine. Sure. The Chinese *don't* want your resources. They just want to trade with you!"

"It's like you're still navigating by maps that have Siam on them."

"*Nooo*, don't anybody listen to what this crazy old cracker has to say. His opinions clearly don't matter anymore."

"They *are* becoming less and less significant, statistically speaking."

"True enough. I didn't even *vote* in the last election. Not for ol' numbnuts there. What's-his-name, the guy with all his money in the Cayman Islands." When he changed his line of sight, his saggy earlobes swayed like drops held pendant by surface tension. "We all have private ails, okay? I just don't see why *now* we have to have public cures for them. I would prefer to still be living in an America of a hundred fifty million people."

"You, the Beav, and George Wallace should build a time machine."

"It used to be a hell of a lot better."

"A lot more DUI deaths, for one thing."

"Absolutely. Who else can lay claim to drinking and driving? Russia?"

"No, their historical soul expects too much absurdity. They mount cameras on their dashboards."

"Getting kneewalking drunk, and then venturing into the night, with a deadly weapon in your hands?"

"Now we're talking. Fucking, refusing to surrender your freedom to pick up and go. Relinquishing to *no man* your right to kill your own fool self."

"And whoever gets in your way."

"Back when you could whomp your kid a good one in public. When he deserved it. When he was being a shit in a restaurant, let's say."

"Cruising for a bruising, in the restaurant's *smoking section*."

"Brings a tear to my eye."

"Goddamn things were made of *steel* back then. Get those tubs of shit up to speed, and the tailfins started shaking off."

"Weaving past wooden billboards that're advertising Edsels. Slogans are like, 'Pulp your body in the crumpled flametrap of tomorrow . . . today!'"

"That's how a lot of the kids in my high school died. Used to be that fifty thousand people would get killed over Memorial Day weekend."

"That is almost certainly untrue."

"Hell yes it's true. Look it up on your Google machine. It. Was. *Great.*"

Lost in his reverie, Dad laughed until his eyes squinched shut. I reached for the wheel but was batted away.

"When I'm gone, what I want you to remember is: *They* didn't build this. You did."

"Also false. I've done no civic dirty work."

"Well, your people did."

"And what would you like me to mourn first at the wake? When I'm gazing out the window above the sink, scraping casserole from dishes? What'll it be? Mayonnaise? Set shots? The Rascal-brand motorized scooter?"

Christ alive do I often want to break through the frozen sea of his certainty. See him plunged finally into ambiguity. But in taking an ice ax to his footing, I would cause us both to go for a swim.

Prejudice is an organic truth, false in itself but accumulated and transmitted over generations. What my father intuits but communicates poorly is: we can't just up and rid ourselves of it and expect to wake up the same. The nation that renounces its foundational prejudices all willy-nilly will then renounce itself until it has nothing left to renounce. Anybody who pines for the good old days pines for a time when this was understood implicitly—that the lifespan of a people coincides exactly with the duration and consistency of that people's prejudices.

"They ain't gonna be playing fucking *ice hockey*, I'll tell you that much," he concluded, pulling us into a gas station. He filled her up, but partially, as he carries only so much cash. He got into a funny little back-and-forth with the attendant, who didn't speak the good English.

Watching him stand there in front of the tank, with his feet, hands, and head positioned urinally, I thought: When you can't get the world to see you as you see yourself—shame. That is the definition of shame.

God. The first time you see your old man shamed? The beginning of the end right there. He can no longer beat up everything. He stops seeming flush with the blood of the world. After that moment, he becomes to you this chastened, over-extended empire of a man. Self-mythology be damned, he has obviously wrapped up his era of misadventure. He will recede. The trouble he stirred up will follow him home.

For me, that happened the day he got dumped overboard on a whitewater rafting trip. A trip that, whoa ho, he did not want to take. For one thing, it had been organized not by him, but by Mom's brother. For another, he had to endure mateship under a nature-boy captain named Gage.

We were washboarding down a fairly rugged class-three rapid. Dad ordered a zag where Gage said zig; we struck submerged boulders; Dad was tossed. Then he just trundled alongside the raft, getting buffeted between rocks and hard places.

I lunged after him, grabbed him under the shoulders of his life vest, tried heaving him into the vessel. I was a fourth-grader, too weak to do it, and the raft was yawing dangerously. Anyway, he wasn't cooperating. He'd gone limp. When I got him half out of the water, he looked me in my eyes, shook his head *no*, and slid back into the froth.

It's a matter of perspective, I guess. You need to get far enough away from your father to see in him the shape of a flawed and fallible man. But you never can get all the way there. It's like that math paradox where, to flee the room, you're allowed one big step toward the door, but each one after that has to be half the size of the last. Eventually, you're just a small distance nearer the exit.

We paddled ahead and waited at the bottom of the rapid. I can still see him as he was when he washed out: bloodied, recumbent, his head above water. Somehow, a lit cigarette was in the right corner of his mouth. When he drew on it, it canted at the angle of gun salutes.

"What you must remember," he said upon opening the driver's-side door. "What you absolutely must remember is this: it's always the darkest before it's pitch black."

Beyond the Pismo Beach pier, the megaton yolk of the setting sun had broken and run into the Pacific. Dad sat next to me on a bench.

"When's the last time you had a perfect moment?" he asked.

"Like . . . ?"

"Like when I used to patrol this stretch of coast, fifty miles out in the destroyer. At night, I'd come onto the deck, and I wouldn't be able to tell where the sky stopped and the water began. I was landless. Moments like that, you cherish. I've had fewer and fewer of those."

"You ever read *Moby-Dick*?" I asked, knowing the answer. "'In landlessness alone resides the highest truth'? Or are you on year eighteen of your twenty-year plan to get through that Blackbeard biography on your nightstand?"

"I still miss it," he said, stubbing out another stick of gum on his tongue. "But now I look around myself and wonder, What the hell is it I'm missing?"

The excitement and the rituals, I thought. Blotting out anxiety while skimming over the surface of a void.

"Well," I said. "For me, it's the opposite. For me, it's the time you took me, Ricky, and Ryan to the Monster Jam truck rally at the old Orange Bowl."

"You mean the jet engine!"

"The very one."

"Kee-rist. During 'The Star Spangled Banner.'"

"They wheeled it out, put an old car behind it, then dropped the hammer. Engine spewed hot fire until that whole jalopy was puddled on the ground."

"Rockets' red glare."

"All of us, arm in arm."

"In all my years, I have never heard scooter trash cheer that hard."

Bloody rare light drained from the few clouds' windward halves. Under the pier, seals were up and barking like they'd stubbed something. I was feeling pretty good. Though I'd learned well enough to bask in these moments without affixing to them anything as dumb or onerous as, say, the expectation of continuity.

"You got a take on things," Dad began again. "Like soccer, for instance. You can see the future. I can only see the past. Still, I find it very hard to believe that Americans—American *fathers*—would give up head-busting for that pussy sport."

We watched the waves hang, break, slide.

Dad snapped his gum, sewing a stitch of muscle in his temple.

They're an energy disturbance, waves. Energy but no matter is moving through them. It's crazy to think about. The ocean is just this big puddle of energy roiling back and forth, end to end, forever.

"For instance, you have no idea the national shitting of the pants that went on when they launched Sputnik," he said. "Thing was the goddamn size of a volleyball. A volleyball with some car antennas sticking out of it. Had one of those radios that kept squawking like how you say I squawk. We thought it was the end of the world. We started sharpening sticks to get ready for it."

Just then, a hurtle of mod lovers on fixed-gear bikes sped between our feet and the pier's railing. "Holy shit," Dad said, shooting up, tracking them as they went. "Someone get me a fucking two-by-four."

I took advantage of the opening. "I think I'm going to try to write stuff full-time," I said. "Support myself that way."

"This mean you're going to quit your job at Yeshiva?"

"Think so. Think I'm going to take a real-ass run at this."

"Just gonna sit at home, make like the constipated mathematician, work shit out with a pencil?"

I stood.

"That worries me," he said, starting back down the pier. "I worry about your discipline. Discipline is the power to say no."

When we parked under the terra-cotta awning at a Super 8, he told me, "Stay in the car. I don't wanna give them reason to suspect some *Lolito* shit here."

Whenever I come home, or what counts as home now, Dad's got a new bottle of Maker's Mark waiting for me. He buys them at Costco; they are comically oversize, 1.75 liters each. I'll open the door, sling down my bag—and there one sits, still sealed in red wax, looking like a large mallet resting on its head.

"Got you that Marker's Mark," he'll say, purposefully mispronouncing it. He swears that in his day, they only ever drank Jack Daniel's. "You gotta finish it, because no one here's gonna."

So I do. Before we left the apartment, I poured up the last of the bottle into a travel thermos.

I know it's not the substance that's addictive. The substance is just another tool. Something to pry open the part of me that was vulnerable, once, back before that part of me curled in on itself like a hand holding something squirmy and potential. Pupal.

Alcohol is a tool, and so is writing. Reporting, too. When getting drunk, or blanking out into a recording consciousness, I'm able to lose myself to time. When getting drunk, or turning reportorial grist into a semicoherent narrative (five hundred words a day, at least, if I'm to have that sundowner!)—I know from fear, anxiety.

When doing either of these things, I am—for the time being, at least—*free*. A worm on sunny open ground, giving zero shits about a bird.

When doing neither of these things, I can hear the rustle of blood in my ears. The kindling crackle of ear hairs trembling. I sort of want to die.

Hence, I do both. Then I wake up—and there it is, the dusty aftertaste of the mortal state—but also this sense of having had my hands on something before it slipped away. I've done to myself what saltwater does to thirst. I get up and do it again.

Find me a man without an addiction. I don't think you can. Whatever it might be that he's addicted to is incidental. It all comes down to the same thing: a means of fleeing yourself and plunging trance-like after transcendence. It's the fulfillment, adulterated or not, of a sincere desire. I want to give myself over, utterly.

9/30/13

The problem is that a sponge can't wring itself dry.

Late morning, we stood in the lacy sunlight of a redwood grove. It smelled sharply of pine needles, tinder. Dad decided that I should be made to explore the ruins of Jack London's wilderness manse.

As we walked toward the visitors' center, he peered upward. His lenses looked alchemized. I held my phone in landscape mode, to take a picture. "Say 'dick cheese.'"

"You put this on YouTube, and I swear to God."

"I'm live-streaming you right now. Feng in Taiwan says you look like a goblin."

We ascended the center's few stairs. "I'll go down swinging," he said. "Believe that."

The one other person there, an elderly docent, opened the door and asked, "Gentlemen, please."

I said, "We know each other, lady."

Dad said, "We're related. It's okay."

The interloper said, "Mr. London is buried here. We ask for a little respect."

Our fists opened and closed, gawping like fish out of water. Then we went inside.

Dad browsed, his hands behind his back. "I look at these other writers—your Jack Londons, your Zane Greys," he said, "and my guess is that these guys weren't family men. Couldn't possibly have been family men, not in a woman's way of understanding the term." He picked up and lightly jostled a ship in a bottle. "I have no idea what you're doing with your life. But . . . it's fucking over when you get married. Writing being no exception."

"Well, that's when I'll sell my soul," I said. "When I've got kids, and they need braces and shit. I'll do celebrity profiles. Buy me a brownstone with a home office."

"What nobody talks about, okay, is the asteroid. Or the dirty nuclear bomb. Both of which are coming."

"Your argument against home ownership in this real-estate climate is *asteroids*?"

"Anyway, it's good you're thinking of that now. It would

make me feel good if you wanted to do that. Then, I'd know there will be more Russells in the world. The long line of Russells"—he gestured unenthusiastically—"prolonged. Otherwise, you're the last one."

"Don't worry. I'll be another stay-at-home dad, bringing in little to *nada* financially."

"No rush. Just don't get all pussified. No Baby Bjorns."

"Until he can tell me he prefers otherwise, my kid's getting clothed in burlap. The amount of research I will do re: area schools—zero."

"Fulfilling the prophecy. From shirtsleeves to shirtsleeves in three generations."

"A reprisal. The sine wave rolls on."

"Maybe he'll make it big with a memoir about what a shitty father you were."

"Oh, I'd murder him first."

We tread lightly through London's ruined manor. It had been made out of the same stuff as its surroundings: redwood trunks, blue slate, volcanic rock. Place had its own hot water, electricity, refrigeration. London dropped about two million dollars on it, adjusted. His life's dream.

He was fixing to move in when it burned down mysteriously one night in 1913. What remains is a maze of fallen beams and roofless, mossy walls.

Dad, strolling apart: "I'm sure that when you *do* write about it, you're gonna conveniently forget to mention all the times I did shit like get my ass kicked by Cuban mothers while snagging you the last blue Power Ranger. Or take you to Toronto, to see the Stanley Cup. Which we never should have touched, by the way."

"Most definitely. It's gotta be life, minus the dull parts. Nobody wants to hear about the week you did nothing but toast up bagels after we all caught norovirus and blew out both ends. Virtue's got no charm, or biographer."

"Right," he derided. "I'm sorry you had such an insufferable upbringing."

Moments later, almost apologetically, he said, "My life now is *only* the dull parts. But, as I've mentioned, I was a piece of shit when I was your age. Make no mistake. The only thing I was up for promoting was myself, and whatever bad thing people wanted to start. They knew where to find me. No drugs involved, of course. But alcohol."

I meandered through the shadows. They were damp as though fresh-peeled. I raised my voice: "It was the style at the time. Three martinis with lunch. A grasshopper after dinner."

"Heavy in my family," Dad sang out. "Yours. You come from a long line of world-class addicts. My mother left me to fend for myself because of it."

The man had *never* mentioned his mother to me.

"And Jimmy. I feel so goddamned responsible for Jimmy's death. James. My older brother. He was such a total fuckup. Fun as hell. But I was getting ready to ask your mother to marry me, and I didn't want her to meet him. I was afraid she might think that he was who I would become."

A faint alarm sounded, a tinkling distant but audible that snapped me to attention. I thought of the cemetery bells they used to twine to the toes of the newly interred.

"I should've been back home, with him," Dad said. "I should've been there. Instead, he passed out alone with a lit cigarette between his lips."

Do we always have to succumb to the malign intelligence of male hurt? Do I always have to destroy the things I love through the very acts that reveal my love for them?

"Kent!" Dad exclaimed. "Look!"

Above us were a dozen birds banking against a faultless sky.

They were flying clockwise and at speed, as if spun centripetally. "What are those," I asked, "turkey vultures?"

"Shitbirds, would be my guess."

Implausibly, on our return, Dad pulled into a Jack in the Box and told me, *Drive*. I hadn't driven him anywhere since the ride back from my license test twelve years prior.

Freed from the wheel, his attention fractaled as such: "That Madonna Inn might've been the first motor hotel in America" → "What's that boat doing there?" → "Which reminds me: the Battle of Jutland . . ." → ". . . and that's how the Battle of Jutland affects us today. Whoa, see that big-ass construction site down there?" → "But *that* machine looks like it could *really* put a hurting on you." → "Remember that Dave Barry column? What'd he say? *'A tool is something that enables you to use the laws of physics to seriously injure yourself'*?" → "Dave Barry is who you should emulate."

For hours, the Hanna-Barbera-ish repetition of commercial roadside landscape ran by our windows. We came to drive in silence but for the soporific purr of tires. Soon, Dad was down for the count. He snored ragged snores. Every now and then something caught and throbbled in his throat.

Rumors of his demise have been greatly exaggerated, by him. He isn't going anywhere. Not yet, at least. Anyway, it's not his call to make.

Cruise-controlled, my mind wandered back to those nights he'd come home late from work either dead tired or wasted, I'm not sure which. He'd throw off his shirt and tie but give up on his shoelaces. He'd announce which game we were to play and then fall face-forward onto his made bed.

If the game was "Aircraft Carrier," I launched toy planes on risky missions from the USS *Dad's Back*. Occasionally, a lock of hair would get caught in an axle and torn out by the roots. I'd shrink into a cringe, wait for it. When I cracked an eye, Dad was still spread-eagled, sawing logs.

If it was "Barbershop," I smeared Barbasol on his shoulders and shaved them. The cream thinned pinkly when I nicked warts and dermal barnacles.

If he decided on "Kent, MD," I was to pour hydrogen peroxide into the bottle's cap and use Q-tips to daub the oozing sun sores on his head.

Afterward, I would untie his shoes and crawl next to him on the crinkly pink cover. He was warm, soft, pale, and reeking. Beached, like. I swear I could close my eyes, open them—and it'd be morning.

I have spent a lot of my life trying to regain this power.

At some point during my woolgathering, the gas needle dipped well below empty. The moment I noticed this felt, face-wise, not unlike the moment the Ark of the Covenant gets opened in Indiana Jones.

I turned off the A/C, feigned like I farted, and rolled down the windows. Dad stirred.

"I was just thinking," he said a few beats later. "You have chosen, by my estimation, a pretty shitty life for yourself."

According to the signage, we were about three miles from his apartment. I leaned over the wheel, goosing the pedal.

"I wouldn't have chosen it. But, as you know, I respect individual decisions."

Big wheels keep on turning, I prayed. *Dear Taurus please.* I would never hear the end of it.

"Everything you are and everything you've done has had nothing to do whatsoever with parental intervention or incursion. I hope you realize that."

The car emptied itself of fumes to burn. We began to glide. Dad said, "I'm proud of you, is what I'm saying. And I guess I don't have a history of telling you that." We began to decelerate.

"I owe it all to you, you know," I said. "The better and the worse."

"You saved my life," he replied. "I'd be dead or in prison still if it wasn't for you. You saved *me*. Thank you."

We petered. Your Priuses, your hybrid SUVs—they zoomed past. I wrung the wheel and threw my weight against the seat belt, trying to inch us that much farther forward.

"On second thought," Dad said. "I take that sui generis shit back. You are, if nothing else, my son."

10/1/13

I was about to age out of Mom's insurance plan, so we all went to the dentist, to see my wisdom teeth off.

They thought Dad was Grandpa. They gave me the gas, which tasted of satin and helped me not freak out when the dentist put his foot on the chair for more torque. My mouth cracked sharply, neaping with blood. My lips went red like wine-mouth, like I'd drunk from my own left ventricle.

After that, we went to Costco, to get us some new glasses prescriptions. As always, I couldn't deal with the glaucoma machine. Started weeping involuntarily while waiting wide-eyed for the air blasts. Tracking the MacGuffin of the optometrist's pen light had me doing likewise. My vision is getting significantly worse, they told me. It's the connective tissue. My eyes are regressing to their cross-eyed natal state.

I was unfazed. I was wearing blu-blockers. I was feeling fucking *phenomenal*, wandering around this, the crown jewel of empire.

Full-size trampolines and St. Louis–style ribs and dry-wicking sportswear, XXL. The bright, continual ringing of registers. Kids hanging off the sides of overloaded carts like Southeast Asian dudes on trains. One liter of Kirkland Vodka was nine dollars, and the bottle's *glass*!

O, give me your poor, your tired, your teriyaki samples yearning to get eaten! Anything you need that is not love: right here.

I had to wipe my eyes.

I was with a sales associate, running down the specs of the Kentucky Rose—Kirkland's finest square-cornered, eighteen-gauge steel casket—when Dad approached with poultry breasts akimbo.

"Feel these," he said. "Which one do you want?"

Is this love? Or is this indirect self-interest?

"They gave you the good stuff, eh?" he asked.

If love means to move outside the black hole of egoism, to will the good of the other *as other*—does he do it? Do *I* do it?

"Look, just pick which fucking bird here."

I'm not sure. Whatever it is—love or its agnate—we each beam ours and run from the other's like two boys playing flashlight tag.

"Why do you keep looking up at me like that?" he asked, breasts sagging.

"That one," I said, pointing with neither hands nor eyes. "Looks delish."

"Which one?"

"The hormonally tumid one."

"The many side effects of nitrous oxide may include trying to flout your fancy vocabulary, eh, Mr. New York Asshole?"

"*Flaunt*," I corrected. "You *flaunt* something you have. Like how we *flaunt* this image of ourselves as exceptional and self-sufficient.

"*Flout* is what you do when you think a thing blows and want the world to know it. Like how we all gotta start *flouting* that shit, even if it means we'll be dissolving the substance that holds us together."

"Decently put," he said, scaling both turkeys one last time before placing the right one in the cart. ". . . for a flesh-flautist."

I was dilated. Everything in my field of vision—blurring from the outside in. When I tried to focus, the red, red crabs and cudgels of olive oil and stacks of Pynchon's latest started wavering. I was dizzy. The ferrous tang in my mouth made me want to retch. By the time you think you need to make a decision, that decision has already been made. We added Stove Top stuffing and a cask of mayo to the cart. We got ourselves in line.

Opening the Taurus's trunk in the bright, denuded parking lot, Dad offered: "I'll make you a deal. If I'm alive and well in the New Year, I'll take you home."

"You sure you want to do that?" Despite the blu-blockers, I closed an eye and saluted the sun.

"Not in the fucking least."

"That's fine."

"No grand adventure?"

"This is fine. Here's fine. Here, but not here yet."

"Here? How you figure you're gonna put *here* into words?"

ACKNOWLEDGMENTS

Thank you to all the editors who helped shape this book into a book: Keith Gessen, Chad Harbach, Greg Veis, Heidi Julavits, Rob Spillman, Cheston Knapp, Jay Caspian Kang, Jordan Pavlin, Sarah Goldstein.

Thank you to the UF and NYU journalism programs, especially Ted Spiker, Renee Martin-Kratzer, Jason Cole, Susie Linfield, Katie Roiphe.

Thank you to Janice Russell, Karen Russell, Lauren Russell, Louis Russell. Thank you to Alan Romanchuck, Fran Romanchuck, Alex Romanchuck. Thank you to Patrick, Filipe, Jon, Collin, Dennis, Liz, Jennifer, Jeanette. Thank you to the Murder Team, and Jonah, and Snatch, and Jim Rutman, and everybody at the Ritz. Thank you, Florida. Thank you, Dad.

A NOTE ABOUT THE AUTHOR

Kent Russell's essays have appeared in *The New Republic, Harper's, GQ, n+1, The Believer, Tin House, Details,* and *Grantland.*

A NOTE ON THE TYPE

This book was set in Janson, an example of the Dutch types that date to the second half of the seventeenth century.

Typeset by Scribe,
Philadelphia, Pennsylvania

Printed and bound by RR Donnelley,
Harrisonburg, Virginia

Designed by Soonyoung Kwon